The Making of New Labour's European Policy

The Making of New Labour's European Policy

Russell Holden
Senior Lecturer in European Studies
School of Lifelong Learning at
University of Wales Institute
Cardiff

First published 2002 by
PALGRAVE
Houndmills, Basingstoke, Hampshire RG21 6XS and
175 Fifth Avenue, New York, N.Y. 10010
Companies and representatives throughout the world

PALGRAVE is the new global academic imprint of
St. Martin's Press LLC Scholarly and Reference Division and
Palgrave Publishers Ltd (formerly Macmillan Press Ltd).

ISBN 0-333-91447-3

This book is printed on paper suitable for recycling and made from fully managed and sustained forest sources.

A catalogue record for this book is available from the British Library.

Library of Congress Cataloging-in-Publication Data
Holden Russell
    The making of New Labour's European policy/Russell Holden
        p. cm.
    Includes bibliographical references and index.
    ISBN 0-333-91447-3 (cloth)
    1. Labour Party (Great Britain) – Platforms. 2. European
Union – Great Britain. 3. Great Britain – Politics and
government – 1979–1997. I. Title.

JN1129.L32 H64 2002
327.4104–dc21
                                                        2001044800

10   9   8   7   6   5   4   3   2   1
11   10   09   08   07   06   05   04   03   02

Printed and bound in Great Britain by
Antony Rowe Ltd, Chippenham, Wiltshire

Contents

Preface

For any observer of the Labour Party over the past two decades, it is evident that the party's behaviour reflects a struggle between the desire to uphold established principles whilst endeavouring to secure electoral victory.

Within this struggle, the European issue has become increasingly prominent as a vehicle for promoting the party and its electoral fortunes, albeit not always explicitly. The Conservative Party, meanwhile, seeks to occupy the ground which Labour previously held when some party zealots preferred to build a set of barricades around the House of Commons. Having become controlled by a dominant faction defining itself by its hostility towards Europe, the Labour leadership has reasserted the party's traditional pro-European sentiments since the mid-1980s and has subsequently guided it to a position where the recognition of the importance of being an active EU player has become a central core of party policy. This has required the party to redefine its policy perspectives in key areas to sustain its claims of economic competence and party unity, an achievement which it has realised both through electoral success in 1997 and its time in office.

In seeking to demonstrate how and why this occurred, this text focuses on the redefining of party strategy between June 1983 and June 1999 whilst dealing with a specific policy area which many previous students of the Labour Party have only partially considered. This is regardless of the fact that the European issue seeps into all aspects of the British political process with immense consequences.

During the preparation of this work, the comments and encouragement of the following individuals has been invaluable: Dr David Baker, Dr Stephen Brigley, Dr Colin Hay, Dr Gerald Taylor and Dr Simon Tormey – each of whom, at various times, has commented on particular chapters. The observations of audience members at conferences organised by the Political Studies Association and the University Association of Contemporary European Studies at which I have aired some of my ideas have also proved to be very helpful. My thanks also extend to those individuals who kindly agreed to my requests for interviews and granted me access to publications and public records.

Ultimately this work would not have been completed without the inestimable help, guidance and calming influence of Susan Richardson and the support and affectionate enthusiasm of my mother and father which have been sustained over many months. Without their help this work would not have been completed. It is to them that I wish to dedicate this book.

1
Introduction

Since the General Election of 1983, the British political system has witnessed a remarkable transformation in one of its key players, namely the Labour Party. Firstly under the managerial style of Neil Kinnock, and more recently under the brief stewardship of John Smith and the evolving leadership of Tony Blair, the party has reconstituted itself into a formidable political machine hardly recognisable from that which contested the 1983 election so ingloriously. The party has undergone the process of both renewal and modernisation.

Critical to this fundamental overhaul has been the decision by the Parliamentary Labour Party (PLP) to reverse its position on Europe, which Mitchell and Heller (*New Statesman,* 26 July 1996) have referred to as the 'rogue elephant' of British politics, in view of its record in dividing the political parties and debilitating government on both sides of the political divide. The reality as far as Labour is concerned is that it has now become the more 'European' of the two parties (George, 1992), a development fully legitimised in the post-1987 Policy Review Process, which the party undertook following its third consecutive election defeat. It was the Policy Review documents that marked the public disavowal of previous negative perceptions and statements on Europe. The official jettisoning of this stance was confirmed in the document entitled *Meet the Challenge* (Labour Party, 1989a). From this point on, Europe was officially viewed as an opportunity rather than a threat, not just by the PLP but also by a very substantial proportion of the Labour Movement, which, for the purposes of this study, will be defined as

1

a set of institutions created by the workers to 'represent their interests as producers, consumers and political citizens' (Minkin, 1991, p. 4)

Given this new reality, made all the more remarkable when considered in the context of the traditional British party perspectives on Europe, a range of issues demand investigation: why this change occurred, what the implications of this have been for the Labour Party and how these changes can be placed in context as the party's European policy has implicitly underpinned much of New Labour's desire and effort to obtain and sustain office.

Between May 1983 and June 1999, it is unquestionable that the positions of the two main parties on Europe were reversed. The Conservatives had long been regarded as the pro-European party in domestic politics, whilst Labour's position had been far more equivocal (Gamble and Kelly, 2000). Yet as Tindale's remarks show, Labour's position has become very clear: 'From qualified acceptance in 1979, Labour moved to outright rejection in 1980, back to grudging acceptance after 1983 and finally to enthusiasm after 1987' (Tindale, 1992, p. 276).

This development needs consideration in respect of how it has altered the nature and face of the PLP in the domestic political environment and as a committed participant in policy discussions with European socialist and social democratic parties. However, it has to be recognised that between 1983 (General Election) and 1999 (the European Parliamentary Elections), the points of reference for this study, there have quite clearly been variations in the level of support given to the idea of Europe acting as an underpinning element of party strategy both within the PLP and other sections of the Labour Movement. The varying level and type of support offered is attributable to a range of explanations that subsequent chapters will seek to explore in the context of examining the renewal, modernisation and continuing transformation of the Labour Party – factors which have contributed to the emergence of New Labour and its European policy.

Remarkably, the policy reversal that was stimulated in response to the poor performance at the 1983 General Election generated little rancour, yet its significance cannot be underestimated. However, many of the leading academics associated with work on differing aspects of Labour Party activity and its history have either underplayed or underestimated the European question in terms of its impact on the future course of the PLP and the subsequent emergence of New Labour. They have also chosen to ignore the influence of this on the domestic political discourse of the subsequent sixteen years, as this study will indicate. Instead, they have tended to focus on issues such as internal party discipline, the link between Labour and the unions and the role and importance of party members and activists. The new stance on Europe which slowly emerged provided a new set of policy parameters around which the PLP chose to position itself as a more respectable political grouping that, in time, could prove itself to be electorally successful. As Davies (1996) remarks, after 1983, Labour began to resemble: 'a snake shedding its skin' (Davies, 1996, p. 415).

This reflects its start in abandoning longstanding policies, notably on nationalisation, the sale of council houses and, of course, Europe. Initially, this was as part of a party renewal programme, but later it became part of the transformation process from a jaded and outdated organisation to a modernised professional party machine.

Accounting for change

In seeking to explain both the policy reversal and how the new perspective on Europe became critical as a driving force for the party's renewal and modernisation, the analysis in the following pages will demonstrate that party thinking and strategy involved more than merely attempting to engage in vote maximisation. After all, Europe has not featured as a prominent concern influencing electoral choice, either during three Parliaments in opposition or three years of government. Rather, choice was determined by leadership change, the role of dominant factions in the PLP and the Labour Movement and, to a far lesser extent, the external environment (in so far as the party is deemed already to have established its primary goal), be it vote maximisation, office maximisation or policy advocacy.

Furthermore, as subsequent chapters will prove, this explanatory approach will be used to demonstrate how the party was able to undertake its policy reversal as part of the renewal process which provided an impetus for modernisation and subsequent electoral victory, as well as the more recent caution displayed in its European policy intentions. This also raises the further question of why the party opted for a less obvious vote winner as a policy to act as a dynamic in driving party change. Subsequent discussion will argue that this was very much connected to the reality of the continuing process of Europeanisation of the British political process.

However, throughout, it will be noted that as a policy issue, Europe does not constitute an area to which the electorate inherently warms, as evidenced by opinion poll surveys. Public opinion on the European issue has oscillated during the period under investigation, as has the passion of the PLP for placing its European policy centre-stage. Yet at no point did the party indicate a tendency to return to the hostile position proclaimed in the 1983 manifesto – a reality explained by an acknowledgement of changing political, economic and social realities as opposed to sheer political opportunism.

Policy changes are undertaken in the hope of securing electoral victory. However, in the period under examination it is evident that in the first instance, Labour was set on restoring public faith in its operations. The shock of the poor electoral performance in 1983 stirred the party and provided the catalyst needed to identify a distinct primary goal and a set of complementary goals geared to making Labour more professional in its conduct and operations. This result marked the point at which the party leadership declared an end to its policy of vehement anti-Europeanism. The Kinnock–Hattersley leadership team represented a new dominant faction willing to acknowledge external environmental change but was not prepared to be driven purely by this in determining its primary and related multiple goals. The party continued to perceive itself as British rather than European in the way it projected itself publicly, keen to protect national interest whenever it appeared threatened. Yet internally, the influence of the evolving process of European integration was starting to mould policy prescriptions. However, the weakness of being in opposition to a government with a substantial majority made it all the more credible to accept what Dunleavy (1991) has termed the 'preference accommodation' approach to policy-making rather than that of 'preference shaping'.

This was based on the judgement that the party was best able to accommodate the political environment created by the Conservatives as opposed to striving to reinfluence the preferences of the electorate. As later sections demonstrate, this became a distinguishing feature of party policy-making on Europe throughout the period under consideration. Although the party's position strengthened between 1983 and 1999, it preferred not to attempt to shape overtly voters' thinking on Europe. It opted to use the European issue as a foundation for the formulation of economic and other policy positions where an acceptance of the value of integration and pooling of sovereignty pervaded policy commitments. Furthermore, it also linked in to crucial concerns of party revival that M. Shaw (1994) identifies when he suggests that European Community (EC) policy overlaps with two key concerns of the party leadership: namely, economic policy and party unity.

These issues represent two crucial criteria for the party leadership in assessing its progress and for the electorate in terms of gauging whether its credibility as a political machine capable of competent government has increased. As a consequence, these concerns will be referred to throughout in explaining party policy change and in tracing the evolution and conduct of New Labour's approach to Europe.

Impetus for change

In many respects, the European issue drove the party's initial policy renewal programme, as the mid-1980s witnessed a new impetus within the European policy-making institutions with the passing of the era of Eurosclerosis, whilst the evolving Thatcher government was sealing off domestic policy channels for Labour exploiting its Parliamentary absolutism. The outcome of this was that by the 1987 election, the first contested under Kinnock's leadership, the PLP had declared its intention to reverse its policy. Labour's policy agenda was increasingly moulded by socio-poltical and economic change at home and abroad.

In practical terms, this provided the impetus for a new economic policy, an ideal opportunity for a new leader to stamp his mark on party thinking. The increasing irrelevance of the Alternative Economic Strategy (AES) gave rise to the possibility of an 'Alternative European Strategy' (Holland, 1983), which acknowledged the increasing interdependence of the British and other European economies. In fact, the party was being modernised around a European axis, a choice consciously made by the leadership. Ideas emerging from the European Community (EC), particularly after the appointment of Jacques Delors as President of the Commission, were increasingly perceived as attractive. Not only was Europe providing a new and welcome front on which to counter 'Thatcherism', but the emergence of concepts such as Social Europe, the Single European Market (SEM) and the progress of integration and co-ordination between states on an increasing range of issues provided a perspective that the PLP leadership was keen to accept rather than merely acknowledge. The reason for this was that these ideas could provide the basis of a new set of policies that a party keen to renew itself could adopt. This was particularly the case for one seeking the trust of the electorate, under a leader spurred on by newly crafted convictions on one level and, on the other, by political common sense that demanded responses to what Shaw (1994) has described as a threefold crisis. This was evident in respect of ideology, governance and electoral failure, whilst Whiteley (1983), in endorsing this analysis, also added the problem of declining party membership to the scenario.

It is clear that throughout Kinnock's leadership and also through that of Smith and Blair, these concerns were always given high priority in developing perspectives on matters like the SEM, the Maastricht Treaty and the 1997 Inter-governmental Conference reviewing the Maastricht Treaty. These responses will be referred to regularly throughout. However, their level of impact is related to the strength of the leadership's position at the time of discussion and the pressures on economic policy and party unity. These developments continued despite the evident reluctance expressed in some quarters of the PLP and Labour Movement, as detailed in Chapters 2 and 3.

The real debate then, and for some even now, especially in the ranks of the PLP (Mitchell and Heller, 1996), remains one of determining how far the new-found support of Europe should extend and at what pace it should proceed. The complexity of this increases by virtue of the very nature of the organisational structure of the Labour Party, with policy-making rights distributed amongst a variety of institutions. This complex structure has to function smoothly whilst crucially securing the support of the trade unions because of the generous financial support and electoral base they continue to provide and the congenital link that uniquely exists in the British body-politic between the two institutions. As Harrison remarks: 'The Labour Party is bound by the Unions not just by cash and card votes but by personalities and doctrines, common experience and sentiment and mutual advantage' (Harrison, 1960, p. 340). However, as the period from 1983 progressed, it became apparent that the trade unions were largely very supportive of a positive European policy position. Although the Labour Movement has long wrestled with the dilemma of reconciling principle with the desire for power, after 1983, the latter perspective gained supremacy. It was the bulk of the trade unions who were the first to recognise the value of exploiting the European institutions for policy-influencing and policy-making purposes, an approach that was either not always evident to other sections of the Labour Movement or still perceived as unacceptable. However, this is not to argue that the unions forced new European thinking on the PLP; rather that they helped to speed up the process of accepting a new line of thought through the promotion of what has been described by Labour Movement members as the 'new realism'. This approach acknowledged the need to work within an existing domestic political environment in which, for the foreseeable future, the Labour Party was to play a peripheral role. In accepting the need for a tone of conciliation rather than confrontation, the European institutional framework provided an alternative forum for policy discussion. However, not all unions were keen to move from the traditional perspective of 'class confrontation'.

Therefore, the policy change on Europe, though occurring early in the period under discussion, was not precise in terms of defining why it was necessary and how wide-ranging it should be. However, it remains clear that moving the position on Europe made it much easier for the party to engage in the wider policy changes that the leadership sought in the light of the 1983 result, where, according to the then General Secretary of the Party, voter apprehension was a factor in Labour's defeat (Report of the Labour NEC to the Annual Party Conference, 1983). This was an important admission so soon after the election. Europe was thus destined to feature prominently in an extensive review of party thinking.

Policy reversal and its significance

It is evident that through the mid-1980s the PLP leadership resolved to become fully engaged with all developments occurring in the EC, in preference to asserting that it represented interests inimical to those of the party and its fundamental principles. This was not notably different to the stance taken between 1974 and 1979, though even in this period the party leadership was wary of accepting decisions that might undermine domestic authority. However, at that stage, the support was less for reasons of true conviction and more for reasons of practicality, particularly after the clear result in the 1975 referendum on continued EC membership. As Kinnock's interest in Europe developed, so did a truer sense of belief in the whole concept (personal interview with Neil Kinnock, 2nd December 1996).

During the course of this study, a raft of explanations will be offered as to why the PLP reversed its European policy. The term 'reverse' will be used throughout, as it best defines what actually transpired. However, it is crucial that the analysis starts from the poor electoral position, the bankruptcy of ideas, the impracticality of exisiting policy commitments and the need to acknowledge and work within the Thatcherite settlement.

This implied the need to respond to majority opinion which was broadly supportive of the government's handling of European policy, recognising some benefits that individuals and the economy could obtain from new policy development. This merely reflected a further manifestation of a country galvanised by the enterprise culture and receptive to the thought of new European markets for business generated by the Single Market. The contours of domestic politics were changing and Labour needed to engage in some form of policy overhaul to demonstrate its vigour and modernity. However, this did not imply a strong sense of support for European economic or political integration; rather a view that involvement in the EC brought positive domestic benefits (Gallup Survey Evidence, 1984–86).

The extent of the change can only be appreciated by acknowledging the chronology of the developments. The 1983 manifesto made a clear commitment to withdrawal:

> The EEC ... was never designed to suit us, and our experience as a member of it has made it more difficult for us to deal with our economic and industrial problems ... It has weakened our ability to achieve the objectives of Labour's international policy. The

next Labour government, committed to radical, socialist policies for reviving the British economy, is bound to find continued membership a most serious obstacle to the fulfilment of these policies. (Labour Party, 1983a, p. 33)

As Rosamund (1994) remarks, the high point of official and public anti- Europe posturing was the 1983 manifesto, with its unequivocal statement that the PLP would terminate membership of the EC. Socialist transformation of Britain was simply incompatible with the Treaty of Rome.

In terms of public opinion, defence issues dominated the foreign policy agenda, with Labour retaining its commitment to unilateralism. Although the Prime Minister's stand over budgetary inequities culminated in a substantial rebate that was warmly welcomed, there is little to suggest that the public was warming to the notion of European integration (Gallup Survey material, March 1984 – January 1985). As Butler and Kavanagh (1984) show, Europe, along with other elements of international policy, hardly featured in the 1983 election. The lack of attention devoted to Europe made it easier for the party leadership to reverse policy, yet this had to remain covert as there was little to attract popular support before the EC generated its own momentum through new policy development. However, the European issue was becoming more significant in relation to its impact on an extensive range of policy areas and rather than confront this complex issue directly, the party recognised the merits of moving towards reversal by introducing change in other areas. The most significant of these was in economic policy. The task of smoothing the change became easier with the advent of the Single European Act (although its passage through the House of Commons was opposed by the PLP), the emergence of the social dimension to Community policy and the evidence of benefit derived from the granting of financial aid through the Structural Funds.

As Kinnock (1994) later recalled, changes had to be made not simply as ends in themselves but also as part of a longer-term initiative to generate a new perspective within the party and the public. This was built upon in the Policy Review Process after the 1987 defeat. The genesis of these ideas was contained in his *New Socialist* article (March–April 1984). Throughout this process, Kinnock emphasised possible electoral success based on policies characterised by realism.

At this juncture, there was also a recognition of the need to respond to new trends notably in the international economy where it was no longer possible, in most cases, for governments to control their own national economies, as confirmed by the events in France in early 1981. However, the commitment to Europe had to be balanced with the delicate issue of retaining sovereignty, a fundamental tradition within British politics, to which many in the Labour Movement strongly subscribed.

The 1987 manifesto limited itself to a few brief lines, different in tone from that of 1983. Though they were not quite as positive as they may have been, the message conveyed was clear:

> Labour's aim is to work constructively with our EEC partners to promote economic expansion and combat unemployment ... We shall, like other member countries, reject EEC interference with our policy for national recovery and renewal. (Labour Party, 1987a, p. 15)

However, by 1989 and the European Parliamentary elections, the party was portraying itself as distinctly pro-European. By this time, the party had endorsed the Social Charter. It had begun to recognise, with the assistance of guidance from some unions, the advantages of being immersed in European institutions and of being aware of the need to build a European element into domestic economic management (detailed further in Chapter 2). In 1989, a Joint Manifesto with the Confederation of European Socialists was used as the manifesto for the European elections. In 1984, this had also been agreed, but not implemented, as the party was not ready for such a commitment.

Although it remains virtually impossible to tie down the policy reversal to one particular date or incident, it is clearly part of a continuum emerging soon after Kinnock's assumption of power, continuing through to the advent of New Labour. Direct support for a policy reversal on Europe was not immediately apparent, yet the party leadership accepted the need to address the wider issue (Holden, 1999; Lent, 1997). Rather than portraying this as a purely electorally driven outcome, the policy change was far more concerned with the promotion of strategic change within the party. The significance of this rests in the foundation laid for future party leaders in promoting the virtues of a modern, responsive and united party. The leadership change and the scale of the 1983 electoral defeat drove the reversal. Europe became more than an issue of party management (Rosamund, 1990) and played the role of mainspring in promoting the reform urgently required for renewal as it acted as both a context and primer for change. This provided an ideal legacy for Blair on his election as party leader and confirms that the origins of New Labour rest in the actions of the Party leadership galvanised into action by the 1983 electoral débacle.

As an issue considered in isolation, the policy reversal on Europe, though significant in terms of demarcating a change in thinking, means very little (particularly in terms of the critique advanced here). It figures as a development in the early period of the Kinnock era in terms of an area warranting attention, though viewed starkly in this light, the importance of the development is not altogether obvious because of the covert dimension to its handling. Nevertheless, the essence of this study is to explain how and why the European issue was instrumental in guiding the party between June 1983 and June 1999. As well as confirming the reality of a policy reversal, the overhaul of European strategy demonstrates that the Blair leadership was concerned with implementation of a strategy as opposed to its conception. As with other areas of policy this confirms the continuum evident in the actions of the PLP from Kinnock to Blair via the Smith interregnum.

Later chapters endeavour to show that the European issue was fundamental to renewal, as it provided a banner under which the PLP could initiate a range of changes, enabling it to respond to the collapse of the long-established social democratic model of politics. This was a model that hinged on strong working-class electoral support, collectivism, a Keynesian welfare state, and elements of corporatism (A.Taylor, 1987) which was showing itself to be increasingly vulnerable. This requirement for change was compounded by the need to react to the increasing influence of internal and external forces such as European integration, the demise of Fordism, changes in the class structure generated via Thatcherism, the increasing internationalisation of the global economy with its concurrent decline in the role of the nation-state and the increasing emphasis on the market and self-regulation. As Grahl and Teague (1988) rightly suggest, the party was also aware that it needed to take another look at economic policy formation, how the EC was developing and the issue of domestic political competition, especially before 1987 with the emergence of the Social Democratic Party (SDP). After 1987, concern switched with the formation of the Liberal Democratic Alliance. Others have argued that the term 'transformation' is more apt as a description of how the PLP changed. However, this implies radical change in terms of party policy in which the European issue was one of a number of areas that were subject to overhaul. Subsequent chapters will go on to show that this did occur but in a more gradual style. Emphasis and priorities changed but this does not equate with the wholesale introduction of new policy ideas and perspectives distinguished by their apparent lack of contact with the party's traditions. However, the tendency to move along this path has increased since the election of Blair as leader. This introduces the concept of 'modernisation' into the discussion.

Modernisation equates with professionalism in terms of planning and organisational techniques, but not necessarily with a set of new ideas. As Heffernan (1994) remarks, this meant that privately the party was highly organised and controlled, contrary to public statements regarding a new style of leadership that stressed it was a 'listening leadership' empowering its membership, permitting it to take part in widespread policy debate. It was decided that this approach had to be avoided following the problems in the period immediately preceding the 1983 defeat. During this period, the PLP was becoming too dominated by activists in the form of amateurs and purists, individuals who were more concerned with taking the appropriate position on an issue rather than the wider view of securing electoral victory. No political party keen to regain office could afford such a recurrence, particularly one as electorally vulnerable as Labour.

In reality, the programme renewal did not offer anything radical. The PLP sought to return to its former familiar terrain, partly as a reaction to the mistakes of earlier in the decade and to the control that the leader was now able to assert over his massed ranks. Moving to preference shaping might have involved compromising still further on existing principles and upsetting traditional supporters. This meant moving in a direction acceptable to its primary support and financial base, namely the unions. Policy reversal on Europe was acceptable to the bulk of unions, many of which were not reticent about further engagement with the European policy-making process.

Alternatively, it has to be asked how Labour could engage in preference shaping, as this was at the heart of the Thatcher government's rationale. Furthermore, this was not being publicly rejected in electoral terms. To shape preferences meant winning back lost Tory voters, some of whom were former Labour supporters, but traditional principles had to be considered for the sake of party credibility. However, with vote winning as the primary goal, by embracing elements of the Thatcher agenda, Labour would become more attractive to a wider range of voters.

Explaining the change

Between 1983 and 1987, the imperative was to rid the party of its unpopular policies, those judged by the electorate to be unacceptable. The leadership quickly recognised that: 'There would have to be profound changes in the policies and organisation of the Party, not simply as ends in themselves but also as contributions to a change in the mentality of the Labour Party' (Kinnock, 1994, p. 36). Amongst the necessary changes falling into this category was European policy. Although not a vote winner, European policy was evolving because of the need to review and alter policy in areas critical to the party standing. This was most notable in terms of economic policy. However, due to internal party constraints and events (Jones, 1996), the leadership did not devote priority status to the issue, as will be discussed in Chapter 2, although a change was deemed necessary (Kinnock, 1984). After 1987, the situation was different and the Policy Review Process provided the legitimisation for the thinking that had been evolving from the earliest days of the Kinnock leadership. The Delors speech to the annual Trade Union Conference in 1988 provided the occasion for the official endorsement of the change, an expression of mass public relief within the Labour Movement (personal interview with Neil Kinnock, 2 December 1996), acknowledging a critical change in policy commitment.

Internally, one has to note the realignments within the PLP which altered the dominant coalition in the party, providing Kinnock with more room for manoeuvre. This was boosted further by the emergence of a set of more pragmatic politicians within party ranks including Tony Blair and Gordon Brown. The support provided by the unions, some of which were very positive in their attitudes towards Europe, was also invaluable. The unions, it must be added, were also keen that the mantle of political leadership remained with the PLP.

Shaw (1994) suggests three interlocking determinants of change: namely, external environmental (political and economic) factors, the leadership's frame of reference (new strategic thinking), and internal party considerations (power structures, alignment of factions and constituent organisations, and party culture). He goes on to state that the prime objective was to restore public faith and trust in the party and in so doing, the most important element was the new 'strategic thinking'. This involved the development of an approach that enabled the PLP both to define policy problems and supply ready-made solutions. In the search for electoral success, organisational issues had preferential treatment over ideological concerns. This implicitly implied a clear slant towards preference accommodation and a lessening of emphasis in those areas where the party seemed vulnerable. Voting patterns were increasingly seen as being the outcome of party image, leadership image and policy preferences. After 1987 in particular, considerable emphasis was placed on perceptions of trust, economic competence and the shaping of public attitudes to the party. Preference accommodation really demanded effective positioning on the political spectrum which ensured garnering of votes from new and established sources. As Shaw maintains: 'The cure followed logically: to provide balm and convey the message that Labour would be safe, pragmatic, and prudent, and eschew controversial policies' (Shaw, 1994, p. 158).

Ideas of returning to an old social democratic mindset were repudiated in favour of what was perceived to be a 'post-revisionist' position. To increase the prospects of electoral success, the party had to widen its constituency of support, noting the emergence of the SDP–Liberal Alliance which included former Labour supporters. In effect, this required that the party went beyond winning the debate in the party, to winning it in the country. Had the leadership overtly declared this intention, it would have made a major strategic and tactical blunder. Instead, it opted in favour of a more covert approach, recognising the need to consult internally and ensure that the party decision-making structure had in place personnel sympathetic to this approach. These were moves geared to instilling and preserving party unity.

Increasingly, international economic trends were casting doubt on existing economic policy ideals. International economic interdependence was now the norm, a fait accompli which the French government, in the early days of the Mitterand presidency, did not fully realise and consequently paid a high price for in sacrificing many of their policy ideals. As George and Haythorne (1996) argue, because of changing global circumstances, governments had to pool resources and share power on a supranational basis. A new paradigm was emerging, as David Martin MEP was suggesting, based on a recognition that:

> Important democratic socialist objectives can no longer be accomplished within the boundaries of a single country. The European Community can open up to the peoples of Europe new areas of manoeuvre that have been and will continue to be lost to the British people. (Tindale, 1992, p. 285)

The PLP had to work within these constraints: hence, the early consideration given to the possibility of ERM (Exchange Rate Mechanism) membership. This was an argument also made convincingly by Tindale (1992) when he acknowledges the reality of policy-making needing to stretch beyond the narrow confines of the nation state, thus rejecting one of the two models of economic management identified by Gamble (Smith and Spear, 1992) as having been used by the PLP since its emergence at the turn of the century.

As regards a new approach to Europe, the union movement began to realise its weaknesses in comparison to its European counterparts, a situation compounded by the low ebb of electoral support for the Labour Party and its consequent lack of influence at Westminster. New thinking was influenced by contact with continental allies who were more aware of economic integration allowing for the preservation of social democratic ideals. These contacts had previously been perceived as a low key objective. The EC could also show itself to be a welcome constraint on the British government, a much-needed fillip in a climate that was emasculating debate. However, by the same token it might prove to be a less welcome constraint on a subsequent Labour government. The emergence of the social dimension within EC policy-making also provided ammunition against an elected national government keen on promoting the free market and self-regulation at every opportunity. The social dimension also helped to convey the view that the EC was no longer a distant and irrelevant collection of institutions with nothing positive to offer the ordinary voter (George and Rosamund, 1992). This presented Labour with a potential new vote winner, and provided an ideal complement to the Single Market programme, more especially those elements perceived as geared to the interests of management and capital.

The other interpretation of developments on Europe which has been aired is that the policy reversal is a manifestation of adversarial politics. This refers to Labour occupying a space not inhabited by the Conservatives (Wincott, 1992). Seizing an opportunity to win a domestic battle whilst being almost politically impotent was a clever move. Rosamund (1994) suggests, however, that this was carried out purely on the grounds of 'oppositional opportunism', the extent of which ran to an attempt to mastermind a defeat of the government on the European Communities Amendment Bill (see Chapter 4). This was justified in terms of adversarial politics. By the same token, however, it has to be recognised that the Conservatives were not negative about every single aspect of European development, particularly the liberalisation of the European economy. This line of thinking seeks to show that the European issue was no different from any other in the arena of adversarial conflict and had to be used for electoral benefit.

It is clear from the preceding sections that numerous academics have looked at how and why the Labour Party refashioned itself under the leadership of Kinnock, Smith and Blair, undertaking programme renewal with a view to securing future electoral success. However, little of what has been written about in relation to these developments has been devoted exclusively to the European question. This begs two fundamental questions: namely, what this indicates in terms of proactive and reactive politics in respect of Labour Party strategy (preference accommodating versus preference shaping), and why such a glaring omission is so apparent within the existing literature on the Labour Party when it is acknowledged how fundamental the European issue was to other elements of party strategy. This is a vacuum that this investigation seeks both to expose and fill.

On the one hand, it signifies that a consensus was not difficult to achieve within the broad swathe of the Labour Movement regarding the inappropriateness of existing policy and the fact that policy change was necessary. Equally, it has to be recognised that the lack of attention devoted to the European question was also due to competing demands from internal pressures and external environmental factors that the party leadership could not ignore. These served as constraining factors on the actions of the dominant coalition at the core of the leadership. However, this still leaves largely unaddressed a host of critical issues. These concern the nature of the policy change over Europe, the motivation behind it, its speed, impact and consequences. Furthermore, the central weakness of much of the discussion of Labour's performance remains: namely that the evolution of the policy is not considered with regard to the centrality of the role of Europe in party strategy and how at different points in the time period being studied its influence has oscillated. For Kinnock, it was central; for Smith, progress was one characterised by consolidation; whilst Blair, particularly as Prime Minister, has erred far more on the side of caution, particularly up until mid-1998.

It appears that Labour Party scholars have chosen to concentrate on what have been perceived to be more controversial areas. Yet on close inspection, the European issue encroaches on all these matters. This oversight ignores the question of how Europe became a vehicle for reinvigorating and rebuilding the party as well as for playing down those areas in which the PLP appeared vulnerable. In carrying out the policy reversal, the leadership was able to demonstrate its newly acquired strength, drawing together the different component parts of the Labour Movement through effective agenda management, with considerable help from a substantial section of the Union movement. Critically, it also helped to forge a new economic policy. The importance of the latter cannot be underestimated in terms of electoral politics and the need to broaden the appeal of the PLP (Jones, 1996). The PLP had to ensure quite clearly that it was more competent than the Conservatives in terms of domestic economic management and it therefore had little option but to accept its policy-making framework.

Conclusion

It is evident that from the mid-1980s onwards, the European issue had begun to encroach on all matters central to what Lent (1997) has described as the Party's 'active vote maximisation ethos'.

Consequently, in seeking to explain and conceptualise the role of the European issue in a period that witnessed a remarkable change for Labour, it becomes evident that the desire for change came from within, though external influences played their part too. However, the explanation advanced duly acknowledges that the electorate holds many negative perceptions of Europe. These revolve around the activities of its institutions and their increasing incursions into the domestic political discourse. Amongst the most important are the worries regarding threats to national identity and culture, exclusion from democratic decision-making processes and centralisation of policy in a largely Brussels-based bureaucracy. These concerns help to explain the anxieties expressed by the leadership at various intervals about appearing to be too pro-European. Sensitivity to these expressions of public concern was built into policy considerations, especially in the second half of the 1990s. Crucially, however, it also confirms that the approach to the policy was based on more than electoral concerns and that the party was single-minded in respect of a distinct primary goal. This, in effect, constituted the desire to modernise the party to ensure the broadening of its appeal to strengthen its electoral base. Furthermore, an emphasis was being placed on the desire to create a professional, trustworthy and competent political organisation. In time, this would be in a position to deliver electoral success as opposed to the socialist objectives desired in former times.

In pursuing the contention of M. Shaw (1994) which will be endorsed throughout, that European policy intersects with two key concerns of the party leadership, namely economic policy and party unity, subsequent chapters aim to explain how and why the issue of European policy has been central to the fortunes of Labour between 1983 and 1999. It also shows how a dominant faction, described as being part of the 'pragmatic centre' (Jones, 2000) of the PLP, wrested control of the party (though initially this was not especially overt) and made Europe a critical dynamic in the party's rejuvenation. Whilst located in a climate of domestic emasculation, Europe forged an agenda for renewal and modernisation that addressed the primary goal identified; it also acknowledged the need to understand a rapidly changing external environment characterised by the internationalisation of national economies and the development of international political institutions.

During the course of the remainder of this text, the analysis will consider the development of European policy within the party in the context of the nature of the change and the initial constraints on the leadership resulting from the two election defeats, before considering the impact of the 1987 election and the subsequent Policy Review Process. In moving from the private to the public statement of change, the latter years of the Kinnock leadership period (post-1987) will be examined in terms of the consolidation of the progress achieved and the confirmation of the party's new position–one that the Blair leadership was content to consolidate. The handling of the European Communities Amendment Act and the brief tenure of Smith will be considered together, prior to an evaluation of the leadership of Blair in opposition and government.

This latter period will demonstrate a slowing down of the European impetus, despite the positive rhetoric often present in party documents and the increasing evidence of the Europeanisation of domestic politics. Common trends will be identified, the theoretical context examined and the application of the new model for explaining the party's renewal and modernisation will be developed to help understand how New Labour sustained and managed its European policy. Throughout, it is clear that the political contours have changed though the imprint of Thatcherism remains strong. However, each of the leaders has remained committed to Europe and the party has shown itself quick to identify the advantages accruing from the Europeanisation of domestic politics. At the same time, it has also varied the pace at which the European impetus has driven forward the party's strategic development from renewal to modernisation.

2
Locating the Dynamic of Policy Reversal, 1983–87

In any thorough examination of how the PLP and the Labour Movement became sympathetic to European integration, it is imperative to identify and explain how far the party moved in such a short passage of time. This development becomes even more significant when it is acknowledged that the European issue acted as the chief dynamic behind the twin processes of party renewal and modernisation. Furthermore, over the period under consideration (1983–99), the policy reversal once declared, has remained unchallenged.

To achieve this objective, a set of explanations will be offered to account for the initially hostile anti-European position adopted by the party in the 1983 election in contrast to the very different approach adopted four years later. Although the public statements surrounding the latter were lacking in great enthusiasm, the leadership had achieved a great deal in altering the party's thinking and fortunes. During these four years, the newly established dominant leadership coalition had resolved how to handle the ever-present dilemma of reconciling a history of ideological impulses with the more pragmatic requirements of being in government and the greater freedoms granted whilst in opposition. The party opted for a reasoned non-radical approach encapsulated in its move towards programme accommodation as the driving-force behind policy adaptation. The growing influence of Europeanisation on domestic politics was duly noted and Labour chose to exploit it as a vehicle, initially to aid and then direct, its strategy towards its desired primary objective.

In the search to recapture and sustain party unity, the new leadership had to imprint itself on both the PLP and the Labour Movement. Political realism, distinguished by a new strategic thinking as exemplified by Kinnock (1985) in *Fabian Tract* 509, provided the rationale for the leadership's actions in the first of the three Parliamentary periods of opposition under scrutiny. In this pamphlet, Kinnock set out his thoughts on how the party needed to change in respect of seeking to shift attitudes and the presentation of policy. This new-found sense of realism did not indicate radical change: in fact, to some degree, it returned to the guiding hand of Tawney (1931), although it addressed the need to operate in new political circumstances.

Effective party agenda management, combined with the drive towards a new economic policy, helped to raise public confidence, with the former proving crucial in galvanising the latter. At the same time, the party realised that the European political environment provided a more effective means of raising issues and questioning the legitimacy of elements of the government's policy programme. As well as concentrating on internal management skills, this chapter will indicate how the desire from within masterminded the process of change in which the ever-increasing influence of the EC was evident, particularly as a domestic factor.

Throughout, references to Europeanisation will use the Bulmer and Birch (2000) view that Europeanisation characterises a distinct process identified with a political discourse and a system of governance. However, the measurement of the impact of this will be qualified by three factors identified by Bomberg and Peterson (2000). These are: the existence of few truly common EU policies, the looseness of rules associated with European policies, and the difficulty sometimes in disentangling the effects of integration from those of globalisation.

This chapter will also show how the PLP was indebted to substantial elements of the trade union movement, notably to the TUC for advancing the new positive perspectives on EC membership amongst different unions (Rosamund, 1993). It was also after 1983 that regular and practical contacts with continental allies increased (personal interview with Neil Kinnock, 2 December 1996), exploiting the Labour traditions of internationalism. However, the adoption of a more positive line of thinking on Europe was designed to maximise influence and credibility on the domestic front, rather than to play a leading role at the European level.

Lastly, the chapter seeks to show how this one particular policy change played a key part in setting the foundations for the Smith and Blair leaderships in advancing the cause of the party. In addition to accepting the Tindale (1992) time frames, due recognition has to be given to the fact that it was only when control over the NEC was secured that the leader's position was strengthened. This permitted him to introduce ideas that he believed were beyond the traditions of adversarial politics and would benefit the PLP in fostering its renewal and public standing. In their study of party membership, Seyd and Whiteley (1992) indicate that the broad swathe of the membership approved of the twin programme of policy reformulation and party reorganisation. Within this overall programme, it was also evident that there was a solid level of support towards EC membership, making Kinnock's task far simpler. This revolved around the plan to modernise the party, and to broaden its appeal and electoral basis so as to prove its professionalism, trustworthiness and competence (Kinnock, 1985).

Over time, this development made it easier for Smith to reinforce his longstanding positive European credentials, whilst for Blair, the policy linked in with his objective of creating a modern and populist party. Most critically of all, each of the three leaders recognised that by pursuing the European dynamic to whatever level of intensity he deemed appropriate, a clear positive European policy ensured a sound economic policy, the preservation of party unity and a projection of competence: critical elements of an effective opposition and governing party. This would help to create an environment suitable for trying to match the achievements of fraternal brothers in France and Spain. In both cases, rapid progress was made in adjusting to the new political climate which demanded compromise positions to be reached on matters of sovereignty, ideology, party structure and, most critically of all, economic policy. These two objectives represented ideals that the party gladly cherished after its electoral maulings in 1979 and 1983. Thus, the first task of this chapter is to set the historical context for the change and how the endorsement of a preference accommodation approach defined how the party intended to secure its primary goal of securing office (Strom, 1990).

The historical struggle over Europe

Throughout the postwar era, successive governments have found Britain's continuing economic decline difficult to deal with and manage in such a way as to minimise disruption to domestic politics. In adhering to the prevalent view of Churchill's three circles of interest, whilst painfully acknowledging the decline from its hegemonic global status, the emphasis of all governments has gradually swung towards Europe. The motivation behind this was a blend of pragmatism coupled with the economic imperative driven by changing trading patterns. For many it remained difficult to retreat from Britain's global position to one in which Europe was the prime interest, particularly when Britain's strategic imperatives continued to be the pursuit of multilateral free trade and the organisation of defence of the capitalist world under the leadership of the United States. Application for membership of the EC therefore indicated a realisation that these objectives were being undermined by the development of the EC without Britain.

For Labour, the issue has an additional complication with rival views evident within party ranks regarding the relevance and acceptability of moving closer to the evolving EC. This reflected the changing configuration of power within the party and the strength of the different component parts of the Labour Movement. Whilst in opposition up to and including 1963 Labour had opposed entry; in government between 1967 and 1970 it favoured and eagerly sought British entry on the back of the increasingly modest performance of the British economy when compared to her European rivals. This was prompted largely by the efforts of George Brown, the party's deputy leader. Under his auspices, the Prime Minister, Cabinet and the PLP were persuaded of the attractiveness of UK membership of the EC. As a result, Britain initiated its second attempt to join with its European neighbours. When it was back in opposition from 1970 to 1974, opportunism was to the fore, with Labour choosing to play adversarial politics. As Young remarks: 'Opposition in short gave control to the instincts of the Party, government gave it to the perceived necessities of the country' (Young, 1998, p. 260).

For the left of the party, Europe provided a vehicle for promoting and establishing a strong coalition against the leadership as well as for targeting the social democratic thinking that was strongly opposed to their principles. For the party leadership Europe provided an opportunity for rallying support and out-manoeuvring the left (George, 1992). It also enabled it to avoid confronting the issue directly, a relief to the leadership which was becoming increasingly divided over the issue, particularly with the appointment of the staunch European advocate, Jenkins, as deputy leader in 1970. Although a socialist programme was opposed by the majority of the PLP it received the backing of a number of constituency parties and large trade unions. This was sufficient to engender concern within the party leadership. Between 1970 and 1973 it managed to prevent the party conference from passing any motion of wholesale opposition to EC membership. Wilson was determined that no single element of the party should commit itself to withdrawal from the EC. Yet on 28 October 1971, 69 members of the PLP voted with the government to pave the way for entry to the EC and a further 20 MPs chose to abstain in the voting lobby.

This approach reflected and confirmed the unwillingness to sell the concept of European integration in other than pragmatic terms as this may threaten the strong sense of identity on which the nation still prided itself. In simple electoral terms this could also mean lost votes. However, when seeking to promote national unity it was not averse to fostering this by focusing on an external foe such as the EC. As subsequent chapters will prove, these are recurrent issues with which the Labour Party had to deal with after the policy reversal undertaken by Kinnock.

When the decision to hold a referendum on Britain's continued membership of the EC was made, Wilson was pre-occupied with retaining party unity in the light of the resolution passed at the 1973 party conference which declared that a future Labour government should withdraw from the EC. This had been reaffirmed at a special party conference convened in April 1975, with the conference judging that the terms of membership that had been re-negotiated by the government were insufficient to justify remaining in the EC in line with a manifesto commitment made in February 1974. This was placed in the hands of James Callaghan, newly installed as Foreign Secretary, whose basic instincts were more Atlanticist than European. He was accompanied in his dealings by Roy Hattersley and Peter Shore (anti-membership faction) representing different wings of the party, though Callaghan's role was predominant. The Cabinet, however, endorsed the new terms by 16 votes to 7. When Parliament voted on the terms, a majority of Labour members voted against accepting the new terms. The wording in the manifesto reflected the lack of deep thought on the whole issue by the party leadership. Consequently, in the mid-1970s Wilson's thoughts concentrated on: 'Trying to manipulate the domestic agenda in a way that presented membership (EC) as inevitable' (Buller, 2001, p. 223).

The idea of a referendum was first mooted by Tony Benn in the hope of appealing over the heads of the party leaders (George, 1992). The debate that ensued, however, followed the lines of an election and the voters ultimately chose to accept the guidance of the leading figures in the main parties, the majority of whom favoured continued membership of the EC. The process of consultation in which the government chose to engage was a strategy to protect its unity and reputation, whilst the voting choices made did not reflect an understanding of these particular issues: rather they represented a view on the personalities involved in advocating the opposing cases. As Butler and Kitzinger remark: 'the referendum was not a vote cast for new departures or bold initiatives. It was a vote for the status quo... The verdict of the referendum was unequivocal but it was also unenthusiastic' (1975, p. 280).

The clear referendum result merely closed one chapter of British politics without galvanising progress in a new stage of British political development, particularly with the rapid departure of Wilson and Jenkins. However, Labour's position was undermined by its weak Parliamentary position, whilst it also acted to protect national interest whenever it appeared threatened. Furthermore, the shifting of the anti-European Benn to the Energy portfolio did not assist the smooth workings of the Council of Ministers. The relaunching of the Labour Common Market Safeguards Committee placed additional stress on the government as it was keen to note any ill-effects of the EC on the UK. However, at the 1977 party conference an NEC resolution indicated quite clearly that elements of existing Community policy ran contrary to British interests as well as to ideas concerning Britain and Europe's future development. This caused considerable offence amongst the UK's European partners, whilst policy wrangles over regional, energy and agricultural policy did not help the UK's cause.

Labour showed little interest in full membership of the European Monetary System (EMS) when it came into operation in March 1979, though it did endeavour to maintain the value of sterling as though it were within the narrower band of fluctuation. This managed to balance the friendships with the US and Germany, yet Britain still had the benefit of more diversified trading patterns than some of its European neighbours. However, problems remained regarding budgetary contributions. The lack of enthusiasm evident in this period also contributed to a series of departures from the PLP by individuals who created the SDP, a more pro-European party. Yet as Labour's internal difficulties intensified, Callaghan was beginning to warm to the benefits of EC membership, recognising the advantages of Britain playing the part of a more constructive partner. At all times, however, he had to guard against hostile domestic reaction, though he favoured co-operation with his European partners on common problems.

The swing from Europe: the seeds of discontent

Bennism

The period immediately preceding the 1979 election witnessed the start of PLP activities becoming increasingly disputatious, thus confirming Duverger's (1954) observation that social democratic-labour parties tend more than other parties to reflect societies' conflicts within party organisation (Jann and Hehn, 2000). The Labour Party contested the 1983 election on a radical programme. This far exceeded any previous social democratic campaigning platforms, with its policies for EC withdrawal and the introduction of measures that were incompatible with continuing membership. These included selective import controls and currency controls.

In tracing the development of the fervent anti-European feeling that swept the party after 1979, two running sores returned to haunt the leadership. Firstly, there was the desire within some parts of the Labour Movement to implement what were deemed to be socialist policies and secondly, the dilemma of how to manage the economy in such a way as to make the first possible. The latter had to be attained whilst ensuring improved living standards for the party's core constituency of supporters.

Although the direct challenge offered by Benn to the leadership crystallised after 1979, his ideas and influence had been gaining support since 1974. This was despite the efforts of the leadership to place him in a peripheral role in government. During these five years, Benn, along with his backers, sought to lead an opposition grouping based on the conviction that continuing EC membership was damaging to the economy. His alternative was to galvanise the economy through some form of Alternative Economic Strategy (AES) which retained control of the key economic levers at national level. His case was advanced by continuing economic decline and the ultimate humiliation of a Labour government having to seek assistance from the International Monetary Fund (IMF) in 1976. However, to make any inroads on these fronts, policy change had to be preceded by structural change in the organisation of both the Labour Movement and the PLP. With the 1979 election defeat, the campaign was launched to target the relevant decision-making structures.

Mounting domestic economic difficulties from 1973 onwards demonstrated the increasing fallibility of Keynesian methods of economic management. These were placed under further strain by the speed of progress towards global interdependence. However, it was not apparent that the government was ready to consider ideas representing a repudiation of Keynesian principles. A policy vacuum was developing which the purveyors of an alternative strategy could exploit. As Jones (1996) observes, the deaths of two major representatives of social democratic thinking, Anthony Crossland and John Mackintosh, combined with the departure of Roy Jenkins for Brussels, left an ideological void to be filled. In the opinion of Featherstone (1988), the British economy was competing less effectively with its rivals, thus providing further ammunition for the anti-EC cause. Economic recovery supplanted EC withdrawal as a policy imperative, yet it made the latter far more acceptable to those advocating a far-reaching alternative approach that could trumpet the EC as the major scapegoat for domestic economic ills. For many, Europe provided a rallying point for those opposed to the leadership, as it was more easily understood by those fighting to preserve national sovereignty. The AES sought to offer democratic national self-government marked by protectionism and vehement anti-Europeanism. Withdrawal from the EC had to occur for a credible

AES to be implemented, as the policy demanded controls on trade, finance and investment to enable reflation via public works and the rebirth of industry. Selective nationalisation, accompanied by compulsory planning agreements, would ensure control over the commanding heights of the economy. These measures contributed to a radical nationalistic form of self-government. Thus, European policy reform was a prerequisite for economic reform, but the latter was easier to attain.

The decision to back EC withdrawal was made by the party in 1980 following a resounding conference vote. However, this decision solidified the link between the PLP's domestic programme and the desire to leave the EC. Yet it did not secure unity within the party, even with the defection of a number of leading pro-European members to the Social Democratic Party in 1981.

Opposition to the EEC was not the sole basis of Bennism. In responding to the breakdown of the postwar consensus, a clear opportunity presented itself to those who felt that too often radical ideas were jettisoned in favour of pragmatism. The reality was that the expressions of party conference regularly gave way to the demands of the party at Westminster. Within this perspective, European co-operation was not entirely rejected: rather, the problem was more concerned with the structure and accountability of the institutions (Benn, 1991).

Acting on the foundations laid prior to 1979, to many, Bennism represented the new face of Labour. On offer was a programme outlining a distinctive set of ideas requiring fundamental institutional reform of the party structure to enable policy change to be enacted. The changes recommended were in the areas of economic, foreign and defence policy (Bilski, 1977). Central to all of this was a repatriation of national sovereignty from the EC, NATO and the IMF. With these developments the goal of socialism in one country became more attainable. It was believed that the existence of a more ideologically driven Conservative Party compared to those of previous eras would help in promoting an alliance where progressive policies were to the fore.

Elliott (1993) encapsulates these plans in a series of interlocking elements. Bennism entailed the adoption of a dirigiste alternative economic strategy for the reversal of national economic decline accompanied by withdrawal from the EC to facilitate an economic programme forbidden under the Treaty of Rome. The nature of internal reforms required were designed to counter the charges of betrayal and under- representation referred to earlier. A redistribution of power in the party was sought in order to make the PLP and the leadership accountable to the party conference and the rank-and-file membership. Developing anti-European policy demonstrated a clear reflection of the wishes of the membership, though it also threatened Parliamentary sovereignty which they were keen to protect and extend.

The alliance that was established was not as strong as the media portrayed, which enabled the post-1983 reconstruction to move more quickly than anticipated, no doubt aided by the scale of the election defeat. Bennism, however, was not laid to rest until 1987.

The seeds of discontent

Sovereignty

As Fella (2000) suggests the 'Old Labour' conception of democratic government was grounded in retaining the absolutist levers of the state, based on the protection and retention of Parliamentary sovereignty. Yet from 1979 onwards the Conservative government was employing these same ideals to undo much of the social democratic consensus achieved between 1945 and 1979. This prompted the party's reflections and recognition of the need to alter its European policy as part of its desire to re-evaluate its attitude towards the distribution of power and democracy within the United Kingdom. This also implied a recognition of a changing international context.

During the 1979–83 period, what had initially started out as an issue of policy quickly transformed itself into an intense debate concerning an article of faith. The depth of the struggle over this issue diverted attention from a range of other policy issues and shifted the Labour Movement into a deep and damaging period of introspection. For those seeking far-reaching reform of the party, Europe became a symbol of considerable importance. The struggle within the party thus became one of asserting control over governing values and policy. Those opposed to EC membership wished to wrest back control over domestic policy issues which had international ramifications. The chief concern in this instance was an objection to the evident trend towards supranational decision-making. This view, however, was not endorsed throughout the Labour Movement. To some, it represented too great a threat to the existing Parliamentary order, whilst for others it signified the possibility of not being able to implement the grand socialist design.

Sovereignty and the Westminster tradition represent critical benchmarks for the Labour Movement, notably for those on the left. Bennites, in particular, were struck by notions of sovereignty (more especially popular sovereignty) and constitutionalism, with the need to ensure as little deviation as possible from controlling one's own affairs. However, this also hints at a paradox in that socialists by tradition are internationalist in outlook, as Nairn (1972) confirms.

Central to these anxieties is the matter of surrendering a policy to a supranational body perceived as antithetical. Jones and Keating (1985) identify three arguments justifying this perspective. The constitutional argument shows that EC membership undermines the autonomy of the British state, the sovereignty of Westminster, as well as the notion of popular sovereignty. For the Bennites, this also conflicted with what has been termed the instrumental argument, as membership of the EC also prevented the introduction of policies required for the establishment of a socialist society. Lastly, through the patriotic argument, Britain's status as a world power would be inhibited by its more restricted role as a member of a tightly knit organisation which prevented a wider global role. This typology was utilised as a means of demonstrating that EC membership was not possible and that moves towards greater European integration had to be halted.

The apparent contradiction within this is that the nationalist dimension should have been more appealing to the Conservative Party (this became increasingly evident in the following decade). The only substantive explanation for this is to be found in the critique offered by Nairn (1972). He offers nationalism as the only available bulwark against the advance of capitalism and its ability to operate beyond the recognised borders of individual states. However, he is choosing to ignore those elements within the Labour Movement which are receptive in varying degrees to the principles of capitalism. The Jones and Keating model (1985) which builds on the earlier work of Nairn (1972) is weak in two areas in that it makes little reference to economic policy-making or the need to retain party unity. Likewise, an explicit recognition of the importance of institutional party reform is also absent from the model. The ongoing European debate is inextricably linked to matters of party organisation, the distribution of powers within the party structure, the role of the leader and the influence of the dominant faction. Though of limited value, the typology helps to provide a framework to explain substantial elements of thinking within the Labour Movement during the late 1970s and early 1980s, a time that witnessed the triumph of activist politics. These resulted in the support of policies which alienated traditional party supporters (Seyd and Whiteley 1992). It also provides a focus for helping to define the primary goal set by the new leadership after the 1983 election in its recovery programme.

The dawning of the policy reversal

With the election of a new leader following the 1983 débâcle, policy strategy was no longer characterised by introspection, but by the realisation of the need to think in wider terms and to respond to the new political environment created by an electorally successful Conservative Party. This was in complete contrast to the situation prior to 1983, with Labour and the trade unions confident that the Conservatives would not secure a second term in office.

Although the election manifesto (Labour Party, 1987a) may suggest otherwise with its cautionary tone, the policy reversal was confirmed by the 1987 election. However, the significant change which did emerge was not marked by a major public debate or period of self-examination. This had been the case in the previous decade with the referendum on EC membership and during the period of Foot's leadership of the PLP.

The result of the May 1983 election ranks as one of the most catastrophic in the history of the Labour Party. In securing 27 per cent of the popular vote (Butler and Kavanagh, 1984), it was recognised that the future course of the party had to alter rapidly if an element of respect, credibility and possibility of being in government was to be restored. In securing such a low share of the popular vote, the PLP recorded its worst electoral performance since the 1918 election. When combining the poor result with the mistrust generated by unpopular policies, the demands for a new stance on Europe began to emerge. In reviving its declining electoral fortunes, the party recognised the need to abandon policies with which traditional supporters were displeased. These included unilateral nuclear disarmament, extensive nationalisation, the unwillingness to sell council houses to sitting tenants and most critically of all, withdrawal from the EC (Seyd and Whiteley, 1992). In seeking to move away from purely national solutions to problems, the party also had to address economic policy as a matter of urgency.

It was clear from the magnitude of the victories secured by both the leader and his deputy in their elections (Kinnock and Hattersley obtaining 71 per cent and 61 per cent of the vote respectively) that if the PLP was to pull back from the more unpopular policies of the immediate past, it would recover some of the lost ground. In electing two figures from differing wings of the PLP it was evident that there was an overwhelming desire for unity. Bennite policies had shown themselves to be electorally unpopular, thus leaving the ground open for a different and new approach. Its tone was moderate, with realism pervading much of the discussion within the disparate groupings that comprise the PLP and the Labour Movement. The Bennites were ironically providing the opportunity for policies which they found difficult to digest and had campaigned vigorously to prevent for a considerable period of time, though sections of them changed their thinking as the decade progressed. The myths of withdrawal had to be exposed, as laid down in the Labour Party Research Department document (1983c). Taking the United Kingdom out of the EC was simply no longer going to help win the next election and opinion poll evidence confirmed this (Gallup Poll Survey evidence, 1983–87 and Riddell, 1983). The leadership's recognition of this was confirmed by Joyce Quinn MP (personal interview, 3 July 1995), who has served the party both at Westminster (as a Shadow European Affairs spokesperson) and in the European Parliament as a staunch advocate of integration.

Through evaluating the private inferences from the public disclosures, it is evident from both public texts (the Strasbourg Speech to Labour MEPs September 1983, the *New Socialist* article 1984 and *Fabian Tract* No. 509 1985) and private conversations (personal interview with Neil Kinnock, 2 December 1996), that the goal of policy reversal was identifiable from early in the Kinnock–Hattersley era. However, the speed and extent of it were not as immediately evident, but were driven by the pace at which the leadership was able to secure control over the party. At the 1984 European elections, Labour's manifesto emphasised the ways in which the party could change Europe from within (Labour Party, 1984b). At this juncture, it was not able to accept all elements of the common manifesto of the Confederation of European Socialists, despite endorsing the document. In 1985, the party did not endorse the Confederation's statement on the European institutions, which it deemed to be overly supranational in tone.

A European dimension was apparent in many of the problem policy areas, yet despite the electoral trauma of 1983, it was not evident that the party lost votes because of its European stance as the issue had a low salience rating amongst voters. Therefore, the decision to engage in policy reversal, but by the same token choosing not to elevate it to public status, suggests both a recognition of the importance of the issue and a sensitivity to sections of the Labour Movement. However, party conference did not even debate European policy at its annual gatherings in 1985 and 1986. The policy change was dependent upon organisational change, and in securing greater control over the party machinery the leadership could start to build the dominant coalition of its choice, enabling the policy change to take place (personal interview with Charles Clarke, 30 June 1995, a member of Kinnock's Private Office).

The 1983 result forced the party to look very carefully at its support base and its future strategy. In so doing, the PLP had to consider whether the root cause of the crisis was driven by sociological or political factors (R. Taylor, 1987). In the case of the former explanation, was it a matter of economic and demographic change eating away at traditional support, with the party's appeal meeting the needs of a declining electorate, or a situation that could be remedied by changing policy? As Crewe (1993) indicates, there was a decline in the traditional support base, as long-established Labour support was affected by economic downturn. Adjustments in the labour market brought about by economic upturn would not be sufficient to restore the lost supporters. Changing the former was exceptionally difficult, with the unions also in some instances likely to prove resistant because of their innate conservatism which could block change (particularly so in the case of the Transport and General

Workers and the Associated Society of Locomotive Engineers and Firemen, unions that played a major role in the party power and voting structure). Altering policy was, of course, easier and had to be the path taken, particularly when viewed against the backdrop of decreasing union membership and influence. As R.Taylor (1987) shows, it was only in 1987 that the PLP was able to regain some of its traditional support lost at the previous two elections. Yet significantly, he goes on to show that support amongst white-collar trade unionists was lower than for the Conservative Party, whilst the rise of professional/managerial groups (18 per cent to 27 per cent, 1964–1987) and the decline in manual workers (47 per cent to 32 per cent 1964–87) indicates an erosion of traditional PLP support. This reality was compounded by the fact that demographic and social trends were increasingly favouring conservative parties and neo-liberal ideas across Europe, at the expense of their social democratic rivals.

The party managers resolved that the problems were primarily political rather than organisational (Internal Report of the NEC June, Labour Party, 1983c), although it was clear that a twin-track approach was needed. This would combine policy reformulation with party reorganisation, but it could only succeed if based on strong party management and a united structure. As a later NEC document (Internal Report September, Labour Party, 1983d) declared, the party had to listen to the electorate rather than make assumptions about what it felt and desired. The electorate, however, was still sceptical about European integration in that although there was no desire to leave the EC, there was concern about the pace of integration and the need to protect national interest at all times even when the threats to it appeared to be marginal (Gallup Opinion Survey evidence, 1983–87). Labour's decision to use the European issue as a pivot for its renewal and modernisation programme was therefore organised in such a way as to respond to international environmental change, with the leadership using Europe as a tool to promote change covertly, in a multitude of areas, without disconcerting the electorate.

What transpired demonstrates that the move was driven more by the forces of pragmatism than by the emergence of a new-found sense of conviction and this ties in with the approach of programme accommodation referred to earlier. The ideological shackles were being released. This was perceived as essential in the effort to boost popular appeal, endorsing the view that in a pluralist electoral system it is necessary to attract as broad a constituency of voters as possible. Furthermore, it is evident that the more a party shows itself able to adapt to new conditions, the more able it will be to retain votes. Had the leadership wished to move towards preference shaping, it would not have had the capacity to realise its ambitions, however modest they may have been, particularly before 1987. Although European policy had to be altered, it was not accorded high priority status: changes in other policy spheres, however, had the imprints of positive European thinking, most notably domestic economic management. Over the medium-to-long term, the leadership did have to ensure that it acquired the capacity to realise its ambitions, and this entailed the need to address the issue of organisational change as soon as possible.

Stimuli for change

Having acknowledged the immediate constraints on the new Labour leadership as well as its desires in 1983, it is essential that the stimuli of the change are identified. The issues of effective party management, economic policy and the role of the trade unions were at the forefront of renewal, as they contributed to the development of a new attitude towards Europe. This contributed significantly to the forging and sustaining of party unity, in turn enabling the realisation of the primary goal as well as endorsing M. Shaw's (1994) paradigm concerning policy and leadership outlined in the previous chapter. None of this would, of course, be permissible without effective party management, which had to be the first priority. Finally, a failure to recognise the changing nature of the EC and the impact of this as a force for change domestically as well as internationally, would be a major defect in any analysis of the policy reversal. Thus, a framework for analysis emerges which differs from the traditional line, yet it does not fully reject the established norms, notably in the work of Shaw (1994) and Grahl and Teague (1988), who both refer to Europe in their analysis of the rebirth of the Labour Party. However, neither uses the European issue as the springboard for explaining the rebirth and modernisation of the party.

For progress to occur in the spheres of economic policy and handling of change, party leadership had to be asserted. This constituted the type of party management of which the PLP had been devoid since 1979: namely learning lessons from defeat, taking advice internally and externally, as well as demonstrating awareness of new political challenges from a potential realignment on the left.

Kinnock's inheritance was that of a shambolic party lacking confidence and harmony. The only way forward was to restore power to the party leader and the dominant faction he was assembling, restoring it from the NEC and undermining those loyal to Bennite strategies. Over and above this was the need to respond to the threats to the postwar consensus symbolised by Thatcherism. This required a response to the new economic priorities and climate established by the Tory government. Old policy recipes were no longer acceptable as far as the electorate was concerned, whilst the alternatives were limited especially if Europe was to be ignored or perceived in a negative light. However long the question of Europe was explicitly skirted, it impinged on the very heart of economic policy and revival, yet prior to 1987 the PLP leadership was able to direct attention elsewhere, by a combination of agenda management and reactive politics (personal interview with Charles Clarke, 30 June 1995). However, in 1986 at the party conference, composite motion 58, recognising that the United Kingdom is politically and economically integrated into the EC, was passed with a clear majority. This was a rare public expression of the policy change that the party was keener to articulate after 1987. The motion also made reference to the needs to support the Single Market programme and construct an EC-wide economic programme to combat unemployment and poverty. In seeking to restore an element of public confidence after 1983, the PLP had to look at the matter of economic management immediately. This was determined by the significance attached to economic policy as a criterion for gauging responsible party behaviour. Approaching this in a new style, distinct from the nationalistic tone that had coloured the AES, could provide the basis for progress and a recognition of a new start. In so doing, the PLP was already beginning its slow march towards accepting the EC as an organisation and institutional structure that offered opportunities to redirect policy, as well as a framework in which to formulate policies that could be used to benefit the whole electorate.

The drive for change was initially inspired by domestic rather than international factors. This included the emphasis on a new positive political deal in the campaign for the 1984 European Parliamentary elections, elaborating on Kinnock's positive public statements referred to earlier. During the campaign, Kinnock made considerable use of backing from colleagues in the Socialist Grouping in the European Parliament who spoke at meetings across the United Kingdom. This provided a complete escape from the scenario described by Kinnock when he remarked that: 'It was almost as if sections of the party measured the purity of their socialism by the distance which they could put between it and the minds of the British people' (Kinnock, 1994, p. 535).

The period of the second Thatcher administration corresponded with the emergence of a new sense of vigour in the EC. The era of Eurosclerosis had passed, with the Stuttgart Summit of 1983 recommitting the member states to the central objectives of the Treaty of Rome. Much of the internal squabbling between the member states over the broad direction and immediate funding of the Community had been concluded, progress on Monetary Union and the Social Dimension was speeding up, and the longstanding British rebate claim had been settled. The climate for the European debate, in so far as one existed within the UK, had altered, partly as a result of the financial deal brokered at Fontainbleau, but more significantly by the sentiments increasingly expressed by Kinnock. Most critical of all was his address to Labour MEPs in Strasbourg in September 1983, during which he called for a 'New Messina', a new European initiative geared to rededicating attention to the aim of economic and political strength and social justice at home and in the workplace. He believed strongly that the EC had a fundamental role to play in shaping the western half of the continent, albeit with modifications to the existing treaties.

Kinnock also declared at this early stage in his leadership that the British Labour Group in the European Parliament was to link up with the Socialist Group. Such progress was clearly going to have an influence on developments within the Labour Movement, as the context for the discussion about Europe had altered and developments within the EC opened possibilities for regulating the market, setting minimum standards for consumers and workers. It also closed policy options formulated by those keen to preserve national sovereignty at all costs. Europe was no longer viewed with derision and cynicism and many in the Labour Movement were starting to convert from being reluctant to more convinced Europeans.

Thus, the domestic and international agenda of the Labour Movement was changing. Welcome opportunities presented themselves and adversarial politics could be played, capitalising on vehement Euroscepticism in Tory ranks. Events appeared to favour the new players in the leadership. This helps to explain the attitude of those represented by the comments of Clive Jenkins, General Secretary of the Association of Scientific and Managerial Staff (ASTMS), who showed himself willing to recant on the European issue whilst addressing Labour Party Conference in 1988: 'We were right in our day' (Jenkins, 1990, p. 138).

The fact that the Community was changing and developing in a fashion acceptable to the PLP is reflected in the manifestos drafted for the elections in 1983 and 1987. The following comments substantiate this development:

> The next Labour government ... is bound to find continued membership a most serious obstacle to the fulfilment of these policies (Labour Party, 1983a, p. 33).

> Labour's aim is to work constructively with our EEC partners to promote economic expansion and combat unemployment (Labour Party, 1987a, p. 15).

The challenge remains one of not simply seeking to establish the impetus for the changes which have been referred to and which will be detailed and expanded on in later chapters, but also to ascertain what, and who, really motivated and drove the changes and for what purpose beyond programme renewal. The reality of change is beyond dispute: the style, timing and influences are subject to much conjecture. The crucial matter is to remember the basis and foundation of change and the vehicle enabling development to occur: namely strong leadership, guaranteed by greater clarity of vision and control of the PLP and the Labour Movement which were increasingly manifest. Most critically of all, this development was being crafted by skilled internal political management, a characteristic of New Labour in the second half of the 1990s.

As Lloyd (1990) suggests, the real issue is one of determining when the PLP converted to full Europeanism, in effect accepting the majority of principles that underpinned the modern and evolving brand of social democracy being offered more widely in other western European governments. This required a sense of conviction as opposed to mere pragmatism and the endorsement of incremental change. In the United Kingdom, progress in the PLP can best be examined by considering, in turn, the issues of party management, economic policy, and the role and influence of trade unions.

Party management

How, then, was the new leader to take up the challenge? From the outset of his leadership, Kinnock had to juggle three sets of concerns in his efforts to lead his party out of the trough of June 1983. He had to cultivate the authority of a statesman and future Prime Minister to ensure that his party management was effective, but in seeking to realise this objective, he also had to carry the political baggage involved in still having to support policies which he did not necessarily accept. This remained the case, particularly as his room for manoeuvre was limited by the nature of party organisation inherited. His predicament was not helped by one of the key elements of his personal manifesto for Europe being published over six months later than originally intended, as this slowed the initial impetus for change (personal interview with Neil Kinnock, 2 December 1996). The basis of his approach to politics was to accept and work within the new political debate dominated by Thatcherism. This implied the need to reconcile the wish to form a government committed to socialist ideals with the fact that this was not acceptable to the electorate.

In responding to this dilemma, the options were either to compromise or to wait for a change in the climate and mood, but the latter was ruled out by the simple issue of political survival and changing socio-economic and demographic trends. Thus, the party opted for a major change and organisational overhaul. Any new leader of the PLP other than a loyal Bennite would have moved in this direction, although the speed and comprehensiveness of the programme would have varied: hence the emergence of a new type of thinking based on realism and moderation, which incorporated elements of what Tindale (1992) has termed 'limited social democracy'. This required the acceptance into policy thinking of the need to move the party towards a more positive perspective on European integration.

Kinnock's immediate challenge on succeeding to office was to defuse the atmosphere of antagonism, a process which could not be completed quickly. However, he could and did begin to orchestrate a realignment of thinking which enabled him to move his supporters into positions of influence. This allowed them to utilise their networks in extending the new mood of realism and constituted what Minkin (1991) has described as 'new loyalism', an influence that grew as Kinnock's managerial style took hold of the party. It soon manifested itself in the support that could be drawn on in discussions and votes within the party structure. In policy terms, this became evident in a new willingness to accept lesser levels of interventionism in favour of the injection of an element of market forces, a reflection of a major change in party policy and an acknowledgement of the importance of the Thatcherite agenda in respect of the political economy.

Regardless of the emergence of a new mood, albeit initially by force of circumstance, it was clear to the new leadership that progress had to be slow and carefully managed (Kinnock, 1994). The very nature of the party structure inhibited change, with the Shadow Cabinet not within the gift of the leader's appointment.

Defeat on the initiative to introduce 'One Man One Vote' (OMOV) in 1984, which the party leader had heavily promoted, confirmed that any major programme of change had to be preceded by the garnering of votes. Otherwise, the leader would be undermined, and the twin-track programme for change would be gravely wounded. Consequently, the leadership chose to tackle the labyrinthine party structures, opting for discussions with representatives from across the range of Labour Movement interests with a view to sensing opinion, policy need and direction. As these needs were imperative, it is self-evident that any policy reversal could only be successfully realised once the desired changes were in place.

As far as European policy was concerned, this was well down the priority list, particularly as it was viewed as a matter of foreign policy (personal interview with Neil Kinnock, 2 December 1996): consequently, progress was going to be slow. This did not, however, imply that the principle of change was being overlooked. In his programme of policy change, Kinnock (1994) identified three sets of policy, all geared to programme accommodation. These were policies that could be changed as a result of decent organisation (Europe), those that needed greater effort and careful timing (policy on nationalisation) and those that demanded more time and the winning of difficult battles (defence). Yet even then his references to Europe only concerned the overturning of the hostile attitude towards the Community. Interestingly, there is no direct mention of economic policy which would have to be reformed first, in order to make a European policy credible. Furthermore, any thoughts of preference shaping policy would have to take a back seat because of the constraints placed on the leader which only began to ease after 1985 (Shaw 1994). At this stage, the issue of Europe was thus a matter of secondary importance, even though it was acknowledged that change was necessary.

It was at this point that the leader played an important card in appointing a team of keen and loyal backers to help with the implementation and sale of policy, the most important of whom were Larry Whitty (Party General Secretary), Peter Mandelson (Director of Communications) and Joyce Gould (Director of Organisation). Meanwhile, in Kinnock's Private Office, Charles Clarke, Patricia Hewitt, John Eatwell and John Reid each played an important role in co-ordinating, presenting and selling policy over a considerable period of time. This helped in creating a dominant faction in the party hierarchy which was central to the introduction and implementation of Kinnock's objectives. This confirmed Harmel and Janda's (1994) thesis concerning party goals and party change which emphasises the critically important role of dominant factions within political parties.

Within the inherited structure, there had to be co-ordination between the key groups at national and local levels, with the arguments having to be won convincingly over the longer term rather than simply being driven by the electoral imperative. As Davies (1996) remarks, what was required and, as the evidence demonstrates, delivered, were the: 'sinuous skills of the party manager' (Davies, 1996, p. 411).

This was in preference to the more widely known evangelistic qualities that Kinnock had often publicly displayed. Healey (1989) remarked that the new leader was set on ridding the party of its disadvantages–the image and reality of division and the inordinate influence of outdated dogma and the role of trade unions in determining party leadership and policy priorities. His campaign for the leadership did not indicate the major changes to follow or the style in which they were to be enacted, because in the summer of 1983 the concern was with re-establishing unity. Naturally he had to secure his position before entering any major schemes and no doubt he was aware of the problems associated with previous attempts at party renewal, most notably under Gaitskell. He was the last PLP leader to attempt a comparable rebuilding programme. As Kellner (1989) comments, Kinnock avoided this problem by virtue of his style: 'Mr Kinnock patiently coaxed the Labour machine into changing its trajectory, whereas Gaitskell handed down the tablets from on high' (Kellner, 1989, p. 14).

This need was particularly pressing in view of the fact that the formal powers of the PLP leadership whilst in opposition were limited. Responsibility for formulating policy and managing the party were very much in the hands of the NEC which could engineer change. Kinnock soon realised that the party had to be steered to a more centrist position which reflected public concerns on policy needs. Social and economic developments were clearly threatening party support and a strong government coupled with a hostile media underpinned the need for positive action. However, Kinnock soon discovered that the state of the party was different from that which he required to bring about the necessary changes. As Shaw (1996) notes, in opposition, the power of the Parliamentary leadership hinged upon a series of right-wing majorities in key bodies. To function effectively, this required consensus over ground rules, principles and policy priorities. In the legacy left by Foot, little of this was evident. It was not until 1985 that through his actions and those of his increasing band of loyal supporters, Kinnock became able to realise his goals on the NEC. This revolved around moving the PLP to a more centrist position, a development which needed not only the backing of the Shadow Cabinet, as it was the NEC that could enforce or deny the change.

Irrespective of the changes brought about, it must be remembered that the significance of these has to be set in the context of the changing perceptions of the leader himself. For the changes to occur, Kinnock had to alter his outlook. During his early years in the House of Commons when he had been a leading figure in the Tribune Group on the left of the party, his thinking was best summarised in comments such as those outlining Labour's central Socialist purpose: 'To fundamentally transform the structure of power and system of ownership in Britain' (Kinnock, 1980, p. 416).

In advocating democratic socialism, he believed in securing control over the commanding heights of the economy. Even at the start of the Thatcher era, he still retained traditional views but they were always based upon constitutional, democratic and Parliamentary methods. Pragmatism soon became evident when he identified two possible routes for future action which he described as socialism by prescription and socialism by plod (Kinnock, 1980), with the latter implicit in its gradualism identifying the course to be followed. This was a decision confirmed when Kinnock refused to support Benn in the 1981 contest for deputy party leader. However, he retained his support for Clause Four and in so doing, distinguished himself from social democratic thinking. Yet he also managed to carve out a niche that would be acceptable to the broad strand of members when it came to the election to succeed Foot as party leader. This was also beneficial to the aim of introducing a mandate to put in place long-term changes to the party so as to prepare for government on the basis of a realist approach extending beyond mere electoralism. These strides also involved an acknowledgement of economic changes, including the meeting of both international and domestic obligations (Kinnock, 1984). Though an oblique reference, this was signalling the rejection of the AES, a further key imperative in the new approach and the mark of a leader who increasingly knew where he wished to take his party and the rest of the Labour Movement.

As has been noted, establishing the ground rules for changes was one thing, enforcing them was a different matter. With the increasing strength of the left during the early and mid-1970s, the NEC had become more of a hindrance than an asset to the front bench, regularly sniping at the party leadership. Consequently, two entrenched camps developed and the power of the leadership was undermined. With the electoral defeat, it was decided that a new system of joint NEC–Shadow Cabinet Committees should be created to promote co-operation between what had become rival groupings. Kinnock, however, did not visualise joint policy determination, rather a reclaiming of control by the leadership. For this to happen, the NEC's role as a proxy player for the Annual Conference had to end, a development that would be greatly helped by the party leader gaining control over the NEC.

Any underplaying of the strength of resistance within the Labour Movement to Kinnock was cast aside after the defeat of the leader in his attempt to introduce the concept of 'one man one vote' for Parliamentary reselection by 3.9 million votes to 3.04 million votes at the 1984 party conference. Two further blows were soon dealt to the leadership in its efforts to redirect the party towards the centre: namely the unwillingness of overspending local councils to set a domestic rate in the face of legislation which could enforce fines and possible disqualification from office for those implicated, and industrial action by the National Union of Mineworkers (NUM) in the face of threatened pit closures. Both issues involved the expending of considerable time and energy and proved to be major distractions for the new leadership. The leadership was desperate to be released from oldstyle conflicts, as it knew that the Thatcher administration would punish them by taking more of the PLP's diminishing core support.

By mid-1985 the situation was altering and at this point Kinnock began to realise that he now had the opportunity to assert himself fully (Shaw, 1994). The miners' strike was over and the non-compliance over rate-capping was also breaking down. Kinnock took the opportunity presented at the 1985 party conference to use these two issues as a vehicle for coming down harshly on those elements that led and galvanised the two disputes. This greatly assisted in his drive to lessen the power of that section of the left which he most deplored. It also demonstrated a determination to manage the party more firmly, an image that could now be projected to the wider public by Kinnock and his increasing troup of loyal backers. Longstanding constraints were now being eased and the leadership was no longer seriously challenged. Few would disagree with Shaw's (1994) comment that: 'Historically, the key to effective leadership has been the ability to institute a system of integrated organisational control which binds together, under the authority of the leader, the main centres of power' (Shaw, 1994, p. 159).

By 1987, Kinnock was well on the way to realising the objective identified above, yet, as the latter section of this chapter will demonstrate, in order to be completely successful he had to call upon support from the unions too. Effective party management, however, was the glue that would hold together all the other initiatives that the leadership desired. In reality, it was the priority, as it underpinned all else that was being attempted. Although Europe did not feature as an early explicit priority objective, it was fundamental as the all-important mechanism for assisting the realisation of the changes deemed necessary after the reflection and analysis stirred by the 1983 election result.

Economic strategy

Within the new party strategy, economic policy was the area most in need of rapid and thorough attention, as it provided one of the first means of reversing the party's fortunes and of fostering positive public attitudes towards it. As John Edmonds, leader of the General Municipal Boilermakers union (GMB) remarked (personal interview, 13 June 1995), economic policy was untenable and had to be overthrown in favour of a more pragmatic position. This comment was endorsed by David Foden of the European Trade Union Institute (personal interview, 20 September 1996), who suggested that changing economic policy was essential as a distinct era had passed.

Over time, the economic policy overhaul provided the launch-pad for the evolving European policy. This was based on seizing opportunities via an acknowledgement of the benefits to be accrued from integration, as opposed to a policy based on the perceived threats presented by the European institutions. This was first evident in the 1984 European election campaign and more so as Kinnock's control over his party grew.

During the first Thatcher administration, the PLP had proposed a combination of devaluation, exchange controls and import controls in order to circumvent capital flight and currency speculation whilst stimulating reflation. What was to be done depended on how quickly existing European policy was to be jettisoned, but the wider question was whether Keynesianism remained a credible option, particularly as inflation had to be controlled at all costs. Even allowing for the removal of AES, there was a lack of clarity about how it was to be replaced. The rapidly-changing environment presented those ill-disposed to capitalism with a series of choices. Could existing strategies be retained, albeit in a much adapted vein, or was a new modern pan-European social democratic approach now appropriate?

Overturning the negative European policy demanded certain urgent changes, principally involving the main elements of AES, the attempt to revive the economy through the regaining of national economic and political sovereignty by ending the dominance of City-based external-oriented finance capital. This would enable the Labour Movement to increase its influence and control over larger elements of the economic and political environment. It would also extend the remit of trade unions in relation to policy-making, re-instituting corporatism and maintaining their longstanding role of providing ballast within the Labour Movement. However, the rest of the economic strategy remained uncertain as the party considered how to formalise its new strategic economic path in a rapidly evolving climate which was challenging the longer term survival of socialism. This threat, as Costello, Michie and Milne (1989) maintain, was based on rapid industrial change, quickly reducing the size of the working class as well as containing the threats from continuing internationalisation and deregulation. Further to these developments were a series of major international structural changes: each of these impacted on the formulation of a competent and credible economic policy, namely the increasing debtor status of the United States, the easing of tensions between the superpowers and the development of the EC with regard to its extending range of policy competencies.

The PLP was presented with a dilemma in so far as socialist objectives could not be met because of the prevalence of international constraints, yet these could be overcome by seeking to use the powers of the sovereign state to insulate the national economy from such constraints. This had been attempted after the financial crises of 1931 and 1970. As Gamble (1992) remarks, however, on both occasions this followed recession and adverse reaction to internal party difficulties and poor electoral performance. In striving to displace the prominence of the rank-and-file, this type of thinking could no longer be acceptable. As a consequence, this resulted in the option being rejected, representing a clear victory for the party hierarchy with the assistance of elements within the trade union movement.

By the time of the post-1987 Policy Review, the essence of economic policy was very different. The groundwork was, however, carried out before the 1987 election. In arriving at the new position, internal and external factors were at work, which impacted on the primary goal that had been identified. International developments and increasing ties with both unions and socialist parties via the Confederation of European Labour Parties provided models for study, adaptation and application. These also incorporated ideas such as those projected by Holland (1983) in his 'alternative European strategy' prompted by the Forum for International Political and Social Economy. This body emphasised a co-ordinated approach to matters of reflation, restructuring and the redistribution of resources: the underlying premise being that Europe is largely self-contained in economic and political terms and that the lynchpin of progress is advancing the process of integration. This had to be undertaken on the basis of programmes deemed acceptable to political parties espousing socialist or social democratic ideals. It was these developments that stirred the first positive thoughts about the practical value of the EMS.

On the other hand, lessons had to be learnt from the French experience. The government had been elected on a ticket of breaking with capitalism, after which there was one year of frenzied economic activity in France resulting in reflation, a doubling of the minimum wage and a 27 per cent increase in public expenditure (Tindale, 1992). It had chosen these policy options in an unfavourable climate, yet the costs were so high that they had to undertake a humiliating policy reversal in the face of a severe balance of payments crisis. Macshane (1991) has most cogently conveyed the real lesson (not the interpretation of those disinclined towards the EC): 'To seek to implement policies without the fullest reference to what is happening beyond national borders is to invite disaster, as the French discovered' (Macshane, 1991, p. 357).

In terms of conventional strategies (Teague, 1989), the national approach demands that the instruments of economic policy-making must be retained at state level. Yet this was the model used by the Mitterand government and by the Labour Party in 1964 and in the 1983 election. European institutions increasingly had to be viewed as the only means of achieving an interventionist policy no longer sustainable at national level due to the power of international capital. The nation-state was therefore no longer able to function as an effective tool in securing and protecting Labour's objectives.

Thus, conventional socialist economic thinking had to undergo major change. The rapid collapse of the French experiment sharpened the sense of urgency to devise a new approach. The impetus and direction of change were clearly enunciated by Newman (1983): 'At some stage it is likely that the relative failure of the left in each country to attain its goals will bring about a transformation of consciousness. No doubt this will only occur where there is a clear change in material circumstances' (Newman, 1983, p. 279).

Others, especially amongst the unions formerly sceptical of the EC, were also prepared to acknowledge the new environment and conceded that there was a gain to be accrued from a supernational pooling of sovereignty. In their view, this had considerable application to the conduct of multinational companies increasing their economic strength and political power through the reshaping of industrial production and the division of labour as well as on environmental matters. A means of control over the dynamic forces of internationalisation was sought and was no longer available via trade unionism alone or through an established national political programme. This was recognised, despite the fact that the level of emasculation in Britain was not evident elsewhere in western Europe. However, this posed two major questions. Could this new arrangement be found, and how in line with socialist principles could it be? For the party, the implication of the change was considerable as it confirmed a severance with the immediate and damaging past and the first important step towards re-establishing itself in the minds of the voting public. The rhetoric of change was quickly evident in the comments of George Robertson, soon to be appointed the Party's European spokesperson: 'We want to see the European nations dealing with problems of growth, unemployment, the recession and the challenge of technology; and we will use any institutions which exist at the moment to make sure it happens' (Robertson, 1984–85, p. 223).

Without this, progress in many other areas would not have occurred. Consequently, the European issue, albeit through the vehicle of economic policy, became the core of the party's policy change. This is a reality ignored by too many academics examining and explaining Labour's recent past and one that is continuously reinforced by the ongoing analysis in subsequent chapters.

Role of the trade unions

A large element of the British political process, in terms of participation and organisation, is predicated on the fact that: 'The Trade Union connection has shaped the ethos and organisation of the British Labour Party ever since the latter's birth at the turn of the century' (Taylor, 1993, p. 424).

With the inextricable historical linkages, party management, by definition, also meant union management. Furthermore, the PLP found itself in a unique position in terms of its legitimate right in giving political form and expression to the collective representation of the British working people, more especially the working classes. The PLP was always concerned with balancing the need to retain the core support of unions and their financial backing. Trade union links were both unavoidable for reasons of finance, yet awkward because of the impact of the block vote. The block vote was, of course, important to the leader in realising policy objectives and in retaining the backing of the Labour Movement, but could just as easily work in reverse. The PLP had always relied on the unions for its sound financial footing and campaign expenditure via affiliation fees. Despite decreases in the 1980s, with affiliation fees dropping dramatically from 6.5 million in 1980 to 5 million by 1990 (Heffernan and Marquasee, 1992), the link has remained important. Declining support for the PLP was, of course, also having an impact on union membership.

It was the TUC, however, that undertook one of the first full analyses of the Single European Market (TUC, 1988b), yet well before the publication of this seminal document, the unions, prompted by the TUC, were attempting to mastermind a change in attitude to their natural opponents, which for many included the EC (Rosamund, 1993).

A dilemma soon presented itself to the party leadership: namely the realisation that the visibility of the unions is perceived as a negative characteristic by the electorate, but the promotion of electora bility for the Labour Movement requires the assertion of union influence at both national and local level. This helps to guarantee the backing of the working-class vote. Thus, change may be thought necessary, but the passage to it was easily blocked by a reluctance to alter the system.

Traditionally, the unions have not been opposed to change provided they have been able to guarantee the link with the Labour Party. In the 1980s, their position was seriously undermined by economic changes more than industrial relations legislation. In terms of government legislation, there is little doubt concerning the impact of outlawing the closed shop and the ending of statutory recognition procedures. The rise in unemployment, decline in manufacturing, changes in the class structure, falling membership, fewer resources and the internationalisation of production all combined to make the environment tough for the unions. This was especially the case for those representing workers in the traditional industries. The diminishing economic power of workers was matched by a similar decline in political influence which could be overturned by the return of a Labour government, though it quickly realised that it was beyond the capacity of the PLP to restore the external environment that formerly prevailed.

As the 1980s progressed, the European question was increasingly framing the domestic political agenda with the tentacles of the Community stretching ever wider. In view of the inextricable links between the unions and the PLP, it is evident that the unions played an important role in stimulating the new policy position. (This allows for the existence of unions still unconvinced by the Community.) In terms of the first Parliament of the period under examination, the issues begging investigation are whether the pace of change was determined by the unions, if so at what speed, and what the implications of this were for the PLP in formulating its European policy. It is also significant to note that the domestic environment was being fashioned to some extent by a changing external environment, where ideals best summarised as social democratic (using the earlier Tindale interpretation) were taking hold and indirectly helping to develop a convergence of approaches suited to integration. By implication, a pooling of sovereignty followed.

The unions were undoubtedly highly influential in promoting the policy change which they ensured came about more quickly than it may otherwise have, with the agenda of most large unions shifting substantially from political to economic issues, so as to meet the changing needs of a declining membership. At the same time, the PLP would not have formulated a policy counter to majority thinking in the unions because of the implications in terms of the dual support they provided. Rather, the PLP was content to build on an inherited foundation, which an increasingly assertive leader could exploit for public and electoral gain, through the processes of modernisation and policy renewal. This points to the need to build on the work of those scholars of the Labour Movement who make reference to the issue of Europe, namely George (1992), Rosamund (1990, 1992, 1993), Grahl and Teague (1988) and Teague (1989). These academics establish a framework for analysis of the change, but one that is restrictive in so far as it treats the key players separately. A complete understanding necessitates a more integrated analysis, making use of the Shaw (1994) model in which he refers to 'new strategic thinking'. In his view, renewal and modernisation were driven by the desire to defeat the Conservatives at all costs which demanded programmatic and organisational changes. In his references to the party power structure, he notes the emergence of a new dominant coalition including union representation bent on reform that manages to assert itself through internal realignments. Yet even in this work, the references to Europe are minimal and the developments are accepted as statements of fact, as opposed to being questioned and used as part of an overarching explanation.

However, during the 1980s, British trade unions underwent a period of crisis, with the election of a Conservative government seeking to end their political role through the passage of legislation designed to minimise their consultative role, curb strikes and complicate recruitment processes. The era of growth, influence and status known as the 'Fourth Estate' gave way to membership decline, whilst technological advancement and the inevitable deskilling that follows gave management more control over the work process. To undermine the PLP, the initial task was to erode the union base, as the Labour Party shorn of this would more than likely be afflicted by internal strife and factionalism. Trade union membership peaked in 1979 when it stood at 13 million, but by 1990 it had declined to just under 10 million (Gallie et al, 1996).

Although unemployment did begin to fall in the second half of the 1980s, the new jobs created did not generate additional members. This was primarily due to the nature of the employment created in the services sector. Yet it can be argued that these trends were existent in the second half of the 1970s: however, the impact was not as negative. This implies a possible change in public mood and a comment on the effectiveness of the unions, most notably in respect of communication channels between the leadership and the members.

To retain any semblance of significance in national life, the unions required a new agenda, one that could also help to secure the electoral victory of the PLP. For the unions, despite the misgivings of some on policy, the PLP remained the only credible political expression of their values and interests. This acknowledged that they still retained an organisational machine capable of effective campaigning, as well as appealing to the backbone of PLP support. In this regard, it is interesting to note the discussion generated at the 1983 TUC Annual Congress by the National Union of Communications Workers (NUCW). Their introduction of the Composite motion 18, which attempted to awaken the rest of the union movement to the new realities and changing parameters brought on by the 1983 election result, was symbolic in beginning a period of reflection.

This conclusively proved that Thatcherism needed to be strongly countered if it was to be overcome. Although Alan Tuffin, the leader of the NUCW, was not striking a 'for or against' pose, this intervention was important as the first positive sign of the need to carve out the new positive agenda. Although the motion was defeated, its significance lies in its inclusion on the agenda, as it focused thinking on the longer-term strategic needs, as opposed to the immediate forces of electoralism. The 1983 Congress legitimised a change of direction, confirming a new sense of thinking most clearly articulated by Alistair Graham, General Secretary of the Civil and Public Services Association (CPSA) when, during Congress, he strongly rebuked the TGWU for their outdated attitudes to future TUC strategy. In his belief, they still assumed that the Thatcher government was to have a short lifespan, thus lessening the need for major reform.

Predominant union opinion had long been insular, with a stiff resistance to the process of European integration. Teague (1989) identifies three camps within the union movement: 'anti-European', 'pragmatic' and 'pro-European'. As the 1980s progressed, the latter became the more significant, undoubtedly boosted by the TUC and the backing for Europe displayed increasingly by its General Secretaries and their longstanding Deputy General Secretary, David Lea, as well as its permanent secretariat. At the start of the decade, the situation was very different, as at the 1981 and 1983 Annual Congresses, resolutions were passed demanding that a future Labour government withdraw Britain from the EC. The notable hostility expressed by some, and led by the TGWU, was founded on the perception that socialist ideals were most likely to be realised in a strong nation-state, free from as much outside intervention as possible. In developing a new approach based on a realistic reading of the changed environment, charges of opportunism were levelled at the unions for their change of heart, albeit more rapid for some than others, particularly on the question of involvement with the EC. However, as Rosamund (1993) correctly states, what transpired was not pure opportunism, but can be explained as the unveiling of a new strategy demonstrating an awareness and understanding of the ever-more pertinent concept of transnational policy-making. This was deemed to have even more to recommend it as a consequence of the marginal influence on domestic policy-making. As the Manufacturing Science and Finance Union commented: 'As the internationalisation of business, industry and the Community itself intensifies, so must the Trade Union response' (MSF, 1988, p. 9).

As Rosamond (1993) maintains, the forces of nationalism (Nairn, 1972) lost out to those of internationalism. This set the stage for the post-1987 era and the removing of obstacles to developments such as ERM entry and the undermining of an ideological approach to decision-making within the Labour Movement. Hostility to Europe largely evaporated and the bulk of trade unions felt able to strike out from the PLP in search of a degree of separation, rather than total independence. The unions were prepared to give leeway to the party leader and Shadow Cabinet in major aspects of policy renewal, provided that they were still actively involved in areas that most impinged on their activities, such as pay policy and labour law.

Historical antecedents prevented a total severing of ties. In Tindale's (1992) second timeframe, this involvement was reduced with the neutralisation of the TUC Liaison Committee and the activity of the less well-defined 'contact group'. In addition, some unions also began to reflect on footing the bill for a party that could not deliver election victory, one that locked them into antiquated traditions. Despite these difficulties, the unions were highly influential until 1987 in forcing the European agenda and, most significantly, many strongly believed in it as they could identify clear benefits from it. Having convinced the PLP of its worth, they were also inclined to play a more reserved role in policy-making within the Labour Movement, though not to the extent that soon transpired.

Equally, the new generation of union leaders were conscious of what Minkin (1991) has described as the 'unwritten rules' which serve to restrict the activities of union leaders. Awareness of their members' needs also made them tread carefully on issues that did not directly affect their members. Undoubtedly, the PLP leadership was also helped by the emergence of a new crop of union leaders whose actions were less rooted in the ideology of class struggle and far more in pragmatism. This enabled them to respond more effectively to the needs of their changing and declining memberships and the wider interests of the electorate. Within the Labour Movement, therefore, the unions could feel a certain element of satisfaction, particularly as leaders like John Edmonds (GMB) and Bill Jordan and Gavin Laird (both from the Amalgamated Union of Engineering Workers) possessed influence as supporters of the party leadership. This provided them with a level of respect previously denied to them by the media and public. They felt able to concentrate more on matters that suited them, which included promoting a European policy that the PLP could and subsequently did choose to use in moulding its own public position after 1987. Not only did these unions have misgivings about the links between the PLP and the TUC General Council, but they were inclined towards co-operation with their employers, the acceptance of management's right to manage free from overt interference, a reduced role for strike action and less direct political campaigning. Although not all management practices were being accepted, the above indicated an acceptance of a new element of realism.

Unions such as the Electricians Union (EETPU), the white-collar Union (APEX) and the National Union of Communications Workers (NUCW) soon recognised the benefits of participating in Europe and they have also played a consolidating role within the Labour Movement. They acknowledged that the electorate was wary of the unions displaying too much power or influence in high politics as opposed to matters of industrial relations, which have a less dramatic impact on a smaller constituency. This problem could be addressed, as Shaw (1994) recommended, by changes in policy, strategy and internal organisation, but equally importantly, this was overlooking their role of trying to preserve electoral support and placating the activist at constituency level. However, after 1983, this had to be carried out in a way other than that previously undertaken, so as to appear less threatening to the broad mass of the electorate. The emergence of Trade Unions for Labour Victory (TULV) in 1979 was an attempt to address this concern. This was a body separate from party machinery, with a stated aim of stimulating organisational and financial support for the PLP. However, after the 1979 election, TULV became a mediator in the struggles between the opposing wings of the PLP. The appearance of Trade Unions for Labour (TUFL) in 1986, in response to the previously cited problems, helped, but as the decade progressed it became an organisation geared more to fund-raising for a diversity of causes in the Labour Movement.

With the 1983 election confirming that the electorate was not happy about the level of union exposure, this presented a dilemma at the core of the issue of leadership control. For their part, the unions perceived themselves as playing a balancing act in ensuring electoral support and in responding to membership demands. Having also become entrapped in the constitutional wrangles of the late 1970s and early 1980s, the bulk of the unions settled for efforts to boost their own and the PLP's electoral fortunes: hence the backing for TULV, and, later, for the 1987 election campaign. The result of this stirred some of the more reluctant backers of change to rethink their strategies, particularly as the EC was offering policies that were attractive and unavailable in the domestic environment. It could also be used as a bulwark against any further attempts by the recalcitrant left to block change.

As the party leader gradually became safely ensconced, it became possible to consider developing a more distant relationship with the unions. In reducing the role of affiliated unions at conference, Kinnock was offering an olive branch to those who felt their leadership was not truly representing their needs. Such a move would, of course, be well received by the media, demonstrating his ability to show resolution in the face of the union barons. He also perceived the unions as a vehicle for the promotion of possible opposition to a future Labour government. In regaining a sense of distance, though not separateness, from them, he and his team believed that by returning to serving the interests of their members more directly, political matters would return largely to the PLP and industrial relations matters would remain with the TUC and other unions. This had largely been the case before the internecine strife had broken out in the late 1970s. The unions did not wish to portray themselves as a weak grouping that could be ignored either. They knew that the latter was not possible because of the multiple links that existed between themselves and the party. They also knew, therefore, that the PLP would not seek to introduce policy proposals that the unions would find untenable.

The response of the unions to this behaviour was interesting. They had to cope with the tough environment in which they found themselves, so they clearly did not want to jeopardise their relations with the Labour Party. At the start of the 1980s, it was evident that union leaders were convinced that the government would have to backtrack on policy in a vein similar to that of the Heath administration. However, this perception was quickly shattered and with the second Conservative election triumph, trade union thinking and more particularly that of the TUC began to alter. This helps to explain the increasing use of language suited to a set of more modest demands allied with an understanding of management's needs. The emphasis became one of conciliation as opposed to confrontation. With the continuing passage of industrial relations legislation and the desire on the part of government to weaken the unions, it was clear that the latter's hands were tied, a reality made all the more alarming with the outlawing of trade unions at the Government Communications Centre (GCHQ) at Cheltenham in early 1984. As was the case with the PLP, the Labour Movement had a choice to make with regard to policy priorities in terms of easing suspicion and galvanising union and public support in an economic and political climate far from conducive to them.

This was not simple expediency but the acceptance of a set of new realities, which only received the full glare of public attention at the 1988 TUC annual congress, with the positive reaction to the speech by EC Commission President Delors. However, an examination of the proceedings of the three previous years (TUC, 1985, 1986 and 1987) reveals that the European question was impinging more and more on the debates. At the same time, these developments must not be viewed as separate from the deliberations within the PLP concerning strategic change and the activities of an organised political opposition destined to play by the rules of adversarial politics.

Traditional explanations tend to view the period in terms of a slow decoupling of the PLP and the unions, setting the precedent for the 1990s. Undoubtedly the seeds of change were sown at the Strasbourg meeting with Labour European Parliament members in 1983 and nurtured further through the mid-1980s by a variety of factors specific to the PLP, as well as through the emerging social dimension and the appointment of Delors as President of the European Commission in 1985. Throughout the majority of unions (both affiliated and unaffiliated to the TUC), there was a need to attract immediate returns for members from an institutional framework that had the potential to offer greater benefits than could be gleaned domestically. The agenda for the PLP was different: it was changing in so far as a broader constituency had to be served and had to be managed carefully (remembering the constraints detailed earlier) because of the wider policy remit and the dual responsibilities of proving economic competence and party unity over the long term.

It is clear from the proceedings of the TUC, notably in 1982 and 1983 (TUC Annual Congress), that the PLP and the TUC shared similar priorities, with the TUC Liaison Committee the declared outlet for co-ordinating anti-government campaigns. This parallel thinking was, however, challenged by the emergence of realism, and the increasing discussions on the process of social dialogue, despite setbacks such as the crisis at GCHQ and the conflicts in the mining and print industries. For instance, in 1984, the TUC made a plea for support on a draft EC Recommendation on the reduction and reorganisation of working time, whilst in 1985, time was devoted at Annual Congress to the impact on working people of an integrated European Community. In 1986, TUC Congress devoted substantial time to the need for measures to open the internal market to be accompanied by policies to extend social development. Two major unions, the GMB and the AEU, were at the forefront of this push, both recognising the value of European institutional involvement and partnership with colleagues on the mainland. The debate had moved on from whether to stay in or come out, and was now focused on how to obtain the best deal as a committed participant. In fact, the issue of withdrawal from the Community was not discussed by the TUC after 1983. Similar progress was not evident in the PLP; however, the inclination of the leader was to move in the same direction, although his intentions were definite by 1984: 'Britain's future, like our past and present, lies with Europe' (*New Socialist*, March–April 1984, p. 9).

In view of the domestic exclusion, it was obvious that the European course had to be selected. This provided an opportunity to apply the knowledge accumulated since the early 1970s (Teague, 1989) and obtain the benefits offered by participating in the European policy-making process. Through the mid-1980s, the pro-European course was furthered by the creation of new contacts between unions, the work of the European Social Committee, Industry Committees via the European Trade Union Confederation (ETUC), and think-tanks, most notably the German Friedrich Ebert Foundation. In focusing initially on issues of social and industrial relations, identifiable and understandable gains could be obtained quickly. Moving in this direction clearly implied a complete rejection of the AES. This was a bold step and charted a course for the PLP to follow in its desire to attain its primary goal through the twin processes of renewal and modernisation, directed by firm leadership. As Macshane commented:

> For the first time in Trade Union history, Unions in different countries including Britain, were confronting the same problems, using the same language, demanding the same solutions, at the same time, and were conscious of doing so in a European as well as national context. (1992, p. 357)

Conclusion

In locating and explaining the dynamic of the European policy reversal which was crucial to the renewal and modernisaton of the party, the 1983–87 period is particularly vital. It is in this short period that the leadership began to reassert control over a party that had lost its direction and acute political antennae. The injection of realism into party behaviour orchestrated by the new leadership and directed through policy change was furthered by groupings within the Labour Movement which recognised the multiple goals the party had to attain if political credibility was to be restored. The party was no longer merely seeking office itself but the realisation of policy goals that would help in securing the vote essential to being electorally successful. Perceptions of competence and trustworthiness were enhanced by the adoption of a new economic policy free of traditional ideological underpinning, though increasingly marked by the tenets of neo-liberal thinking.

Whilst Kinnock and Hattersley were active in reshaping the PLP to match their objectives, they were helped enormously by those within the Labour Movement who identified the benefits available from a positive European policy. The work they carried out enabled the party leadership to address internal matters in the knowledge that certain unions were effectively carrying out a lobbying campaign on behalf of policy reversal which generated little ill-feeling. The lack of real opposition to the impending change which became fully public after 1987 reflected a lack of tension within the PLP and Labour Movement indicating that the leadership was establishing control. This provided the latter with a valuable inheritance and time to address their domestic priorities, which were being enhanced by the developing EC policy agenda driven increasingly by social democratic ideals. This also made economic policy reform easier to enact, whilst effective party management achieved considerable internal results as well as portraying the leadership as responsible to potential supporters. However, without the union leadership it is difficult to conceive that progress would have been as rapid, as the leadership agenda was so overburdened with the domestic agenda. Yet, it was the party leader who ultimately had to deliver the policy change in a way that was acceptable to the diffuse strands within the PLP and the Labour Movement.

It was the combination of a slightly improved electoral performance in 1987 with an increasing control over the internal workings of the party which enabled the policy reversal to be publicly
declared and legitimised via the Policy Review Process which began
after the election. With the full endorsement that followed, it
became increasingly apparent that European policy was to be
central to party strategy as Kinnock continued to apply the politics
of programme accommodation in his strategic thinking. This, after
all, was the most realisitic path that a weakened chief opposition
party could follow, whilst acknowledging the critical role of the
trade unions in advancing the European agenda within the Labour
Movement. This was despite the tension that still prevailed concerning the issue of sovereignty (Jones and Keating, 1985).

3
The Policy Review Process: Legitimising Change

Despite the slight improvement in performance of the PLP at the 1987 election as a consequence of the professionalism injected into party operations, Labour made limited inroads into the Conservative majority in the House of Commons. This third consecutive defeat proved even to those recalcitrant elements in both the PLP and the remainder of the Labour Movement that further significant reforms in respect of policy and organisation were needed to convince the electorate that the Labour Party represented a potential alternative government. As many maintain, the post-election review provided a focus for the leadership as a means of promoting policy change and renewing the party through the furthering of organisational adjustment in the policy-making machinery. This constituted a confirmation of the increasing strength of the leadership and the ascendancy of the new dominant faction in the party.

It is against this background that the subsequent Policy Review Process needs to be viewed as a key stage on the path from renewal to modernisation and ultimately electoral victory in 1997. The need for a review was not questioned within the Labour Movement (R. Taylor, 1987). As Merkel (1990) comments, no other socialist party in western Europe suffered such a dramatic vote loss in the 1980s and the need to address the problem was self-evident. Rather, it was a matter of how far the review should extend, how radical it was going to be in its recommendations and the degree to which Europe was going to be central to its conclusions. These were issues that only the leadership could resolve.

The review was fundamental in formalising and extending the process of change begun in the 1983–87 period, an era that witnessed the reuniting of the PLP, the first stage in the rebuilding of a decaying institution. It was a process in which the European question was very much the catalyst in determining key changes in other priority policy areas, particularly economic policy. In completing the political somersault on Europe that Rosamund (1994) outlines, Labour was able to use a new language concerning Europe in the final Policy Review document:

> The Conservatives are so bitterly divided on the European question that they cannot speak for the nation ... We believe Britain must be a leader in Europe, not a follower ... Europe must indeed be a community for people as well as a market for business. (Labour Party, 1991, pp. 52–3)

The European issue became the focus for unity and the driving force, albeit implicitly, within the Policy Review Process: it was no longer an isolated issue, as Rosamund (1994) argues. As Gamble and Kelly (2000) claim, Europe was presented in the Policy Review Process as: 'the framework within which any future Labour's governments efforts to improve British economic performance would have to be pursued' (Gamble and Kelly, 2000, p. 3).

This chapter will therefore seek to show how and why the Policy Review Process was an essential step in the renewal of the Labour Party, noting from the outset of this period that the position of the leader had been strengthened to some degree by the progress made in the 1987 election. Having identified a primary goal – namely that of office-seeking (Strom, 1990), a clear thrust for organisational and policy reform as well as the means for advancing change – the review provided the leadership with the means it required to further its objectives.

However, as with the analysis of any aspect of policy-making, the role of external events must never be excluded. Through the application of Harmel and Janda's (1994) theoretical perspective throughout the text in addition to those of Strom (1990) and M. Shaw (1994), it is clear that although influential, the external environment did not determine the impetus for the Policy Review Process in the eyes of the dominant party faction. Yet, it did play a part in determining some strategic decisions concerning policy emphasis and outcomes in accepting new political realities. The process provided the mechanism for altering and confirming the party's new policy profile and for confirming the strength of the leadership. Europe, by implication, had become a domestic issue.

The preservation and strengthening of party unity was critical in this regard. This enabled it to build on the foundations laid in the previous Parliament which were consolidated during Smith's brief tenure as leader (see Chapter 4), and advanced by Blair from 1994 onwards, as will be demonstrated in Chapters 5 and 6. Thus, the origins of New Labour's European policy were to become increasingly visible.

The four-year period of the Policy Review Process (1987–91) demonstrated how the party was modernising in respect of the control the leadership acquired over party organisation and policy, whilst displaying a clear European dimension to its policy intentions, even allowing for the evident caution needed in assessing the level of Europeanisation of domestic politics (Bomberg and Peterson, 2000). In accepting the continuing Europeanisation of the political process, Labour was using external intervention to a limited extent in moulding progress towards programme accommodation as its underpinning rationale for policy-making. However, the number of sections devoted exclusively to Europe in the Policy Review documents were limited. This development will be analysed by assessing the essence of the review process, its underpinning principles, the role of the unions within the discussions, the policy outcomes generated and most critically of all, the role of the leadership in directing the operation.

In tracing and explaining the steps taken by Kinnock and his team in creating a more professional party less weighed down by its ideological heritage, the party was moving away from what Lloyd (1990) described as its isolationist status. This marked a further step in arriving at a new blend of policy that drew upon traditional Labour thinkers and virtues, a process begun in 1984 with Kinnock's *New Socialist* article. In this approach, the EU was recognised as important in terms of its enduring power and its status as a potential economic and political superpower. Consequently, deeper involvement in this body as a means of prospering on a competitive level dictated that economic policies and priorities had to alter.

Acceptance of this helped to consolidate unity in the ranks of the Labour Movement. This helped to ensure a European foundation to policy aims and objectives across a wide range of areas, as Europe was no longer deemed to be a stand-alone issue or a peripheral foreign policy concern. It was now perceived as critical in the formation of economic policy and wider party strategy as its concerns increasingly cut across a range of policy competencies.

Essence of the review

The initial suggestion for a Policy Review came from Tom Sawyer, Deputy General Secretary of the National Union of Public Employees (NUPE). From his position on the NEC as an increasingly central figure in the dominant party faction, he argued the case for a review. This addressed the perceived gap between the party and the electorate on a considerable range of issues. Furthermore, as Taylor (1997) suggests, the review could be used to put an end to disunity, which would help in the contest to secure popular support. Kinnock endorsed these intentions (*The Times*, 14 July 1987) when he remarked that far-reaching changes were needed to match party policy with the demands of the electorate. The 1987 party conference set the process in motion in approving a resolution moved by John Edmonds, General Secretary of the GMB, demanding a review of the party's future activities that ensured its attractiveness and relevance to the needs of the working people. Furthermore, he stressed that the documents produced emphasised Labour's traditional values and collective approach to politics (Labour Party, 1987b).

When Party General Secretary Larry Whitty spoke to the party conference in 1988 (Labour Party,1988b), he projected the review as a forward-looking study designed to match the party to the needs of the voters, as well as pointing out those areas where a detailed examination of existing policy was needed. The former had already been established internally in a document entitled *Labour and Britain in the 1990s*, presented in November 1987 to the Joint Executive and the Shadow Cabinet. This had helped to push the party in the direction of a review, which always had victory at the next election as the ultimate goal, supplemented by a series of interlinked multiple goals designed to maximise the chances of this happening. However, it was appreciated that the Policy Review Process alone would not guarantee the desired result.

Recalling Seyd and Whiteley's (1992) proposition that after 1983, the PLP engaged in a two-track approach to recovery via policy reformulation and party reorganisation, the Policy Review Process was an essential step in fulfilling the former objective, whilst the latter was more concerned with providing a focus for the post-Kinnock era and the long standing concerns which had recently served to undermine the Labour Movement. These were in the spheres of finance, organisation, unity, image and electoral decline. Thus, renewal would enhance electoral appeal provided the policy package was well-conceived and market-tested. This was essential in the efforts to appeal to as broad a swathe of the electorate as possible. As Rubenstein (2000) remarks, this hinged on policy being popular and practical. Private polling suggested that Labour was viewed as outdated and identified with an old agenda (Hughes and Wintour, 1990) in so far as existing political techniques enabled this to take place. Critically, this also showed that voters were essentially happy to stay within the EC though they were not overly keen on the institutions (Labour Party, 1987a). Evidently, the Policy Review Process was geared to electoral considerations, yet at the same time, its intrinsic aim was not to distance the party totally from its previous traditions but to arrive at a new blend of policy ideas based upon a revision of long-held principles. It was intended, therefore, to satisfy short- and long-term needs. In creating this new blend, the leadership had to acknowledge that Europe had a low electoral salience for voters in the 1987 election (Gallup Opinion Survey Material, 1987). As a consequence, direct references to Europe in new policy formation were limited, though this is not to deny the increasing centrality of the European issue in strategic thinking. It was central to the range of goals identified by the leadership and could not be disaggregated from the domestic policy-making process.

Consequently, as Shaw (1988) has pointed out, the Policy Review Process's importance also revealed a sense of symbolism in so far as it was demonstrating a willingness to listen and respond to new developments. The emphasis was clearly, however, on the latter and on ideas that the newly reorganised party machine described by Hughes and Wintour (1990) as the 'new model party,' were putting in place. The role of the newly empowered Leaders' Office and the Shadow Communications Agency was important in this context and was fully compatible with increased leadership control of the party. This was a process not geared to the notion of inclusion though it did encourage widening popular appeal by overturning electorally unappealing policy, as the party had divested itself of Militant and other destabilising elements.

The Policy Review Process did not constitute a complete break with the party's past traditions and history as suggested by Elliott (1993) or Smith (1995), though the latter refers to the obtaining of a new identity in a form of extended revisionism. Rather, it was a case of taking note of continental influences and developments without totally forsaking domestic traditions. In acknowledging such influences, the leadership was building on existing links and seeking to marry ideas from successful continental cases to established tradition as part of restoring credibility and defining an internal response to British domestic priorities. Kinnock stated that: 'The review will ensure that the programme we develop is directly related to the conditions which we will encounter before, during and after the time we next have the opportunity to bid for power in a general election' (Labour Party, 1987, p. 3).

This choice constituted a compromise acceptable to most: one that attempted to balance longstanding virtues with the requisite level of openness to the rapidly evolving European social democratic approach to policy-making. Thus, as a number of observers, most notably Garner (1990), state, the Policy Review Process did not mark a totally new beginning but a development of ideas which implicitly, though not always uncritically, continued to lead the party in a positive European direction. Wilton (1990) goes further in suggesting that the documents represent a rehash of the 1964 election manifesto, with the only significant difference being on the issue of Europe. However, it is on this very issue that he helps to destroy his own argument, as it is the constant implicit reference to Europe and the policy demands it was making that mark the Policy Review Process out as a major point on the road to the establishment of a modern party, recognising its encroachment on virtually all aspects of policy. The review confirmed that the EC was no longer perceived as an insular and exclusive club of rich nations (Labour Party, 1988a). This was in no small measure due to the changing priorities of economic policy that the review articulated, most notably with the acceptance of a greater role for the market in determining the provision and distribution of goods and services and the need to avoid the repetition of previous economic policy mistakes that contributed so much to the defeat in 1979.

Europe became a convenient banner under which reforms could be initiated and gradually introduced. Whilst the documents produced did not provide an explicitly bold new vision for the party, they amounted to far more than a public relations exercise. However, the final outcome did not have the level of detail to be found in a policy statement such as the party's 1982 programme, sanctioned by the Annual Conference. Clearly, the emphasis was on producing a moderate approach capturing the middle ground: hence the continuing endorsement by the PLP of preference accommodation. The style of the documents did indicate a willingness to appeal to the broad range of voters, but this does not imply that the documents amounted to mere publicity handouts on the lines of an election leaflet. Rather, they built on the central thrust of *Fabian Tract* 509 (1985) that was suggesting a broadening of approach for the party. This implied updating existing ideas, retaining established principles and not just jettisoning a raft of long-existent ideals.

The essence of the Policy Review Process was determined by the unstinting efforts to avoid the policy and organisational mistakes made after 1979 which contributed substantially to three consecutive electoral defeats. These problems intensified and are not fully explained by the disunity within the ranks. Equally important was the degree to which the review confirmed the authority of the leadership that was boosted further with the final convincing victory of the modernisers over the traditionalists in 1988. This was an imperative defined by the new leadership as soon as it acquired office in 1983, whilst in a wider context the procedure has to be viewed in terms of the history and continuing development of a party which only managed to secure a substantial working Parliamentary majority for the third time in 1997.

In 1987, it was still coping with the electoral decline identified by Whiteley (1983) as part of the three-fold crisis that the party had to resolve. However, it also has to be recognised (and not underestimated) how much external events and trends, and the ability to respond to them, also contributed to this record. Thatcherism had brought about economic, social and institutional changes, most notably the decline in manufacturing industry, a shrinking in the size of the industrial working class, changes in occupational structure, an increase in the size of private sector and spread of home ownership. Coupled with what Smith (1992) has termed as Labour's 'ideological failings', the party had to consult as widely as possible within its ranks on its future course. New voting patterns amongst the working class (Worcester, 1991) added substance to the thoughts expressed in *Fabian Tract* 509, ensuring that the party had to change course and place more emphasis on Kircheimer's (1966) recipe for political success. Hence, Kinnock's comments at the 1987 party conference about the nature of the review are notable. He warned about offence being taken by those who have perceived the activity of re-examining ideas as constituting a betrayal of fundamental principles.

Wickham Jones (1995) is correct in stating the full complexities of the changes undertaken by Labour. This does, however, extend beyond the notion of placating the concerns of the electorate and the City. Nevertheless, the outcomes of the Policy Review Process did not harm the efforts to win over sections of opinion and influence, which had long cast doubt on the validity of much of what Labour was advocating. This confirmed a return to consensus politics, part of the 'catch-up' process identified by Hay (1994) as critical to Labour's revival. His analysis extends to the recommendation of a preference shaping (in contrast to preference accommodation) strategy for Labour which is not what transpired or was intended or possible. Although there was a broad sharing of ideas, values and sentiments, too many differences persisted within the Labour Movement regarding the speed, nature and extent of reform necessary to have made this attainable.

To Kinnock, betrayal constituted a failure to undertake the above tasks. In so doing, he also made it clear that he had no plan to veer from socialist principles, notably community, democracy and justice. Yet as early as the 1986 party conference, he went significantly further in incorporating a clear reference to the positive elements of the market principle as a tool of economic policy, though not as a means of altering priorities. Pragmatism was clearly the path down which the party was being taken, acknowledging the changing economy, changing society and changing electorate. This was a sentiment identified by Jones (1996) in his analysis of Labour Party conferences during the 1980s.

The thrust of the change was one of programme accommodation, with realism manifest through the electoral considerations directing the process, as opposed to providing an ideological underpinning. This was the thread running through changes recommended by bodies such as the Commission on Social Justice and the thinking behind much of the PLP policy approach to the 1997 election. At the same time, the PLP was reluctantly acknowledging the increasing entrenchment of the Thatcherite settlement. With the outright rejection of dated policy approaches (notably nationalisation, exchange controls, tariffs and the unwillingness to sell council houses), the electorate was also able to begin to visualise a new style of party with which it could identify and for which it could vote. This occurred in the 1989 European Parliamentary elections and constituted the first major test of public opinion since 1987. Although the turn-out was low at 36 per cent of the electorate, the importance of the outcome cannot be overlooked, with the PLP securing forty-five out of the eighty-seven seats available. The great unknown within the result was the level of disenchantment with the Conservative Party and the reaction to division within its ranks. For the Labour leadership, this confirmed that the party was moving in the right direction and it served to provide a path which it continued to follow in the build-up to the Maastricht Treaty. This direction was continued in discussions concerning advancing European integration and the subsequent issue of how to manage domestic sovereignty. Thus, the Policy Review Process was significant as part of a long-term strategy to turn the party round which extended beyond the decisions made between 1983 and 1987 and the contents of the 1987 manifesto. A further stage had to be completed in the process of fully legitimising the change. Yet it was also one that could pay some short-term dividends in the struggle for credibility, helping to make the party more attractive to less obvious Labour supporters, without being seen to move too quickly in too short a time and upsetting traditional supporters.

As a consequence of the above differences regarding the terrain of the Policy Review Process, the outcome was always likely to be a little muddied, if only to preserve the new-found unity within party ranks which the European issue was promoting (Shaw, 1994). An overtly radical document would not have proved popular with potential new voters and could only be tried once the leadership was fully secure and if the government was riddled by in-fighting. With the removal of the opposition's sworn enemy, its leader, in 1990, Labour's task became all the more difficult. However, by that stage the bulk of the policy review was complete and the remaining documents did not introduce new policy prescriptions. This undoubtedly helped to set the tone for the emergence of New Labour perspectives later in the decade.

Leadership and the policy review

Labour's renewal and modernisation processes are largely about the leadership being able to exercise control over the direction and future actions of the party. Consequently, the critical role of the leadership in providing impetus needs to be considered under the headings of ideology and political practice. This also constitutes a response to the common dilemma of a party leader who seeks to encourage freedom whilst preserving the cohesion needed to be effective in opposition and government. Responding to this difficult challenge was central to Kinnock's strategy of moving the party on from its weak status to a position of strength that remained loyal to its history though not to all previous policy decisions.

This infers organisational and ideological mastery of the party which, in this instance, required victory for the forces of pragmatism and electoralism over a body of ideas purely reflecting the interests and principles of the Labour Movement. The idea was to adjust principles and alter policies in line with evolving external conditions, which would help to rebuild the party following defeat in 1987. It could also tackle the continuing decline in the popular vote evident over the previous fifty years.

It was therefore a matter of urgency to broaden the base for support (*Fabian Tract* 509), yet it was also possible by now to trace an element of continuity in the leadership's actions, with the emergence of the new dominant faction in the party possessing a specific agenda for change. This faction had already declared its approach to be one guided by programme accommodation in which Europe was to provide a clear focus of attention. The Policy Review Process presented an opportunity for a more thorough overhaul than had been possible before 1987, one that sought to address issues of socialist thinking and philosophy, a concern speeded up with the rapid discrediting of socialism in central and eastern Europe.

(a) Ideological impulses

Throughout the endless discussions preceding production of the Policy Review Process documents, it is clear that the party was keen on devising an electorally successful agenda. This was in preference to one steeped in the progressive thinking that could be traced back to the full politicisation and participation of the Labour Movement in the domestic political process at the start of the twentieth century. What became evident was a form of revisionism driven by the demands of economic policy and, where relevant and appropriate, the need to reconsider and rework the inheritances of Keynes and Crossland. The intention was to tie in with the changing environment driven by the continuing development of the global economy and the strengthening of the EC. The electorate was no longer won over simply on the basis of dated policy prescriptions, notably Keynesianism, or continued hostility towards the market (Worcester, 1991). The concern of the leadership became that of determining a new approach, addressing short- and long-term needs. Certainly, in the first instance, it was valuable to secure the most appropriate electoral mix of policies, but the overriding objective was to create a modern and politically relevant organisation for the longer term fully in tune with public needs. This required a structure able to deliver realisable objectives, for the latter were self-evidently crucial to the continuing electoral success of the Conservatives.

Although immediate agreement prevailed after the 1987 election on the need for more than a merely routine post-mortem, the nature and extent of it were subject to much discussion, with attempts to reconcile short-term factors with longer-term implications. In conceptual terms, this meant addressing the two sets of needs identified by Harmel and Janda (1994), the primary goal and the associated multiple goals. The first offering for consideration was that of party stalwart Geoff Bish (Labour Party Policy Director) in his document *Policy Development for the 1990s* in July 1987. This was a bland and evasive document that was questioned most critically by Bryan Gould, Labour's Campaign Co-ordinator in 1987, whose influence had increased since securing the highest vote in the recent Shadow Cabinet elections. He was particularly concerned with the issues of the origins of policies, the stimuli for them and the ends they were serving. As the review progressed, Gould's influence declined, yet the issues he identified remained central to the discussions. The real debate about future strategy was underway, yet Kinnock was not immediately certain of what he wanted, sensing that more reflection was needed prior to firm commitments being issued.

Sawyer injected an element of calm good sense into the proceedings (another figure whose reputation in the Labour Movement was strengthening). Fundamental to his thinking was the need to address the process for delivering the end product as, for him, this also marked a move from an ideological grounding to one underpinned by a greater element of pragmatism. Sawyer's case for a multi-disciplinary approach won the day, forming the basis for the subsequent Policy Review Process, which at all times was governed by the need to remember what the old and potentially new voters deemed important. The issue was one of balancing the need to retain principle with a commitment to rethinking critical areas (Hughes and Wintour, 1990). Sawyer also suggested that the process be co-ordinated from the leader's office and that policy prescriptions could no longer be separated from the issue of how they were to be communicated. He knew full well that the left was more inclined to an open, critical discussion, yet he argued the case of the leadership that was driven more by electoral considerations and the adaptation of the party in line with strategic thinking.

Although the power of the leadership was increasing, it could not force the process too quickly as the party was continuing to consolidate its strength. It was only in 1988 that none of the eighteen union-influenced places on the NEC contained a committed member of the far left (Kellner, 1989): hence the two clear stages evident in the Policy Review Process and the increasingly astute use of developments in the EC to mould policy. On one level, responding to the progress in the Single Market programme was pragmatic in recognising and accepting market capitalism, whilst the support given for the emerging social dimension had a clearer ideological ring to it in ensuring backing from traditional supporters. This served to lessen the worst excesses of market capitalism. Both approaches were also in tune with the majority opinion in the ranks of northern European socialist and social democratic parties. This certainly helped to raise the prestige of Kinnock's leadership amongst his continental allies, who campaigned vigorously for him in the European elections of 1984 and 1989 (personal interview with Neil Kinnock, 2 December 1996).

Deep down, however, the Policy Review Process lacked a coherent theoretical basis and was not rooted in an extensive socio-political analysis of the previous twenty years. Neither did it intend to try anything as far-reaching as the reform programme Gaitskell attempted in the 1950s. As Shaw (1994) suggests, the emphasis was neo-revisionist, reworking and updating where possible and advancing the ideas of individual freedom, the legitimacy of the use of market and reducing state power. This was in contrast to the radical Bad Godesberg approach introduced by the German social democrats in 1959 in response to their continuing poor public reception. In presenting the party as pro-European, the party would be perceived as fully accepting the Treaty of Rome, whilst in accepting the emerging social dimension, it was able to placate its more traditional supporters. Yet as this analysis shows, this does not equate with a strong ideological underpinning (an issue clearly still very relevant in considering the behaviour of New Labour). As Marquand (1991) implies, the thinking was more inclined to have been determined by opinion survey than doctrine. However, as maintained earlier, the PLP was making greater strides than those suggested by Crossland (1956) whose *Future of Socialism* did not address the issue of European integration even though it was published in the same year as the Treaty of Rome.

In establishing some form of philosophical slant to the Policy Review Process, it is clear that the document entitled *Democratic Socialist Aims and Values* (Labour Party, 1988a) signifies an important statement of the party's declared intentions and boundaries. This document, based largely on Hattersley's 1987 text *Choose Freedom*, was by no stretch of the imagination radical, but it did confirm and legitimise Labour's final rejection of ideas and policies which had dogged Kinnock's inheritance, though its references to Europe are minimal. These represented obstacles in the path of modernisation. As Shaw's (1994) remark suggests, *Aims and Values*

(Labour Party, 1988a) enabled the party to continue to consign ideological considerations to the sidelines. The publication revolved around the 'Rawlsian' concept of freedom and the need for the state to protect and extend liberty, by means of promoting equality. Quite naturally, *Aims and Values* was also acceptable at this point (Taylor, 1997) because of the strength of leadership which had enabled it to overcome many of the fundamental difficulties that had recently riddled the Labour Movement. Thus, electoralism was deemed to be important and the opening Policy Review Process documents did not provide a real basis for an ideological overhaul. The final outcome of this stage of the Policy Review Process did not represent the detailing of a new set of views: hence the limited interest in the debate at the 1988 Party Conference. However, astute party management, a further assertion of increasing leadership control, can just as easily explain the behaviour. The significance of this was more for outside consumption, public image and the demands of electoral considerations, which, at this juncture, were deemed as priority concerns.

The Policy Review Process was intentionally devoid of a clear ideological thread. *Aims and Values* did not galvanise the party or constitute a driving force for the Policy Review Process, but it did mean that Kinnock had struck first blood in his drive to legitimise fully his new path for Labour. Previous efforts going back to the work of Blunkett (Hughes and Wintour, 1990), who in 1985 had recommended 'participatory democracy' as the guiding principle, had also been flatly rejected. This, however, was not what Hattersley intended: his strategy was concerned with the rebuilding of the party. In so doing, one could choose to try to fill the vacuum created by the failings of the left and the inappropriateness of their approach to policy, or develop a significant idea and use this as a framework around which to construct a new approach. This problem resurfaced in 1988 when the campaign management team was trying to pull the review together. Patricia Hewitt, a key Kinnock assistant, was particularly conscious of this and made reference to comments from American Democratic Senator Bruce Babbitt in communications with her closest colleagues: 'The Party has succeeded in scrubbing the graffiti of its past off the wall, but we still have not painted the mural of the future' (Hughes and Wintour, 1990, p. 167).

Uniting the party did not have the same impact, yet this was the route taken by the leadership. There was no definitive alternative idea to the challenges presented by 'new right' thinking. Unity was fostered and the desired changes were legitimised, but the public was clearly not overwhelmed with the outcome, as opinion polls suggest. Furthermore, increased support for Labour in the polls between June 1987 and April 1990 (most notably at the 1989 European elections, the point at which they peaked before the 1992 election) must also be seen in the context of increasing weakness in the Conservatives, largely attributable to its own internal divisions over Europe (Taylor, 1997).

Thus, the Policy Review Process lacked a significant idea, but instead, the party opted for a move towards the evolving social democratic scheme of thinking evident in Germany where the neo-liberal challenge was being taken up. This ensured that the problem with the revisionist approach, which revealed the vulnerability of the social democratic state to the pressures of economic change and the growing welfare bills grounded in Keynesian tools of economic regulation, were no longer adequate and required a major review. When these realities were combined with the evident failings of ideas propounded by the left a clear opportunity for change was presenting itself. In responding, the leadership preferred to opt for more modest objectives and circumspection became the benchmark of the Policy Review Process. This resulted in limited explicit references to Europe but European contacts were increased and exploited, as the EC was moving on a path that delighted Labour, particularly in view of its emasculation in the domestic political process. The most important contacts established were with the French Socialists and the German SPD-linked think-tank, the Friedrich Ebert Foundation. Further valuable links were initiated by the pro-European MEPs led by David Martin, who took on the leadership of the Labour Group after the more Eurosceptical Alf Lomas in 1987.

Kinnock's response to his quandary was to develop a style of managerial leadership devoid of major ideological content, enabling the PLP and the Labour Movement to advance in a controlled fashion. Uniting the party did not equate with the establishment of a clear sense of ideological purpose for either internal consumption or as a response to 'new right' policy prescriptions, yet it was the preferred approach of the party leadership. This was the course pursued also by Kinnock's successors.

(b) Political practice

With the Policy Review Process lacking an ideological foundation, the review was driven by a combination of leadership stirred by new opportunities, political craft and electoral priority, combined with an eagerness to portray the right kind of public image. This was under the guise of strong internal control approved by the leader and also exercised by aides and advisers, but always with his full agreement. This level of organisation made the Policy Review deliverable in terms of its tight organisational timeframe and in its adherence to declared objectives. As Shaw observes: 'The leadership and the increasingly influential strategic community saw the purpose of the Review as adapting the Party to the new social, economic and cultural realities of Britain in the 1990s' (Shaw, 1994, p. 84).

This focus, combined with recent experiences of division, promoted a sense of unity within the ranks and also demonstrated what a newly confident party could aspire to. Unity became more critical than the passage of a radical programme. This undoubtedly had a bearing on the final published documents.

The leader was definite about how to reconstruct the party by means of appearing to spread internal democracy and broadening its appeal. This implied an endorsement of many social democratic principles, the adoption of a pro-European stance, accepting collective security within the Atlantic alliance and an acceptance of the market economy. However, it also implied democracy in the sense of instilling transparency, which did not necessarily equate with a substantial tolerance for opinion that conflicted with the leadership platform. Critically, as Heffernan (1994) suggests, what transpired was a shift in the focus of power from the party ranks back to the Parliamentary leadership, albeit extended most importantly through the use of the leader's office at the expense of the extra-Parliamentary bodies, particularly Annual Conference and the NEC. Power was being concentrated in a smaller group of individuals, though it was not quite as limited to the inner circle as Heffernan (1994) proclaims (personal interview with Neil Kinnock, 2 December 1996). Whether this tactic is judged to have been successful, is dependent upon whether it is viewed as better to consult with all strands of opinion as a means of retaining unity, or by opting for unity on the basis of excluding those who may jeopardise it. This is regardless of whether or not they may have positive contributions to make and is very much a question of chosen leadership style. At this point, the consolidation and preservation of unity was paramount and this message had to be conveyed to as wide an audience as possible.

The conduct of the review and its findings show that the party was being firmly led. Ideally, this also implied listening carefully to the needs of the membership, yet this is where the intentions of Sawyer proved to be weak. Such a process was started but it amounted to little, except in the case of the separately organised women's consultation group which collated substantial quantities of information that was directed into a number of the review groups. This was despite the fact that moving in this direction could have helped to project the party as modern, responsive, proactive and progressive. It was as if the leader deemed the process unimportant. Sawyer attempted to address this weakness by instigating a political education exercise into the second stage of the Policy Review Process, but this only served to endorse the leader's objectives, rather than generate real discussion.

In contrast to Gaitskell, Kinnock more subtly redirected the party in line with his intentions, capitalising on his increasing authority after 1987. This enabled him to begin to influence surrounding conditions, especially within the Labour Movement, to a greater degree than previously. This was further strengthened by the outcome of the elections in 1988 for the leader and his deputy, confirming the final defeat for the traditional left and the full authority of Kinnock and Hattersley.

Kinnock was initially able to secure unquestioned control of the party; then he ensured the backing of key unions in his confrontations with the recalcitrant left before finally tackling the party machine. In this, Kinnock was continuing a tradition at which previous leaders had proved themselves adept. This required the appointment of favoured candidates to key offices. In terms of Shadow Cabinet appointments, he was greatly assisted by the emergence of a group of loyal and able figures, many of whom now occupy places in Cabinet, notably Gordon Brown and John Reid.

Such personnel were vitally important in publicly delivering the policy changes in the Policy Review Process which enabled Kinnock to consolidate his position of strength. These tasks were further made easier by the bankruptcy of much of the left's thinking and by the need to respond to the gauntlet thrown down by the sheer confidence and aggression of his chief political rival. Thatcher acted as a perverse asset and a catalyst for considerable aspects of the party's resurgence. Her hostility towards the EC naturally aroused the interest of some Labour supporters in an institutional structure with which they were unfamiliar (personal interview with Joyce Quinn MP, 3 July 1995).

The organisation of the Policy Review Process groups reflected the wishes of the leader and the issues that he believed to be central to his approach. The review groups were instructed at the outset of their work to take full account of the existing state of public opinion in formulating party policy. This was done by means of regular presentations from the Shadow Communications Agency. Recognising areas of weakness enabled the party to remove those policies detrimental to the new stance, an image it was keen to cultivate.

In terms of mechanics, the review was organised into seven distinct areas, each with its own specific terms of reference, with four out of the seven focusing on economic policy issues. (For this study the most relevant are the *Britain in the World* and the *People at Work* groups.) Kinnock took the most important decisions influencing the outcome and supervision of the Policy Review Process at the outset, with the selection and appointment of the members and group convenors. He also placed a member of his own staff on each group to prevent deviation from the tasks set. Potential opponents were very much on the sidelines, both within the PLP and the unions. In fact, the latter were only dominant in two of the groups, though they were involved in policy preparation groups set up before the 1987 election. In these the input of Tony Clarke (National Union of Communications Workers), Sam Mcluskie (National Union of Seamen), and Alex Kitson (TGWU) were the most important (personal interview with Neil Kinnock, 2 December 1996). Consequently, the course of the review was clearly defined. Electoral considerations were to weigh far more heavily in discussions than the desires of the rank-and-file, a reality that leading trade unionists were also willing to accept in return for co-option on to the review, as was the case with Rodney Bickerstaffe (NUPE), John Edmonds (GMB) and Ron Todd (TGWU), each of whom headed their respective unions. The review also brought together the PLP Secretariat from Walworth Road with the Parliamentary-based secretariat serving the Shadow Cabinet. Thus, the party bureaucracy was being centralised, making it easier to isolate potential dissent. Over and above this were the regular meetings of the campaign management team which closely monitored developments. This ensured, as Hughes and Wintour (1990) remark, that in the newly refashioned party, political demands became inseparable from the imperative to communicate effectively.

The above structures ensured that when presented to Shadow Cabinet, the three major Policy Review Process documents were accepted and endorsed by majority vote at the NEC. Each was then accepted with minimal change by party conference, with the support of the block vote mechanism. In the case of *Opportunity Britain* in 1991 the same procedure was followed, but this time the Shadow Cabinet (Heffernan, 1994) heavily influenced the document. Throughout the process, every Policy Review Process group report went to the leader's office before reaching the NEC.

The review enabled the party to undertake a smooth but vital operation in political transition which is most clearly evident in the document *Meet the Challenge, Make the Change* (Labour Party, 1989a). However, without the strong imprint of leadership the transition would not have taken place as smoothly and worthless wrangles over ideological concerns would have continued. This style of leadership was also responsible for the undermining of group convenors whose review findings were deemed unacceptable to party leadership, as was the case with Bryan Gould and Michael Meacher (Heffernan, 1994). In the case of the former, this also helps to account for his decreasing influence on the party leadership despite his best efforts to formulate policy prescriptions.

Trade union impact

Having noted the role of the unions in changing party behaviour between 1983 and 1987, their influence on the Policy Review Process must also be considered. Their significance is evident in terms of their earlier positive display of recognition towards the

EC, both amongst those affiliated and unaffiliated to the TUC. This served as an impetus to much of the thinking behind the review process.

As the evidence of the previous chapter shows, this was far more explicit than that shown by the PLP and motivated by more than electoral and economic considerations. It was also under-pinned by a substantive case that revolved around the conviction that European integration offered a credible alternative policy framework in which to work, one which could help to refashion domestic politics. This perspective would also help to bring benefits to paid-up party and union members. British trade unions began to tread a more European path in response to both an increasing sense of domestic failure and a growing level of contact with continental counterparts via the European Trade Union Confederation and its various sub-committees. They also recognised, with the increasing Europeanisation and globalisation of capital, that it was important for them to have representation in a wider set of policy-making forums. This helped to spawn a new approach amongst a group of key senior figures epitomised by the thinking and actions of Bill Jordan, President of the AEU in 1988:

> As organisations eager to secure balanced economic growth, full employment and a strong Trade Union movement throughout Europe, we must do our best to shrug off our old Euro-inhibitions and commit ourselves to pushing to the real improvements 1992 could bring. (Tindale, 1992, p. 297)

Such concerns were fully spelt out in the 1988 document *Maximising the Benefit, Minimising the Cost* (TUC, 1988b), and were developed further through the creation of a committee dealing specifically with European strategy. As Taylor remarked: 'The politics of programmatic renewal were concerned with finding a new intra-movement and inter-organisational consensus' (Taylor, 1987, p. 149).

For understandable reasons, all unions had an interest in the elec-tability of the PLP, although the tradition of unquestioned support for Labour had been undermined by the level of electoral support members had given the Conservatives since 1979 (Worcester, 1991).

They were still largely concerned about the possibility of the rise of third party politics and had a deep distaste for the Conservative government. In backing the PLP, the hope was to restore the balance from the employers to organised labour in such a way as to insert an element of social justice in public policy provision, industrial relations and workplace organisation. The emerging European social dimension added a further impetus to this cause (personal interview with Joyce Quinn MP, 3 July 1995).

Although the last Labour government had collapsed on the back of union militancy, as the 1980s progressed, the desire for a return of a Labour government scaled new heights and the PLP leadership recognised that it was increasingly able to rely on union support in key sectors for party renewal. As for their part, the unions were seeking to regain some national influence in policy-making on issues extending far beyond the traditional areas of dispute such as recognition, pay and wage bargaining. This was part of the approach termed 'new realism'. As A. Taylor (1987) points out, the unions began to see that the so-called traditional social democratic project was being undermined by the challenges of high unemployment, industrial restructuring and the emergence of neoliberal ideals. The greatest changes had occurred in manufacturing with a decline of two million jobs: replacement jobs in the services sector were far less unionised (Davies, 1996). Unions therefore had to change their thinking to accommodate such developments and to attract new members: hence a desire to foster the case for programmatic renewal in their closest political ally.

Kinnock's increasing assurance as leader was in no small measure due to union backing. The interests of both sides were best preserved by the unions pursuing a form of self-denying ordinance, as the more they were seen as determining the content and direction of party policy, the more the PLP was perceived as a mere mouthpiece for them. This was despite the fact that trade union membership and affiliation to the TUC declined through the 1980s (Heffernan and Marquasee 1992). The PLP also had to be conscious of not being too closely linked with declining unions as it was also seeking to broaden its appeal by attracting the non-unionised majority. This was illustrated by the leadership's decision not to provide unconditional support for the miners in their 1984–85 dispute.

In choosing not to display their full potential muscle, those unions who could best be described as being of the new modernising tradition recognised their longstanding role as a stabilising influence on the PLP (notably the GMB, AEU, USDAW and APEX). This implied that within the Labour Movement, the dominant party faction had the upper hand.

It was John Edmonds of the GMB who increasingly allied himself with the Kinnock leadership and its aim to reform and update the party structure. He played a valuable role for the PLP in the speed with which he was willing to issue severe reprimands to anyone displaying disloyalty to the PLP leadership (personal interview with John Edmonds, 13 June 1995). Although Union leaders like Edmonds could not prevent a challenge to party leadership, they were ill-disposed generally to the Benn–Heffer ticket in 1988, but in choosing to back Prescott for the position of Deputy Leader, they reminded the leadership not to take them totally for granted. This ensured that the Policy Review Process did not offer too unacceptable a package of proposals. Benn and Heffer's support was most pronounced amongst constituency activists. Even so, Edmonds was still able to reassure his union conference in 1988 that: 'The Policy Review was not a betrayal of basic principles' (*GMB Journal*, August 1988, p. 6).

Although input from the union rank-and-file to the Policy Review Process was low-key, Kinnock ensured that trade unions were involved in the process, albeit on his terms. This was all the more significant in view of the diminishing role accorded for the TUC–Labour Liaison Committee. The TUC was very reticent about its involvement in the *People at Work* group as it feared that this would be deemed harmful to Labour's electoral fortunes. The chief implication of this was that once the final documents were presented to the NEC, they had already been approved by these union leaders despite the fact that there was little recourse to discussion at internal party conferences or with their respective memberships. This demonstrated a further manifestation of the leader's new level of control over his domain which was endorsed by a number of key union leaders.

Although the Kinnock leadership relied heavily on the block vote, it also knew that the process had to be reformed. Trade union leaders cast over 90 per cent of the vote at all Labour conferences between 1987 and 1991. In fact, with the support of the four largest unions, Labour's Parliamentary leadership could win any vote at party conference during this period, as Heffernan (1994) and Minkin (1991) confirm. In many respects, the unions were both part of the problem of political adaptation as well as part of its solution. With their role in the NEC diminished and their limited influence as group convenors, the unions had conceded considerable ground. However, the whole process had largely been inspired by a union figure, Sawyer. Although on a formal level, the structural and constitutional changes were to the detriment of union influence, there remained, as Minkin (1991) pointed out, a considerable degree of private dialogue between the PLP, the TUC and union affiliates over a wide range of issues. This was most notable through the informal Contact Group. This arrangement was convenient for both sides who could demonstrate gains from this arrangement to their respective constituencies which, of course, overlapped considerably.

Policy outcomes

The Policy Review Process did lead to significant changes in party policy, most particularly on the economy, industrial relations, Europe and defence (Driver and Martell, 1998), yet as has been argued throughout, in two of those four areas – economic matters and Europe – much had been achieved by 1987. The documentation produced over the four years served to legitimise publicly what had already been attained by an increasingly confident and assertive leadership. Substance was, in effect, added to agreed positions. As Garner (1990) confirms, much of what the reports detailed had already been outlined in a range of interviews, speeches and publications produced by Kinnock, or on his behalf by individuals in the dominant faction.

What transpired was the product of a steady and lengthy process, representing an organised way of drawing together a whole range of propositions which, once endorsed, legitimised the start of a new era that the party leadership was keen to sanction. The chief outcome as far as the Labour Movement was concerned was the re-establishment of a climate of internal consensus driven by a clear primary goal. However, beyond this was a carefully conceived response to the political environment created by

Thatcherism. A new economic policy emerged and Westminster isolation was eased by the emergence of a new European perspective on all major issues though still not always sufficiently explicit because of the PLP's unwillingness to examine how to deal with challenges to national sovereignty. A new sense of balance was evolving in relation to the application of the principles of equality, choice and liberty in order that both short- and long-term gains could be achieved. All too often, though, the former was accorded priority status in the application of the aforementioned principles. All of this served to represent a foundation from which New Labour developed.

Any meaningful consideration of the substance of the Policy Review Process and its implications has to begin with an analysis of the economic programme offered. After all, four of the review groups focused on economic policy and it was in this sphere that the basis of the new consensus was created, driven by the European issue. At the heart of all the statements about economic policy was the final burial of any ideas of creating a socialist economy, whilst on the subject of Europe, the Policy Review Process laid to rest all remaining fundamental misgivings about the EC (Tindale 1992). With the clear links between economic and European policy, the latter could no longer be approached as an isolated and distinctive concern. This was an important admission and one that Kinnock had been keen to promote as early as 1984 in his *New Socialist* article.

Acceptance of the centrality of the market to issues of domestic economic management and the creation of wealth is central to an appreciation of the significance of the Policy Review. The market was now perceived as a means of overseeing resource allocation, but differences did prevail over how to realise this objective. The state still had a potential role to perform and this difference managed to distinguish the PLP from the government on a range of policies, though in many ways the PLP was keen to imitate the competence of government economic policy. Throughout the Policy Review Process, however, the disadvantages of over-reliance on the market were stated. The conclusion of this was the acceptance of a supply-side doctrine for socialism. Yet as the Policy Review Process maintained, the economic role of modern government was to: 'help make the market system work properly where it can, will and shall and to replace or strengthen it where it can't, won't or shouldn't' (Labour Party, 1989a, p. 6).

Acceptance of the market also implied the endorsement of the SEM programme, a further example of pragmatic influences at work and a demonstration of programme accommodation. In so doing, the PLP also realised it had to work in existing conditions and was probably incapable of constructing a credible alternative economic programme to that of the government. However, as the Policy Review Process progressed, the commitments to state intervention decreased and this of course reduced the possibility of tax hikes, another issue on which Labour had often been criticised.

In phase two of the review, the critical *Meet the Challenge, Make the Change* (Labour Party, 1989a), the emphasis had slightly altered to favouring supply-side oriented policy. Improving overall competitiveness with the encouragement of a more flexible labour market best attained the broad economic goals desired by the electorate. There was also a commitment to investment in research and development and an examination of the future of public ownership. In effect, nationalisation was being displaced by a mechanism involving regulatory commissions and statutory frameworks, whilst the medium-term economic strategy promoted was again not a new idea.

On Europe, the case was a little different. The need to refashion thinking was driven also partly by external dynamics, which, though taking account of the encroachment of Europe on all domestic matters, still gave the Policy Review Process room for manoeuvre. This clearly makes it difficult to disentangle economic from other policy areas. The emerging social dimension filled the ideological vacuum: witness the remarks of Chris Smith MP: 'We were stuck with Thatcher's reactionary social policies: the EC began to appear as a haven of progressive ideas' (Tindale, 1992, p. 295).

The Delors speech at the 1988 TUC Conference created further opportunity which the PLP was keen to seize upon in the light of increasing friction within the government over its European stance. This was an opportunity a more traditional party would not have taken on and Labour was very keen to endorse the principles encapsulated in the Social Charter. The programme served to control the neo-liberal elements of the Single Market, proving attractive to both the PLP and the Labour Movement. It also confirmed participation in and acceptance of the EC as a positive and tangible mechanism in constructing economic strategy. This was built upon in the 'People at Work' review group. Its brief was to concentrate on employment issues and the collective rights of trade unions. It also overlapped with discussion of issues such as social regulation and social ownership. Whether this chimed with the public perceptions is, of course, another matter, as the electorate was unlikely to change its long-established views on unions and their contribution to industrial strife and economic decline (personal interview with Neil Kinnock, 2 December 1996). The leader of the Labour Group in the European Parliament, David Martin MEP, confirmed this with his remarks that:

> Important democratic socialist objectives can no longer be accomplished within the boundaries of a single country. The EC can open up to the peoples of Europe new areas of manoeuvre that have been and will continue to be lost to the British people. (Martin, 1988, p. 3)

In charting the developments of the review group addressing Europe, any assessment of what was achieved is coloured by the lack of time devoted to primary European matters. Security, trade and development issues were global and time accorded to them was evidently perceived as more important because of changing economic conditions coupled with the emergence of new security needs in a post-Cold War Europe. As has been argued earlier, movement on a pro-European outlook had been generated elsewhere in the Labour Movement and the PLP was more inclined through the review to refine attitudes developed elsewhere, capitalising on the broad statements of the Phase One Report produced in 1988. Therefore, the review had nothing fundamentally new to say about the EC: instead, it opted to use it as a vehicle for promoting change in other areas. In so doing, it was capitalising on the increasing satisfaction expressed by the public in its attitude to EC membership. The British Social Attitudes Survey (1992) reveals how public acceptance of the EC had risen from 61 per cent of those interviewed in 1986 to 76 per cent in 1990. What is of more significance is how by 1991 a document was produced that laid out in detail how the Community could develop in a way that was beneficial to all interests, not just Britain's. These sentiments are best characterised by the statement:

We believe Britain must be a leader in Europe, not a follower. Our strong links with our sister parties in Europe forming the largest group in the European Parliament mean that a Labour government will be able to work with our European partners to defend Britain's interests and build a stronger community. (Labour Party, 1991, p. 53)

It is at this juncture that Labour recommends progress on enlargement of EC membership, the development of a common Foreign and Security strategy and the need to address the democratic deficit evident within the policy-making and institutional structure. Ultimately, it was a case of merging the respective findings into a manageable and coherent document. Much of this had already been recommended in *Looking to the Future* (Labour Party, 1990). In fact, the final proposals were moderate and again influenced by electoral considerations: hence the greater attention devoted to controlling inflation and the acceptance of entry into the ERM. However, the latter smacked of adversarial politics. This seemed to be undertaken more for political than economic motives.

A reassessment of party thinking had being carried out, and however flimsy this may have been from a philosophical point of view the thinking was now geared totally to the identified primary goal and the multiple goals that encroached on electoral considerations. Kinnock's views on the health of domestic economic institutions and practices (Labour Party, 1991) were remarkably conservative, with the blame for national failings resting almost entirely on twelve years of poor government. In choosing these words, the policy slant was again about consensus and the ardent wish to avoid reopening old wounds: hence programme accommodation and the willingness to advance debate from a purely government-led agenda. The final document was conceivably a document too far: after all, the process had been going on for four years and despite the language used, public interest and knowledge of what was being done was bound to decline (Taylor, 1997).

The other way of judging the impact of the Policy Review Process is by means of looking at electoral considerations. This assesses how much the party hierarchy was in line with public thinking, namely moving from a class-based party to one more in tune with continuing social, economic and political change in formulating appropriate policy. Although the electorate was convinced that the party was less extreme, this was hardly sufficient to elect it to office. Polling evidence (Taylor, 1997) shows that Labour's appeal varied considerably between July 1987 and December 1990. This can be explained by the impact of particular parts of the review, notably in terms of the 1989 European elections, yet one has to recall problems faced by the Conservatives on Europe and the Poll Tax, as well as the implications of the resignation of Thatcher. Thus, it appears that the polling figures, though positive for Labour, were not necessarily engineered by them, as Heath and Jowell (1992) suggest, and this development was built on the negative force of public reaction to the government. As regards the election, it is quite conceivable that though the public admired the PLP and its leadership for carrying out the review, they were not sufficiently convinced of its merits or the ability of a Labour government to implement its contents. This was irrespective of the lack of radicalism in them. It also needs to be stated that the PLP did not contest the 1992 election on the Policy Review Process alone and a range of other factors explained the defeat at the polls. Hence, there has to be some doubt expressed at Heath and Jowell's (1992) calculation that the Policy Review Process gave Labour an additional 1.1 per cent of the vote in 1992, a claim based upon changes in Labour's perceived position and new policy preferences.

Conclusion

The Policy Review Process was designed to indicate a party making a break with its recent past. It was, without doubt, significant to the development of the modern Labour Party that successfully contested the 1997 General Election. This significance lies less in what the document advocated and more in terms of what it symbolised at a vital stage in confirming the public rebirth of what had appeared to be a decaying institution due to the actions of the new dominant faction. It is all too easy to be critical of the lack of radicalism in the documents produced and to decry the lack of a 'Bad Godesberg' approach, which Marquand (1991) suggests was needed to cure the ailing Labour Movement. However, the leadership would not have wished to enact this type of programme, despite having the power to do so, as it acknowledged the need to work within the Thatcherite settlement as well as acknowledging the element of conservatism evident within the ranks of the Labour Movement.

In taking policy issues out of party politics for the period of the review (Thorpe, 1997), the leadership was able to concentrate on organisational change. All the emphasis on short-term electoral needs cannot, therefore, override the longer-term strategy of renewal in which the Policy Review Process was a necessary stepping stone. Although it is evident that the review process was more akin to tailoring a programme rather than a set of principles, the party did confirm its new position on Europe as well as on a range of other key issues. This impacted on all elements of policy and the Labour Movement, as well as the domestic political discourse with the Europeanisation of domestic politics continuing and Labour choosing to embrace this ideal. Consequently, Europe became the driving-force of party thinking, contributing substantially, though not always overtly, to the new sense of unity and purpose throughout the Labour Movement. The lack of discussion at party conference during the mid-1980s both confirmed this development and demonstrated an endorsement of the strategy.

The Policy Review Process was clearly a pragmatic response, built on political craft, good organisation and the seizing of new opportunities. As the review progressed, the language used in referring to the EC became increasingly positive, whilst the evolving detail of European policy signified an understanding of its importance as a vehicle for promoting change. At the same time, there was a growing recognition of the value of being integrated in a developing policy-making framework that presented many potentially exciting opportunities. The key to unlocking this full potential was to convince the electorate of the gains on offer, a difficult challenge in an environment that was becoming ever-more anxious about the extension of the EC's influence (Gallup, November 1991). However, there remained limits to what a single-minded and highly dedicated leadership could hope to achieve with an election looming. The Policy Review Process did not constitute, and was not intended to represent, a complete break with the party's rich heritage.

It undoubtedly helped to prepare the ground for New Labour: the modernisers were directing the course of the party but it remains foolish to equate this with a later slavish adherence to Blairism.

Between 1987 and 1991, the only major rebuff that the leader received was over his attempt to revise unilateralism in 1988 (Heffernan, 2000). This internal strength did not necessarily equate with a position of wider strength, as manifest in poll ratings (Taylor, 1997).

The 1992 election was essentially fought on Conservative terms, with Europe receiving a low salience rating. Labour's disappointing performance, however, has to be explained more by this than the impact of the Policy Review Process. The one year gap between the publication of the final document and the calling of the election reduced the discussion on the party's new policy position. However, the process was not carried out simply to gain victory at the next election; rather it represented one of a series of electoral devices implemented with longer-term objectives in mind. In receiving 7.6 per cent of the vote less than the Conservatives (Curtice and Steed, 1992), this was the fourth election in a row that Labour were 7 per cent or more in arrears. Thus, in a limited sense, the Policy Review Process had not made the party any more electable, though on an assessment of voters' views on parties' governing abilities, Labour's rating on Europe climbed 2 per cent between 1989 and 1992 (Gallup Political Index, 1991). This leads into the issue of assessing the desirability of policy as opposed to that of the leadership.

The next challenge on the road to electoral recovery was to engineer a response to the ERM crisis and the Maastricht Treaty which consolidated earlier gains and retained the central status of Europe to policy-making without alienating existing or potential new supporters. These two events came so soon after the election that the party was hardly prepared for the shock and magnitude of these developments. It soon became evident that despite remaining implicit to party thinking, Europe was viewed as one issue that could not be proclaimed too publicly despite the openness that had emerged surrounding the discussion of this issue since 1987.

It seemed as if the party was losing confidence: however, the contrary was true. Effective party management and economic reform enabled the leader and his allies to continue the process of modernisation on their own terms despite the loss of one year in the modernisation process because of the miners' strike (Kinnock, 1994). Policy change had been legitimised, party strategy mapped out and the external environment acknowledged. At the same time, party unity had been restored. This represented a fundamental principle for New Labour gaining even more importance when coupled with economic and financial prudence.

4
The Challenges of the Maastricht Issue

With the completion of the Policy Review Process, the Labour Party was keen to contest an election as soon as possible, in order to confirm its fitness for government. However, this wish was not immediately granted and the result at the 1992 election proved to be a major disappointment to the party and all its supporters. This was despite having enacted the main thrust of the recommendations of *Fabian Tract* 509 (1985). In essence, this had moved the party from being a class-based to a 'catch-all' party, seeking to extend its electoral appeal as much as possible. It had also ensured that the party recognised its need to move away from those regions and socio-economic forces subject to secular decline in its efforts to catch up with those modernising trends that the Thatcher government had harvested and encouraged (Callaghan, 2000).

The outcome of the election and its wide-ranging implications for matters of party strategy constitute the essence of the discussion in this chapter, as these two concerns dictated the style of leadership and policy priority given to Europe until the election of Blair as leader in 1994. Furthermore, in assessing the impact of European policy on the renewal and modernisation of the party with the Policy Review Process complete, the focus shifted to how the established leadership could continue to pursue the European issue as a vehicle to promote ongoing modernisation. A dilemma was soon evident in that in seeking to explain the poor result, it was clear that the European question was not a significant contributory factor to the outcome. In addition, the party had to consolidate its new policy position which was soon to be tested by two major external events, the ERM crisis in the summer of 1992 and the Parliamentary discussions over passage of the European Communities Amendment Bill. Both these events had enormous domestic implications as a consequence of the growing political and economic Europeanisation of British life.

In advancing the central proposition of this study, whilst at the same time addressing the aforementioned dilemma, this chapter will take the following course. The European issue will be scrutinised in terms of its influence during the election, the post-mortem that followed and the external challenges that presented themselves to the party leadership. The respective roles of Kinnock and Smith as party leaders will be included in the discussion. In the case of the latter, due to the brevity of the leadership period, comments on the impact of Smith's stewardship will be incorporated into the main body of the discussion. The objective was to continue to reinforce the arguments central to this study, that show how the influence of Europe has been central to party strategy between 1983 and 1999. With the changes in party leadership, although the centrality of Europe has never been questioned, the tactics conceived and the language used have varied in advancing the European argument for party renewal and continuing modernisation. Consequently, the intensity at which the European issue drove party strategy varied, particularly during this period. This reality has been evident throughout the emergence of New Labour's European policy.

New opportunities

As Young has remarked: 'The existence of European Union is a condition infusing the bloodstream of every British official and politician' (Young, 1998, p. 412). Yet for the Labour Party, more so than for the remainder of the Labour Movement (due to its declining influence), the burning issue was how the European discourse could be used or blended into a discrete vehicle for promoting and achieving more than advancement of the party in Westminster terms. As Macshane (1996) correctly suggests, discussion of party policy on Europe had always been limited to internal and tactical concerns and now an opportunity to recast party thinking was presenting itself in terms of indicating firm commitment to the European integration process. The 1992–94 period, from the General Election through to Blair's accession as leader, gave Labour an opportunity to consolidate its new position further and build on its newly established equanimity over Europe.

However, as events showed, this was difficult to achieve. The decision to prioritise party concerns over a matter that was issue- and conviction-based was very difficult, especially when coupled with the recognition that although Europe would never be an issue that could win an election, it could be responsible for an election defeat if poorly handled. Thus, it soon became apparent that internal factors, national considerations – notably playing the game of 'oppositional opportunism' (Rosamond, 1994) – and the reservations of public opinion were likely to be victorious over wider issues in the search to be the dominant influence in European policy thinking. As Wincott (1992) suggests, the former drove the party to occupy a policy space vacated by the government in its efforts to secure office (Strom, 1990).

Strong party leadership evident throughout the whole review process culminated in a policy position that suited the needs of the dominant leadership faction, yet with the replacement of Kinnock, the distinct European foundations which he put in place were not developed further. This was not due to Smith's convictions, rather his choice of priorities: hence the identification of ebbs and flows in Europe's role as the central dynamic in party policy-making and the need to explain why this is so. This occurred despite the intense unpopularity of the Conservative government in its fourth term, initially stemming from perceived economic mismanagement following the ERM crisis. Much of this unpopularity was generated by the increasing divisions stirred by the European question, which Labour was more than happy to exploit for its own end, undermining the Conservatives by using the tactic of effective oppositional politics. This detracted from the party's efforts to construct a clear and tightly argued pro-European strategy.

In a number of respects, the PLP was hamstrung as it essentially backed the thrust of the European Communities Amendment Bill, the Parliamentary progress of which it did not wish to delay. The ERM crisis placed considerable pressure on the party and its European credentials for the first time since the adoption of its very positive European perspective, particularly after the shattering blow of the election defeat with its clear display of sound economic principles. It was difficult to respond to the public dissatisfaction with government economic policy whilst wishing to reinforce the newly established legitimacy and respectability of its economic policy by endorsing the ERM. Paradoxically, it led to an endorsement of the policy of creating a single currency. Labour clearly had to play the role of chief opposition party yet it also wished to consolidate its achievements, a task all the more difficult to achieve as Conservative unpopularity was due largely to its mishandling of the economy than to its stance on Europe. By its very nature, treading this thin line implied lessening the European impetus cultivated by Kinnock, despite the possibilities of longer-term disadvantages to party policy-making and credibility. The party leadership had built up a body of healthy support, most notably through the strong personal relationship established between Kinnock and Felipe Gonzalez, the leader of the Spanish Socialist Party (personal interview with Nick Siegler, Labour Party International Secretary, 14 February 2000).

However, the leadership and the dominant faction also had to remind itself of the concerns of party unity, democracy and internal management in conducting a serious election post-mortem which had to extend beyond the needs of its own membership (internal factors). The outcome of this represented a victory for the internal and national pressures (opposition politics and public opinion) over those emanating from European, American and global sources (external environmental factors). This was irrespective of the fact that shortly after the election, the party voted into office a leader with a longer-standing European pedigree than Kinnock, dating back to the early 1970s. At the time of the European Communities Amendment debates, Smith was one of the few Parliamentary survivors of the sixty-eight Labour MPs who had defied the party whip and voted for UK membership of the EEC in 1971.

Political courage on a European scale was not in evidence as the party wrestled instead with domestic issues. Most notable amongst these were economic matters, which, although increasingly tinged by European connections, were not primarily driven though by them. In the contest between domestic policy choices and external national interests, the former was the clear victor as this was the route to electoral success and an 'office seeking' strategy (Strom 1990). Policy principle was not compromised but policy detail was increasingly overlooked as the shock of the election defeat made the party all the more determined to ensure victory at the next opportunity. The 1992 election result had generated a considerable shock that was destined to make a serious impact on policy-making and, more immediately, on the plans of Smith as the new leader, as well as on Blair's inheritance.

This chapter will conclude by showing that the party strategy was essentially unchanged and strong enough to resist the challenges confronted, especially the ERM crisis of September 1992. European policy was not advanced in a strategic sense in so far as the issue was not deemed a means of recasting politics, despite the continuing Europeanisation of the domestic political process. Between July 1992 and 1994, the foot was taken off the European accelerator pedal with the leadership unwilling to confront directly some of the issues generated by a policy that incorporates issues of sovereignty, identity and political economy. These are issues that, by their very nature, generate heated discussion and controversy which the party leadership was desperate to avoid. This lack of progress can be explained by consideration of a range of factors. These include the response to the divisions in the Conservative government over European strategy, the pressures of domestic political competition, the reservations on Europe apparent amongst some party members, and, to a lesser degree, the continuing public disinterest concerning the realities of economic and political integration. However, it should be noted that although the period spans two leaders who shared the same primary goal and chief European spokesman in the House of Commons, Kinnock and Smith did not conduct their leadership responsibilities in the same style, or surround themselves with the same team of advisers. Yet, both sought to prove Labour's European credentials beyond doubt. During the leadership of Smith, the party began to set the tone of caution that has continued under Blair, with Labour fearful of pushing the European issue too strongly for fear of electoral disadvantage.

Implications of the 1992 election

As Butler and Kavanagh (1992) remark, the 1992 victory was a remarkable achievement by the Conservatives. Its success, when viewed against the backdrop of a range of unfavourable domestic indicators besides electoral European trends where established governing parties were experiencing voting reverses, clearly disappointed and unsettled Labour. Yet this was the benchmark that the party had to use in order to assess its progress on the continuing path from renewal to modernisation. At this juncture, it had completed its policy reversal on Europe and expunged from its commitments policies perceived to be damaging to its cause.

The party had endorsed ERM in 1988 well ahead of the government, whilst in 1990 it indicated support for the single currency and a European Central Bank. In 1991 it agreed to the recommendation of acceptance of EMU by its economic subcommittee, on the back of encouragement from the party leader and the newly established Institute of Public Policy Research (IPPR). This further entrenched the position on Europe, confirming a clear stance, though one in need of further fleshing out in respect of policy detail. This was all part of its move towards being more of a social democratic party based on the increasing levels of partnership with its fraternal colleagues, most notably in Germany, Sweden and Spain. These pro-European sympathies were illustrated by fully endorsing the market as a means of creating wealth and by supporting new labour legislation, giving rights to workers rather than unions.

ERM membership and subsequent support for EMU provided Labour with a vehicle for being tough on inflation, despite misgivings that extended beyond the predictable sources. Between 1989 and 1992, Labour moved from an explicitly anti-EMU position to one of qualified support for the process. However, this remained more difficult to explain and sell than policy related to the social dimension, as the benefits were not immediately apparent. For Kinnock and Smith, however, ERM membership was critical to Labour's anti-inflation strategy as it indicated to the financial markets that the party was paying due deference to budgetary discipline, fiscal rectitude and careful economic management. Thus, as was the case for the government, attacking inflation was deemed more of a priority than unemployment, (Labour Party, 1990). This was because Labour needed a tool to overcome pressure on sterling and the usual crisis of expectations and demands from economic expansion programmes that await incoming Labour governments. ERM entry was welcome too as a means of improving the capacity to overcome economic shocks (Labour Party, 1990).

The party also wished to play a role in crucial decisions affecting the whole of the European economy. Political realists such as Kinnock, Smith and Brown and chief economic adviser, John Eatwell, were also patently aware that Britain was never going to be able to remain outside a European monetary system and continue as a substantive player in matters of European political economy. For the 1992 election, the Shadow Chancellor was even willing to go before television cameras and pledge party support for the ERM and protection of the pound in the system.

Thus, for the first time in nearly twenty years, the Conservatives were faced by an opposition party with an essentially united view on Europe. This was a party more able than it ever had been to take the grand strategic view of Europe, despite the limitations indicated. Labour now posed a threat to the political system, which as Young (1998) remarks, allotted Europe an auxiliary and increasingly negative status. This provided an opportunity to change the tone and nature of political debate, with the Conservatives increasingly divided over significant aspects of political and economic integration, a problem intensified by weak leadership. This was manifest in its desire to be at the centre of Europe, though in reality merely playing lip service to the concept. This simply served to contribute to reinforcing Labour's potential position. The social dimension provided an issue that enabled Labour to open up a clear divide that the public could both acknowledge and understand, particularly as it also gave them the chance to round on the relevant opt-out clause in the Maastricht Treaty. As Lord Eatwell indicated: 'The Social Protocol defines the dividing line between those on the government benches who regard labour as a cost and those on our benches who regard it as a resource' (House of Lords, 22 July, Volume 548 Column 841).

This created a new political space that Labour was willing and able to exploit, using the device of 'oppositional opportunism' (Rosamund, 1994). The question became one of determining how the Party could act on manifesto commitments such as the desire:

> to promote Britain out of the European second division into which our country has been relegated by the Tories ... We shall fight for Britain's interests, working for Europe-wide policies to fight unemployment and to enhance regional and structural industrial policy. (Labour Party, 1992, p. 35)

Between 1974 and 1991 (Mori Polls 1974–91), inquiring into 'the most important issue' and 'other important issues', there was not a month when the European issue had more saliency than prices, law and order and education. Having reversed its policy on Europe securing public acceptance at the 1989 European polls, this did not imply that the electorate was won over to its pro-Europe position, though the implicit underpinning of the party's modernisation was deemed more attractive now that the party publicly displayed its pro-European credentials. This is something the party had feared doing before 1987 and now it had to win over the electorate as there was no desire by strategists to turn back. It was doing so at a point where it was able to capitalise on Conservative divisions and the issue of union recognition and rights through the Social Chapter. Even during the most intense period of Conservative in-fighting whilst the European Communities Amendment Bill was in its passage through Parliament, Europe still did not preoccupy public thinking in terms of its impact on everyday life. This reality was confirmed by Young (1998) who suggests that the election was underpinned by scepticism surrounding Labour's competence and the party's challenge until the next series of polls was to overcome this sentiment and its debilitating impact on domestic politics. This challenge has continued to feature in the Labour Party agenda, with the party under Blair unwilling to confront it directly.

For the first time since 1979, during the 1992 election campaign foreign policy concerns were once again to the fore, a dividend of the post-Cold War era and the new political and economic environment created as a consequence. Defence, though, had been a critical election issue throughout the 1980s. However, the issue of Europe did not capture the public's imagination (Butler and Kavanagh, 1992). Public interest had not been developed and nurtured, a requirement demanding leadership from the dominant coalition. Having experienced the Maastricht negotiation and the signing of the Treaty of European Union in February 1992, the public required explanation of its content and shortcomings, as well as an indication of how it could be built up in the hope of resolving Britain's longstanding ambivalence towards Europe. This represented a substantial challenge, one that merited Labour's serious attention. In the run-up to the 1992 election, the position of Europe in the policy priority order declined. The fear of electoral defeat short-circuited any plan to promote Europe more strongly on the policy agenda. This was a situation that intensified after 1992, particularly with Smith's accession to the leadership and the displacement of some of Kinnock's more enthusiastic European advisers, most notably Peter Mandelson.

Labour did not lose the election because it took too few risks on Europe, displaying a lack of nerve. Rather, it correctly judged that the public was essentially disinterested. The concern was how to prove its new sense of responsibility to the electorate and this required the leadership to promote the value of its new European stance. The Policy Review Process had, after all, publicly laid to rest the party's hostility to Europe. It actually committed the party to a social community in which key rights were to be protected. However, public interest needed to be directed to the European issue in a way that extended far beyond the bickering and tactical manoeuvrings of Westminster. This would enable it to acquire the status it merited as a policy worthy of serious and detailed attention placed in a full global context, rather than being subsumed by concerns of national politics (Taylor, 1997).

Proclaiming social democratic virtues within the Labour Movement and receiving their endorsement was one thing; converting this into understandable public expression and support was another challenge. This required not just clearer public communication but also a distinct value system to underpin and guide the future course and progress of the party. This represented a reality that the Policy Review Process had chosen to overlook. However, the arch-modernisers (most notably Philip Gould, who was later to play a key role as one of Blair's closest advisers), keen to promote further reviews of policy and strategy, did not favour the extolling of European policy or any innovative approach to this issue. The leadership preferred to consolidate its position, perceiving that Europe had not harmed its cause, but that it could do so in the future. This further manifestation of programme accommodation was continuing the trend confirmed by the Policy Review Process, yet now the situation had moved on and the PLP had a further challenge to take up. However, as Young (1998) remarks: 'The European Union had long ceased to be a litmus test of whether a Labour politician was sufficiently red or blue' (Young, 1998, p. 484).

The issue was now one of ascertaining how far and how quickly the party sought to move towards playing a more direct role within the integration process.

In the light of this new reality, which indicated a major policy achievement, the party began to display a sense of complacency over Europe in respect of policy development. This was fostered by the ease with which it could exploit the weaknesses of the government without having to formulate its own definite vision beyond the broad statements set out in the Review Process. However, this also enabled a consolidation of existing achievements by the leadership, the preservation of unity and the advocacy of an economic policy that demonstrated competence and an understanding of economic change. Europe was destined not to be an overt lynchpin of policy strategy in the post-Kinnock era, though it remained essential in defining policy parameters. It was not a case of the election influencing the most European of senior Labour figures to defer on this complex issue, preferably to electoral needs, but rather a continuation of a long Labour tradition of placing party needs before issue and policy significance. In so doing, the leadership, more especially under Smith, was succumbing to internal and national influences rather than external ones. As an agenda item in its own right, Europe's status as a second-order issue was confirmed. Moreover, it was a case of publicly playing down the role of the European question in framing policy and securing party unity because of the concern that this approach may generate amongst existing and potential supporters. This was also an outcome of the Policy Review Process and its lack of substantive overt reference to Europe, and the awareness of public misgivings (interview with Dr R. Berry, 13 December 1999). Dr Berry, a leading backbench supporter of the party leadership, expressed considerable reservations regarding EMU at the time of the European Communities Amendment Bill debates.

Maastricht and modernisation: the dilemma

Having confronted the electorate in a contest in which Europe did not receive the attention it merited, the first direct test for Labour's policy reversal was the handling of the European Communities Amendment Bill as opposed to the Treaty itself. This was where the party could intervene. Although it was Kinnock who directed Labour's initial response to the Maastricht deal in December 1991, his role was limited due to the Parliamentary timetable and the subsequent election. It was his successor who masterminded the challenge to the government, with the help of the party's longstanding European spokesman George Robertson. It was through their choice of tactics that in treading a delicate path Labour was not going to enter into a direct confrontation with the Major government. The rhetoric was positive: 'Britain has to be in Europe's first division and we have to have the ambition and the policies to be sure we get there' (Robertson, 1992, p. 5).

However, the events of the Parliamentary passage of the Bill and the ERM crisis of 1992 made this task more complex. Irrespective of these developments, as this chapter shows, the positive rhetoric used was not matched by deed.

Labour had to ensure that it did not jeopardise its newly established respectability and it chose to pursue the tactics of *realpolitik* and consolidation. In seeking to avoid any diminution of its newly legitimised credentials at the same time as playing the role of an effective chief opposition party, it found itself embroiled in the longstanding postwar discourse which framed much of British politics. This concerned the readjustment from loss of empire, the inevitability of Britain's place in Europe and her ultimate political and economic destiny. Healthy debate over the realities of European integration was acceptable, yet this had to be tempered by awareness of the multiple influences on the party as well as the desire for the prize it was seeking: electoral success and political office (Strom, 1990). Much could be made of the fact that the Conservative Party appeared to be far clearer about what it disapproved of, as opposed to what it favoured. This constituted Labour's rationale of oppositional politics and a policy-making approach driven by the forces of preference accommodation as it provided Labour with an easy target on which to focus. It was geared to securing short-term advantage in its appeal to the broad electoral constituency that it was seeking to win over. A sense of complacency was creeping into this policy, slowing the evolution of a critical area of concern, and this was to prove to have some damaging implications for the formation of policy. However, issues of political sovereignty appeared to no longer worry the majority of members of the Parliamentary party.

Labour's initial reaction to the deal brokered at Maastricht was based on its key strength, namely exploiting the fundamental tension between the government's desire to play a central role in Europe, whilst choosing to opt out from two significant policy areas. One of these areas, EMU, was fundamental to full economic integration and possible political union and this weakened Britain's bargaining position within the EU. In presenting the Conservative position as a hollow victory, both Kinnock (House of Commons, 18 December Volume 21 Cols 286–7 1991) and Alistair Darling (House of Commons, 18 December Volume 21, Cols 394–400, 1991) stressed the missed opportunities likely to manifest themselves as a cost of the desire to maintain Conservative Party unity. In making these statements, Labour was setting out a convincing case, yet one has to ask whether this was for electoral consumption or motivated by considered attention devoted to the UK's future European course. Rhetoric suggested the latter: the reality, though, was the former. This was to set the tone for the remainder of the decade, particularly during the time of opposition, as the PLP chose to exploit Conservative division over Europe in preference to focusing on its own distinct and long-range strategy.

In the second reading of the European Communities Amendment Bill (House of Commons, 20 May, Volume 28, Cols 273–280), Kinnock clearly indicated his support for the broad thrust of the Treaty because of its necessity in terms of furthering national interest. Labour was happy to endorse the principles of subsidiarity and economic convergence, the policies offered through the social dimension and the emerging common foreign and security policy. These were issues that were identified as important in the Policy Review Process documents. All of these developments tied in with its broad strategy and the paradigm for party change being argued, as they presented important constituent parts of the multiple goals which the leadership had identified and wished to attain in order to realise its primary goal (Harmel and Janda, 1994). Shadow Foreign Secretary Gerald Kaufman (House of Commons, 21 May, Volume 21, Cols 520–2) placed considerable emphasis on the consensus between the parties, commenting that the Treaty contained more Labour than Conservative Party policy elements This served to heighten further internal Tory dissatisfaction.

Policy responses were evidently moulded by internal and sometimes national forces, rather than by a sense of innovating capacity. It was evident that a sense of policy dynamism, as manifest in the second half of the 1980s, was no longer possible, as developments of the magnitude of the initial reversal were not feasible, bearing in mind the changes already made. One critical goal was, however, attainable: namely that of converting the links between external influences into an understandable message at a domestic level with respect to economic policy, employment, taxation and market access. As Bob Waring MP (House of Commons, 20 May, Volume 208, Col. 381) maintained, opposition to the Treaty would have sent the wrong message to sister parties on the continent and to the working people. Furthermore, it would have denied the opportunity for Labour members to improve the Bill. This comment was endorsed in the same debate by Giles Radice, a Party colleague, who went further in remarking that:

> There is no salvation for Labour as an anti-European or even a reluctantly European Party. We must continue to develop our strategy and our policies within a European framework. Labour's future, like that of Britain as a whole lies in the European Community. (House of Commons, 20 May, Volume 208, Col. 545)

However, this was a Treaty that aroused displeasure within certain sections of the party. Yet, to have opposed it would only have served to undermine much of the progress achieved by Kinnock and Hattersley, largely directed by Robertson. Consequently, the strategy adopted by Kinnock and, more significantly, by Smith was to support the Treaty as the best available treaty at the time. This did not preclude setting about its improvement during the ratification process so that it more fully reflected Labour values and priorities. The distinction between the Treaty and Bill was vital and stressed at regular intervals. In the Upper Chamber, Labour Leader Lord Richard made it abundantly clear that debate on the Bill provided an opportunity for the government to consider its overall strategy (House of Lords, 20 July, Volume 548, Col. 667). This provided strong evidence of the concentration on opposition politics, whilst Labour could attempt to integrate its own values and priorities into the final measure.

Critical to this was the demand for the United Kingdom to be part of the Social Chapter, favouring state intervention as opposed to limited government in work place legislation. This was merely adding credence to the conclusions of the Policy Review Process *People at Work* special group. This provision of the Treaty was critical in converting a portion of the anti-European faction to the leadership's point of view. The Treaty championed the rights of workers, women and pensioners and in reality it became very difficult for anyone in the Labour Movement to oppose, The leadership was thus asserting its control and ensuring that basic party ideals were being upheld. This was the weapon constantly used by Labour against the government, culminating in the Conservative government's defeat in July 1993 over the Social Protocol, though this was essentially a symbolic victory.

Where the party failed to capitalise was in placing more emphasis on the wider issues the Treaty raised, in terms of the future direction of Europe. This was particularly the case in respect of monetary union and key theoretical premises concerning the future structure of the EU. Ideas such as intergovernmentalism and supranationalism, which remain central to the future organisation and powers of Europe's institutional policy-making structure were neglected as Labour chose not to devote substantial time to its vision of the future shape of the Union it favoured. This failing created a further policy vacuum to which Blair was slow to respond when these issues re-emerged later in the decade. This represented a lack of dynamism and innovation due to the continuing low status granted to this crucial area. Yet, in its concentration on the social dimension, the party managed (Gardiner, 1996) to make the passage of a piece of European constitutional law a domestic political success in contrast to the Single European Act, where its behaviour had been far less constructive. This enabled the party to retain its European credentials, but misgivings within the ranks remained evident, with sixty-six MPs defying the party line and voting against the Bill on the third reading.

Maastricht and modernisation: the tactics

Having established the nature of the dilemma presented by the Maastricht Treaty, the key issue regarding tactics is to explain how the leadership chose to handle this next stage of the integration process. In opting to concentrate on the weaknesses of the government in contrast to developing a clearer substantial policy of its own, Labour chose to maximise the concept of 'oppositional opportunism' focusing on programme accommodation.

Although Rosamond (1994) refers to two forces driving this strategy – the intellectual challenge of devising appropriate policy and the progress towards European integration – one must also add the realisation that the European dynamic was driving almost every conceivable element of party policy. This was most notable in domestic economic management, foreign direct investment and environmental concerns. However, this was not made immediately apparent to the greater bulk of party supporters, as it was clear that public opinion was concerned about the increasing impact of the EC institutions and their policy reach (Gallup Opinion Survey, 1991). In many respects, this was an effective, though slightly cautious, approach, yet one that appealed to a strategy based on office seeking (Strom, 1990). In opting to focus on domestic issues, the party was aiming to build a constituency of support that would be more difficult to achieve by simply concentrating on Europe. Furthermore, it was easier to carry the party machine by taking this line, whilst it also catered for differing perspectives on European integration. This constituted the politics of transition that Smith also preferred, as he believed the domestic constituency would prefer to see progress in other areas, notably taxation and price stability. In following this through, Smith was willing to engage in wide-ranging consultations and the creation of effective communication channels to promote a more collegial and consensual approach than his predecessor. In addressing the lessons of the election defeat, he was keen to concentrate on what he deemed to be central concerns. The European flame was not being snuffed out: rather, the evolution of policy detail was slowing and its second-order status was being reinforced. Smith recognised that the public perception of Labour's record on Europe was poor (Gallup Opinion Survey, 1991), and in countering this he needed to maximise opportunities to create a sense of potential government linked to a perception of competent economic management.

The Parliamentary consideration of the European Communities Amendment Bill coincided with the British Presidency of the Council of Ministers in the second half of 1992. For the government, this evidently added to their embarrassment, with the public disagreements within the party receiving more attention than they normally would have. This had a major impact on the Parliamentary agenda. Although the office of President is vaguely defined, it does provide an opportunity for leadership and a natural focus for developing a policy agenda. Administered poorly, it generates confusion and is publicly damaging, particularly in respect of the external environment, reinforcing long standing negative images of British thinking. Labour could have applied pressure in seeking the placing of issues on this agenda. The reality for Labour was that this provided an additional problem: having to tease out a clear policy when the party evidently did not have something either sufficiently specific to convey or the desire to make this policy more than a second-order issue. Dwelling on public embarrassment had a limited value as it was unlikely that an internal Conservative revolt would be large enough to bring the government down, despite the consistent record of the Liberal Democrat MPs. Labour tacticians must have realised this and therefore chose to work within those limitations. All the time, it was conscious of how it could retain a non-controversial approach which could be defended, yet one that also retained the credibility which was so crucial to its overall strategy.

The Bill which dominated the 1992–93 Parliamentary session also caused some problems internally for Labour, though the public gaze was elsewhere, primarily focusing on domestic concerns. As well as maintaining the balancing act outlined earlier, there was a further problem for the party: the fact that a new leader was not immediately in place to act as a focus, particularly during the awkward period of self-examination into which the party entered following electoral defeat. Initially, serious problems occurred in respect of the stance to be taken over the second reading. The Shadow Cabinet decision to opt for abstention was not universally welcomed, and at the end of the second reading debate, the party vote was split three ways with sixty-one MPs voting against the agreed party line. Further difficulties ensued in respect of demands for a referendum on ratification in a small number of member states. However, this idea was flatly rejected at the 1992 annual conference. The problem for the leadership was that this represented a reasonable position when set against the opt-out clauses negotiated at Maastricht. This was where the differences between perspectives on the Treaty and the Bill were magnified, a crucial distinction that the whole of the Labour Movement and segments of the public failed to appreciate. This complicated Labour's tactical dilemma still further, which Brown highlighted in his contribution to the debate on the third reading (House of Commons, 20 May, Volume 235, Cols 455–61). Thus, internal factors proved to be highly influential. In playing the 'oppositional opportunism' card, the PLP chose to vote against the government in the 4 November Paving Debate. From December 1993, Labour appeared keen to urge a rapid completion of the ratification process (Alderman, 1993) and was not going to engage in proposing wrecking amendments to the Bill. However, further problems occurred in terms of voting on the third reading, similar to those at the previous legislative stage. The situation would have been far more difficult had Bryan Gould been successful in either of his bids for Party or Deputy Leader following Kinnock's resignation. As Callaghan remarks: 'His defeat cleared the way for those who saw the defeat of inflation as the necessary focus of macroeconomic policy' (Callaghan, 2000, p. 156).

Alternatively, had the leadership election been later, this would have posed very considerable problems for established policy, especially in respect of domestic economic management on Europe. This was because much of Gould's election platform would have been vindicated. The party was also able to claim success with three amendments introduced during the third reading debate, as these ensured that the Bill contained proposals that Labour was keen to incorporate. Yet one does need to ask whether this approach helped to sustain the Major government in office.

Although Gould's twin-pronged campaign for office failed, it did provide an opportunity for airing some of the ill-feeling regarding the Maastricht proposals, notably over economic policy. It also marked the end of the challenge from a fundamentally anti-European perspective, culminating in the statements that the party was willing to endorse in the 1994 European elections (Labour Party, 1994a). Gould, in part, was aggrieved by Labour's support for ERM, which he maintained made it difficult to criticise effectively government economic policy, a problem compounded by the ERM crisis in September 1992. However, this was in contrast to the thinking of the bulk of the rank-and-file who preferred the Smith option (Seyd and Whiteley, 1992). Gould's thinking was based on

Keynesian convictions and misgivings, as opposed to deep antipathy over European integration (Gould, 1995). However, as far back as 1989, he was arguing for a more proactive approach in terms of a clear policy position involving substantial government intervention in the running of the economy, though this went against the party line. This was completely contrary to the changes that were in place by the 1992 election, best summarised by Eatwell (Michie et al., 1992).

Equally evident within the party were other members who were dissatisfied with the leadership attitude to the Maastricht Treaty and thus capable of posing problems at Westminster. What was especially interesting and potentially problematic was the criticism from those who did not revel in the Eurosceptic role. The most effective representative was the newly elected secretary of the Tribune Group, Peter Hain. His concerns (Hain, 1995) were primarily geared to the degree to which economic and monetarist matters were receiving more attention and prominence than those relating to social harmonisation, thus failing the party and Labour Movement on a key aspect of its social democratic credentials. In effect, he was claiming that the leadership had opted for monetary over social convergence, and he articulated this at every available opportunity. This represented a more realistic view to which Smith could have subscribed, but he was a shrewder political figure, recognising the damage that could ensue from this stance. It would also cast a shadow over the party's unity which he was so keen to preserve, recognising the virtues identified earlier in M. Shaw's (1994) analysis.

This symbolised a different type of opposition to Europe – not that of principle, but of policy. However, its content was not driven purely by electoral factors but by an element of conviction. This has to be contrasted with the persistent and deeper objections of MPs Tony Benn, Peter Shore, Denzil Davies and Ron Leighton with regard to the adverse impact (as they perceived it) on domestic economic policy, price stability and sovereignty aired at every opportunity during debate.

The tactics displayed represented a consolidation process for the party. Although the consideration of the Bill overlapped with the electoral post-mortem, it was never going to change fundamentally the approach or essence of the party's handling of this issue. Even the chief protagonists of modernisation paid scant attention to the process of European integration, failing to recognise its importance as a vehicle for defining Labour more clearly in the public view. Smith, however, never flinched from his basic principles but judged that the party was going to be better off by focusing less directly on an issue that stirred emotions and cultivated serious misgivings. In so doing, the party did not fully exploit the opportunities created by Kinnock, but gravitas coupled with leadership authority were victorious over political dynamism and public promotion of the virtues of further European integration. External factors, though clearly evident as influences, capitulated to internal and national concerns in terms of the decisions taken by the newly dominant faction.

Conclusion

In the months immediately after the election, the party's stance took a battering, most notably after the orgy of speculation that forced the pound out of the ERM. The government was harried but never fundamentally challenged on this or the main bulk of the Maastricht provisions, as this flew in the face of Labour's interests. Any thought of exit from the ERM was tantamount to a critical undermining of party progress on economic policy, as well as the issue of Europe. In fact, the party was willing to endorse the concept of a single currency based on the realisation of real economic convergence. As regards orthodox economic policy, this demonstrated the capitulation of Keynesian strategy in favour of the centrality of price stability.

The period covered by this chapter shows the consolidation of Labour's newly established European credentials, yet also indicates the extent of the difficulties it faced in trying to cope with a very delicate issue that could, if mishandled, produce damaging results. This chapter demonstrates that the overarching set of explanations advanced by this text remained intact, yet reticence and pragmatism slowed the evolution of European policy. This was evident in the 1992 election campaign, the post-mortem that ensued and Smith's leadership campaign, as well as his time as party leader. However, many also realised that the moves towards Europe implied the longer-term approach. Yet they were not ready or prepared to take this line, despite the uncertainty about how to respond to a post-Thatcherite Conservative administration that lacked the ability to sustain and implement a coherent European policy programme. The problem was that Labour's response was based on the belief that the Conservative government would rapidly self-destruct as a result of the fractures generated by the European issue. As events turned out, the wait proved to be a long one.

Although the dominant faction that assumed control of the party following Kinnock's resignation shared his sentiments regarding the direction in which the party should move, the impetus generated in the 1983–87 period was not sustained at anywhere near the same pace. Broad support for the EC did not equate with backing for rapid progress towards integration nor the move towards the single currency, as these concerns touched on the sensitive matter of sovereignty. The primary concern was to ensure that rhetorical issue support was converted into concrete support and although this had been achieved in respect of education, health and unemployment (Gallup Post Election Survey, 1992), there was the realisation that it would be far tougher to achieve over Europe. However, by the time of the occasion of his death in May 1994, his popularity was at a peak, with the party united and modernisation sustained. The latter had been achieved as a result of the decision to confront the issue of union strength with respect to party policy-making in the hope of improving the position of the party in terms of domestic competition.

The Smith era clearly marks an interregnum, during which the avoidance of direct confrontation with the government over Europe resulted in Conservative Eurosceptics still retaining their allegiance to the Conservative leadership. The 1992 election and the handling of the European Communities Amendment Bill did, however, prove to the electorate that the PLP had overturned its anti-European stance. Prior to this, it had only been apparent to those in the Labour Movement. This goal had been attained at the same time as being able to exploit Conservative disarray whilst emphasising Labour unity, despite the evidence of differences with the leadership on issues of European principle and policy. The European issue was proving to be important, yet it was not at the core of the party's thinking during this limited time period. This was a characteristic still prevalent in Labour's behaviour on the advent of the Blair era, despite the adoption of the prefix 'New' in 1994.

5
Blair's Leadership: New Labour in Opposition

With the election of Blair as party leader by a convincing margin following the death of Smith in 1994, Labour's process of modernisation continued apace, albeit increasingly through the lens of the Thatcherite settlement, substantial elements of which had already been endorsed in the Policy Review Process. In view of the 1992 election defeat and the desire to inject a dose of renewed vigour, competence and trust into the domestic political machine, Blair was determined to create and impose a strategy on the party that would generate an air of proficiency prior to entering government. This, he believed, would help to guarantee electoral success. At the same time, it confirmed Blair's intention of acting as an agent for continuing change within the party.

As Philip Gould (1998) observes, the air of competence that was being sought implied a building of trust with the electorate, achievable by instilling a sense of purpose rather than via the advancement of a clear policy programme. In declaring his intentions during the leadership campaign in June 1994, notably in a document entitled *Strategic Principles* (Gould, 1998), Blair was keen to introduce the issue of 'national renewal' into political discourse. National renewal was deemed to be the natural follow-up to the process of party renewal achieved by his two immediate predecessors. It enabled Labour to buy time with regard to presenting detailed policy prescriptions whilst capitalising on the increasing vulnerability of a government riddled by leadership uncertainty and dissension. This was most evident in its handling of European policy. Consequently, it featured substantially in the leader's speeches to party conference in 1994 and 1995.

In setting out broad policy principles, Blair was continuing the political modernisation process begun in the mid-1980s, using it as a catalyst for building trust with the electorate. This represented an extension of the Cowell and Larkin (1999) thesis in which they have argued the case for the identification of a motivating impulse to explain the party transformation. Blair was seeking to continue the process of modernisation as a means of asserting his control over the party machine at the same time as ensuring that the party developed a distinct public identity that would be perceived to be electorally appealing. In forging this, the party confirmed its acceptance of the basic assumptions of the Thatcherite counter-revolution in political economy (Marquand, 1997). It was able to confirm its directional change and adjustment through its wider programmatic appeal and its presentation of identifiable objectives and political strategies (Heffernan, 2000).

Blair wished to ensure that, from the outset, the capacity and power to do this was firmly in the hands of the party elite and the new dominant leadership faction. In reality, this needed the development of a 'winning rhetoric' (Bale and Buller, 1995). As the rest of this chapter will demonstrate, this became the party's chief concern in the build-up to the next election. Europe was not used as the primary vehicle for promoting change, yet neither was it an external influence on the political discourse as a consequence of the continuing Europeanisation of domestic politics manifest in the ever-widening reach and impact of EU legislation. However, in seeking to explain party behaviour, it is also a matter of observing how external pressures are internalised and processed by the party itself, particularly with regard to domestic policy.

The party was seeking to promote itself as a progressive and modernising force responding to a changing environment; however, running through the veins of New Labour there was still a reticence concerning movement towards a more overtly public European position for fear of jeopardising potential electoral support. Throughout the 1994–97 period, despite the small changes of emphasis in its European policy, the party preferred to defer on the European question wherever possible. It opted not to extend the policy agenda beyond the domestic arena, as the business of winning an election was perceived to be more critical (the party's primary goal) than the process of preparing a strategy for government. The 1997 election manifesto's ten-point contract with the people confirmed this with its reference to international issues in only one area and then it was exceedingly vague: 'We will give Britain the leadership in Europe which Britain and Europe deserve' (Labour Party, 1997, p. 5).

From 1994 onwards, it became evident that the pivot around which party strategy revolved was one in which trust and public identity were to the fore. Risks and radical ideas were eliminated, with prudent economic policy and the protection of national interest as major concerns, even though a positive influence abroad was always desired. This, however, proved to show that even in a less than positive context Europe remained a means of harnessing the chief concerns of the leadership: economic policy and party unity (M. Shaw, 1994). However, it also confirmed that the party remained convinced of its need to maintain its British identity in order to create a policy that demonstrated a strong Britain within the EU. This fulfilled the continuing need to address and placate two distinct political communities, those in Britain and the rest of Europe.

In absorbing the shock of the 1992 election defeat, Labour had to reconcile the twin forces of modernisation and caution, whilst recognising that ultimately the dynamic driving the party's future fortunes and primary goal was the need for respect and wide-ranging public trust. To achieve this also required the leadership to consider how the issue of national interest and the handling of Europe would best reflect the representation and protection of such an objective. The appointment of Robin Cook as Shadow Foreign Secretary in 1994 reflected the duality of this approach, as he was keen to express his belief in a Europe of separate nation-states, each of which, through diplomatic and political bargaining, was able to provide identifiable gains for its citizens (Anderson and Mann, 1997). At the same time, this provided conclusive proof that the party had shed its previous image and hostile anti-European policy.

All of this suggests another period of modest development, though in comparison to the Smith era, Blair and Cook did sketch out a framework of thinking indicating a very positive perspective, albeit essentially based on winning rhetoric. This was most forcefully expounded by Blair (1996) in his work *New Britain – My Vision of a Young Country*. However, this was always marked by the caution inherent in Blair's early statements and the fear of losing support from key sections of the voting public, as the party was working hard to extend its voter base. As Panebianco (1988) observes, this constituted the reality of a shift from being a 'mass bureaucratic' party, stressing ideology, to an 'electoral-professional' organisation, stressing issues and leadership. At the same time, the close links with the United States were important and were reflected in the appeals to national interest and neo-liberal ideals. This was mostly in respect of economic thinking and the preference expressed for deregulation, flexible labour markets and welfare reform. As the election approached, it became clear that the party was creating a strategy that differed from the EU in certain policy areas, most notably those that possessed high voter saliency.

As far as evolution of policy was concerned, Blair was keen to build on Smith's tenure but he had an essentially domestic agenda in line with recognising the low salience of non-domestic issues at election time, aside from that of defence. Little was to be gained from campaigning strongly on Europe (personal interview with Dr R. Berry, 13 December 1999). However, Blair was aware that Europe was destined to be one of the most sensitive areas of policy for the party in its efforts to project itself as a credible alternative government. The pro-European rhetoric was favourable and this won him support, yet he also knew that he could fare no worse than the Conservative government in the handling of this issue. This lessened the pressure to act, though the PLP also wished to avoid being labelled soft by a government keen to play the politics of patriotism at the first opportunity (Falla, 2000). Unity was to be preserved, preference accommodation was favoured and party discipline was rigid, though on Europe the task was simplified because the discussion no longer concerned the basic principle of membership and continuing involvement with the EU. The focus was now on the pace and extent of integration.

Expediency was to the fore in place of ideological conviction as part of the political modernisation process that Blair was keen to continue. Economic modernisation had been completed as a consequence of the implementation of the Single European Act, the SEM and the incorporation of the main tenets of essentially Anglo-

American neo-liberal economic thinking into party policy formulation. The impulse for progress was injecting a sense of trust, moderation and responsibility into a political party which had been absent until Kinnock had assumed the party leadership. Consequently, the remainder of this chapter will show the impact of the election of Blair as party leader and how he managed and used Europe as an election issue. This is analysed by means of reflecting on his political priorities. The reality was a balancing of positive rhetoric (including references to 'Third Way Politics') with imprecise commitments on substantive issues in which the tactic was to juggle pro-European thinking with patriotic sentiment.

The impact of Blair's election

In examining the period between Blair's assumption of power and the 1997 election, it is evident that the party's efforts were concentrating on preparation for the election. The evidence indicates that although the party was not inclined to rescind on the achievements of Kinnock and the consolidations of Smith, it chose not to push the European question up its list of policy priorities. The party, as Lent (1997) notes, was disposed to an 'active vote maximising ethos' strategy in which Europe played a lesser part, more as a consequence of the changing domestic political environment, than as a pivotal element. Yet there was a substantial element of continuity with much of what had passed in the 1980s under previous Labour party leaders. As Smith (2001) remarks:

> Many of the elements of Blair's New Labour project are found in Kinnock's policy review; the reconciliation with the market, a new conception of the role of the state, a new relationship with the trade unions and close integration with Europe. (Smith, 2001, p. 257)

This justifies the claim that to fully understand New Labour's European strategy it is imperative to return to the 1983 election to detect its roots: the approach pursued throughout the course of this text.

The margin of victory influenced by the lack of real opposition in the leadership contest certainly strengthened Blair's position in a party that was frustrated, though convinced of its short-term objectives and unified as a consequence. However, some differences manifested themselves in respect of the method and style to be used in attaining the desired ends. These revolved around fears concerning what has popularly become known as the 'Clintonisation' of the party and the difficulty in balancing both middle-class desires and its traditional social conscience (Keating, 1999). However, with regard to Europe, unity was evident in respect of continuing commitment to the policy reversal undertaken by Kinnock and consolidated by Smith. There was, though, evidence of concern over specific issues, notably threats to sovereignty, the issue of subsidiarity and monetary union (Baker, et al., 1996). Intriguingly, the survey conducted by the aforementioned academics identified near unanimity of thinking on only one issue – that of collectivist and interventionist values. This study also identifies the differing views of front and backbench MPs on elements of national economic policy management and taxation. When viewed against the multitude of interests and opinions prevalent amongst those questioned (MPs and MEPs), the findings were not unduly alarming to the leadership.

In respect of the party transformation to which the modernisation process was central, the significance of the size of the leadership election victory was important, particularly in terms of Wilson's (1994) observation on party leadership. He suggests that: 'Despite pressures from socio-economic change, institutional reforms, and altered terms of party competition, political parties do not respond with changes unless their leaders order them to do so' (Wilson, 1994, p. 275).

Blair did not have an entirely free hand; however, he was fortunate to find himself in a favourable political climate in which he could maximise the Smith goodwill factor, and a sense of freshness, dynamism and youth in comparison to the jaded and increasingly divided Conservative Party. Furthermore, Blair was keen to continue the process begun by Kinnock to transfer power from sovereign institutions within the party to a core elite made up of the leader, his private office, and trusted campaign professionals and leadership colleagues; membership of this grouping was not fixed (Heffernan, 1997). After all, without the groundwork of Kinnock, it was possible that Blair would not have been elected party leader.

Early opinion polls (Sopel, 1995) following Blair's victory served to magnify his strong position, yet Labour was equally constrained by the new reality of voters being less bound by the restrictions of class-based politics and tribal loyalties. This pointed to the advantages of consensus politics, an approach that was never far from the leadership's thinking. However, as far as Europe was concerned, the reality was different, particularly with the Conservatives claiming, whenever possible, that the PLP was unquestioning in its support of Europe. This required Labour to think constantly about how it could effectively trump the nationalist card of the Conservatives.

However, it is not altogether apparent whether the bulk of party and Labour Movement members perceived what the essence of Blair's thinking was, particularly with regard to the continuing transformation of Labour beyond that of modernising the party and preparing it for government. It was not certain to them whether he was to be the initiator or continuing agent of change, or whether he wished to be seen as the figure completing the programme which a less secure leader was unable to risk. An alternative view suggests it was a case of a change in the direction of policy as an alternative route to securing the support of an essentially moderate electorate through the application and adaptation of traditional values to a modern setting, coupled with the promotion of a new ethos. The presentation of the leader and his plans by the aforementioned elite grouping makes it easy to recognise that Blair was very much part of a programmatic continuum acting as the agent for ongoing party change geared to ensure electoral success. Yet beneath the winning rhetoric, it was increasingly evident that Blair was sustaining a process begun in the previous decade, albeit from a position of greater strength in a far more favourable political climate when compared with his predecessors.

Yet, the leader and his newly installed dominant faction, strongly influenced by the cumulative impact of four electoral defeats, had distinct ideas concerning the party's future direction. The response to the 1992 election defeat which spawned this thinking was merely a reflection of how Labour had internalised and coped with its external experiences. As Heffernan remarks: 'Electoral defeat does provide an external stimulus provoking party change by leading the party to interpret the rationale for change where electoral pressures convey political impacts to parties' (Heffernan, 2000, p. 98).

In reality, the leadership was showing itself very keen to accept and modify elements of excess in Thatcherite thinking. Although, as

Hay (1994) and Wickham Jones (1995) have maintained in a detailed debate in two articles on the notion of 'political catch-up', it was a case of responding to changes in the political discourse, accommodating economic change and furthering renewal as a route out of the political wilderness. This also had to capitalise on the limitations of the Policy Review Process, which, as Taylor (1997) suggests, neither failed to address adequately the links with the natural constituency of support and the question of clear ideological principles, nor provide a critique of the role of the state in a neo-liberal economic order.

The cause of those regarded as modernisers was reinforced by the 1992 defeat as they firmly believed that one of the major explanations for the disappointing outcome was that the party still needed to undertake further reform, notably in respect of its internal procedures. In this context, Blair was quick to seize on the findings of a series of studies undertaken by the Fabian Society (1992) under the auspices of Giles Radice MP, that pointed out a lack of trust within the electorate towards Labour. To the traditionalists, this smacked of what Leys (1991) has termed 'market research socialism' with its origins in the Shadow Communications Agency established by Kinnock. This had only been disbanded on his resignation as party leader. However, it is interesting to note that within this study and the focus groups established by Philip Gould (1998), the attention devoted to Europe was very limited. This setting of parameters undermined the European issue, indicating its lack of centrality from overt party strategy, yet at the same time this marked a failure to regard publicly its evident linkage with other critical policy concerns. In reality, the perspectives offered by New Labour demonstrated the lessening of ideological concerns within the party, in response to the dominance of new-right thinking prevalent since the mid-1970s in framing many of the domestic political priorities. This helped in the fight to secure a wider support base for electoral activity.

With the Blair victory, one of the key agents of modernisation, Mandelson, was restored to a senior position in the party hierarchy, whilst Philip Gould also regained a critical role as a strategic policy adviser and communications expert. Both individuals had played important roles for Kinnock in his reforms and drive towards programmatic change. It was Phillip Gould who, whilst working with

Kinnock, had coined the term 'New Labour' in a campaigning note in February 1989. This was based on the need to draw a line between a new and old party and was geared to promoting attitudinal change towards Labour. His calls for modernisation in the late 1980s were equally relevant in 1994. With the party having moved on in respect of reform, though insufficiently in terms of acquiring public backing, the response was likely to be more positive. More importantly, as Macshane (1994) commented: 'For the first time in half a century, Labour has a leader fascinated by what can be done in the future more than he is obsessed or frightened by what has been done in the past' (*New Statesman*, 22 July, 1994, p. 20).

As Gamble (1996) observes, Thatcherism had enshrined detailed statements on freedom, law and order and trade union powers into the domestic political debate and political culture. Blair was ready to accede to these from the outset as part of his programme of instilling popular trust into a party deprived of power for nearly a generation. To do this clearly implied a continuing programme of modernisation that incorporated the basic ideals of the neo-liberal paradigm as well as recognising the diminution of state power and the increasing impact of transnational actors that threatened national sovereignty. In this respect, Labour was moving beyond the simple acknowledgement of mistakes such as those made by the French and Swedish governments in the early 1980s and 1990s (Shaw, 1998). Political modernisation had to accompany economic modernisation so that it was possible to work around the increasing restraints on the authority and policy-making capacity of the nation-state. Consequently, this implied an implicit recognition of the importance of Europe to policy-making considerations. However, much of this was very heavily camouflaged and determined by the overarching desire to defer on the European issue wherever possible, in order to help achieve a positive electoral outcome. These developments point to a continuation of the strategy instigated by Kinnock and consolidated by Smith.

In one area, Europe, there appeared to be a change in practice: namely a return to the pre-1987 days (under Kinnock) of displaying great caution in drawing too much attention to the European issue. This reticence is not explained by electoral fear or political weakness, as Blair did not have to counter the obstacles that Kinnock had to overcome. However, in both instances it is clear that the leadership had defined objectives, though in the case of Blair there was a reluctance to add substantive detail to broad statements of concern. As with Kinnock, Blair quickly surrounded himself with a team of key advisers who guided his thinking and orchestrated the party and its public projection, very carefully strengthening the managerialist and media-oriented perspectives that had developed during the Kinnock years and lessened under Smith. Nevertheless, in the search to appeal to as broad a constituency as possible, it remains unclear to what extent Blair's real views on Europe were shrouded by the impulse of electioneering yet spurred on by the catalyst of consolidating public trust.

Contextualising the change

Many in the party, including some at the highest levels, were aware that Labour's defeat at the polls in 1992, however disappointing, was also linked to the public recall of what the party had represented and its accompanying record. Blair (1993), too, commented at length on this dilemma and, in this, he made the case for modernisation rather than political adjustment. However, the 'winning rhetoric' revealed little concerning Europe as part of the new culture of Labour and its policy programmes were more inclined to favour populist ideas and policy adjustment. Where possible, this was applied to Europe, most notably in the tone used in the 1997 manifesto (Labour Party, 1997).

The term 'new' actually appeared some thirty-seven times in the leader's speech to the party conference in 1994 (Butler and Kavanagh, 1997) and was still used heavily (107 times) in the '*Road to the Manifesto*' document (Labour Party, 1996a). In his declaration of New Labour faith at the 1995 party conference, Blair, praising Kinnock, recalled that: '1983 was, for me a watershed. New Labour was born then.'

This reference to newness recognised an acceptance of the new global political economy, which, as Hay (1999), as well as Smith and Kenny (1997) rightly remark, reflected the difference between the modernised party and the traditional party that grew out of the Labour Movement. In the latter, emphasis had always been placed on the concepts of egalitarianism, corporatism, collectivism and expansive welfarism. Blair rapidly acknowledged that a distinction had to be drawn between the policies of earlier eras and those appropriate to contemporary conditions, yet he also made references to the successes and values of the past wherever possible. This was most notable in his speech to the Fabian Society (1995) commemorating the fiftieth anniversary of the 1945 election victory, whilst as early as 1991 (*Marxism Today*), he emphasised his desire to learn lessons from Labour history as opposed to being shackled by it. In effect, this was still part of constructing a new party out of the shell of the old, ending Conservative hegemony and Labour's minority status. Traditional values were being retained: however, the means of attaining these were destined to alter swiftly, reflecting social and cultural change as well as policy priority. As regards Europe, the internationalist tradition still had to be reconciled with the issue of how European the party wished itself to be. This represented an issue the party was reluctant to confront directly.

The opportunity also enabled Blair to emphasise the issue of national renewal and maintain the support of the disparate elements in the Labour Movement. In reversing the nature of the relationship between capital and labour, he was exploiting a further opportunity to engender the trust required to capture a larger section of the electorate's backing. This reflected his desire to play the long political game so as to realise the objective of leading Labour for two full terms of consecutive government.

However, the advent of Blair implied more than a continuation of the Thatcherite hegemony. Firstly, the new leader was not bringing with him any ideological belongings, though he had a clear legacy which he could not afford to overlook. His approach was based on the conviction that party values had not changed but the means to realise these had to be more modern and inclusive in order to attract more voters. He was therefore keen to pursue the continuum of change ushered in by Kinnock and consolidated by Smith. However, early on he was choosing to say little about policy, preferring to establish internal consensus on values prior to seeking agreement on policy objectives. Blair was, of course, fortunate in not having to reconstruct the party and furthermore, his relative newness to Westminster left him unscathed by longstanding party bickering.

As far as the new leader was concerned, ideological battles had been fought, with the victors and vanquished evident. Capital had proved itself victorious over labour whilst the era of grand ideology had also passed (Fukuyama, 1989). Efficiency appeared to be favoured more than equality, with the market-oriented order the constraining force on policy-making rather than the public sector. In effect, the old debates were sterile and issues of dogma had been removed from the Labour lexicon. As Shaw (1998) maintains, the old distinctions between state and market and public and private were over at the same time as the promotion of individualistic and consumer-oriented values were becoming more prevalent. A paradigm shift was evident in the domestic political discourse with the increasing Europeanisation of widescale political debate, yet for New Labour the rhetoric demanding change was far more prominent than the actions claiming it had transpired.

For Blair, the viability of traditional social democracy was questionable and the transformation of Labour into a credible electoral force led him towards elements of Thatcherite thinking. In his eyes, this linked conveniently with the reality of a modernised party. This applied most notably to economic strategy and enterprise capitalism, though differences over market fundamentalism and Europe were evident. New ideas such as 'stakeholding' were quickly rejected due to their rapidly fading electoral appeal and links to outdated ideals. The Conservatives had attacked 'stakeholding' as a euphemism for a return to corporatism and a revival of trade union power.

As regards Europe, no breach with the historical experience was favoured, though the promotion of more market-oriented societies was evident. This triggered tension in seeking to accommodate the demands of maintaining warm relations with the United States whilst supporting the great majority of EU policy initiatives.

A new, more dynamic style of oppositional politics through leadership use of the media and a broad appeal to public opinion became apparent. This tied in with the leader's real objectives, which Held and Goldblatt (*New Statesman*, 10 January 1997) described as the creation of a populist party destined to transform into a populist government offering economic efficiency and social justice. This enabled the party to capitalise on the disarray evident in the government. By 1994, this was manifest in a number of areas. The government had suffered a substantial devaluation of its currency, a rebellion on the Maastricht Treaty, the loss to the party whip of a further eight MPs and the dismissal of a Chancellor previously responsible for running the Prime Minister's leadership campaign. New political realities were accepted and these were the impulses behind the continuing programmatic development of New Labour. These realities had then to be linked into an approach that ensured a clear electoral focus with flagship policies, generating a sense of economic optimism, part of a scaling down of ambitions and expectations. This implied the triumph of pragmatism and caution where trust and confidence could be instilled through the delivery of a non-radical policy programme. The upshot was the avoidance of voter disillusionment, a focus for a manifesto programme offering change and positive action, as well as the reinforcement of a new sense of responsibility and competence. This was underpinned by the notion of spill-over generated from the process of European integration. European matters were fully camouflaged and, when potentially awkward, as with the Social Chapter which contrasted the promotion of equity in the workplace with threats to competitiveness in the market, the issue was played down. Core support had to be retained, yet it had to be offset against the possible loss of support from newly acquired backers in the business sector. At the same time, it was a clear point of difference between the two main parties over Europe.

From the moment Blair resoundingly defeated his leadership rivals, the party began to prepare for the next election. In maintaining the application of the modified Downsian (1957) tactics of Kinnock and Smith, the leadership recognised the continuing need to convince a wider element of the electorate of its merits in order to help to win its first election in nearly twenty years. This merely increased the urgency to extend its appeal beyond the narrow coalition of supporters that naturally supported the party. Yet it had already undergone a major policy review, two substantial membership drives, a series of consultation exercises and an ideological restatement of principle. Policy convergence with the Conservatives became more apparent, as evidenced in Blair's 1995 Mais Lecture (22 May) where he stated categorically that expansionary fiscal or monetary policies going against trends and global conditions would not be introduced. However, the European issue, central to the renewal and modernisation of Labour, has to be viewed in a different fashion, as it reflected the contrasting principles of nationalism and internationalism long manifest in party thinking and the determination of policy that reflected where the UK's allegiances lie.

Active vote maximisation

Any consideration of the policy priorities set by the Blair leadership faction must be viewed in terms of the contribution to active vote maximisation ethos (Lent, 1997), yet in respect of Europe the issue is a little more complex. Critical analysis has to go beyond a consideration of the policy approach to include an assessment of what understanding the party had of Europe as a vehicle for and symbol of change and continuing transformation.

Although Blair spoke of a more positive role in Europe as a basis for promoting international co-operation for mutual benefit in the 1994 *Strategic Principles* document (Gould, 1998), he recognised that the real issues in the domestic political debate concerned economic policy competence, fear of increased taxation, endorsing the virtues of popular capitalism and trust. In its efforts to regain electoral respect and trust, Labour required a sound economic strategy, a task made all the more difficult in the light of its commitment to the ERM and its comparative silence over the issue of EMU following its public proclamations in 1990 and 1991 concerning the European Central Bank.

Public disquiet on Europe (Peterson, 1997), stirred up by the ERM débâcle, made it all the more urgent for the party to camouflage its European policy, which it chose to wrap up in other concerns especially economic, investment and business matters. However, as this chapter indicates, it resulted in the party neglecting a key issue, in that it failed to develop a clear strategic overview with defined intermediate and long-term policy objectives. At the same time, there was negligible discussion of the magnitude of the European question in respect of Britain's role in the global political economy and in resolving issues of destiny and identity (personal interviews with Dr R. Berry, MP, 13 December 1999 and Dr D. Macshane MP, 14 February 2000). Europe remained a legitimate, though lesser, priority defined by domestic concerns, notably the need to balance internal party, national and international requirements. The party also had to be conscious of public unease as this contributed to the shaping of a set of limited objectives determined by the desire to promote national renewal. The latter was fully documented in the British and European Social Attitudes Survey (1998), which drew particular attention to the fact that: 'voters in all main parties have become more Eurosceptic in the period 1992 to 1997' (British and European Social Attitudes Survey, 1998, p. 185)

In seeking to implement an active vote maximisation ethos, Labour clearly had to ditch an appeal geared to an electorate based on class or traditional party identification. At the same time, it had to placate core support to protect itself from further possible electoral disappointments. Although this implied a loosening of ties with the Labour Movement which, in large part, showed itself to be very supportive of a strong European strategy, it was clear that Europe did not galvanise the party in the same way as it had during the Kinnock era. However, the party was far more united on the issue, despite some reservations on aspects of the integration process (Baker, et al. 1996). It still provided a context for encouraging change as it underpinned a raft of policies. However, it was no longer the chief primer for change. In opting for the politics of consensus and inclusiveness demanded by the forces of psephology as recommended by key policy advisers, policy prescriptions had to cater for as wide a range of interests as possible. This evidence indicated, according to Butler and Kavanagh (1997), that Labour's normal vote had declined to 33 per cent of the 1992 electorate, compared to 40 per cent for the Conservatives. Consequently, preference accommodation was still to the fore in policy creation and, as Shaw (1998) remarks, Labour was becoming 'adjustive' in outlook. To the traditionalists, this implied capitulation to many of the party's best traditions as the leadership was showing itself as cautious and unwilling to pursue radical initiatives. This has to be seen also as one of the limitations of an opposition party desperate to re-enter government, lacking the authority or confidence to enter into preference shaping as a means of generating policy change.

The one exception to the reticence expressed over Europe lay in the constitutional realm, with the party having no qualms concerning the pooling of sovereignty that European integration requires (Mandelson and Liddle 1996). This was rationalised on the basis that full sovereignty could only be claimed by the ability to tackle common problems in a European context. There was now recognition of the reality of the political and economic spill-over resulting from progress on functional integration in key policy areas. Yet at the same time, Labour, like any political party seeking office, had to realise that European integration, as Geddes (1994) remarks, was beginning to bind political parties into an economic and political agenda over which they had decreasing influence. Explaining the realities of the new trends of practical interdependence and interconnectedness to the electorate was a tough challenge, one that the party was showing little inclination to tackle.

On succeeding Kinnock, Blair was set on consolidating the programmatic and structural changes of his predecessors, yet as a result of the 1992 defeat, he was keen to modify the party ethos. This required the full implementation of the ideas of Kircheimer (1966) expressed some thirty years previously. In seeking to appeal to a far wider electorate, the leadership was happy to use techniques geared to identify public feelings and aspirations which it planned to convert into policy commitments, underpinned by pragmatic rather than ideological impulses. This also implied policy reform and a substantive acknowledgement of a new external environment pushing for renewal and change. This had been the case with the US Democratic Party in its successful 1992 presidential campaign and required resolute leadership, which the reformed party structure was designed to promote. In seeking to update party traditions whilst distancing Labour from traditional northern European conceptions of social democracy, pragmatism was to the fore in the search for a more effective means of achieving party goals. This demanded strong internal management and an emphasis on programme accommodation in seeking a broader electoral appeal, issues that Blair was keen to address from the moment he took on the leadership mantle.

In respect of the priorities New Labour was keen to promote, policy had to be deemed to be in the national interest. The challenge on Europe was to achieve this whilst acknowledging the implication that it was also linked to non-domestic issues. This accounts for the emphasis on promoting sound economics and rekindling the trust of the electorate. Most critical of all was the advice of the American pollster Stanley Greenberg (Gould, 1998), who spoke of the need to convince the middle class that the Party was devoted to enlarging rather than restricting opportunity in society, thus favouring the politics of inclusion. In view of the recognition of cumulative changes in the social structure, accompanied by class and partisan dealignment in forcing a change in electoral strategy (which militated against a Labour victory), the challenge was to arrive at a policy programme which was identifiably different from the Conservatives, yet which had to appeal to segments of the electorate who previously voted for them. It was clearly going to rule out any substantive development on European policy, as the party leadership was tending towards an increasingly sceptical position as a consequence of public expressions of belief (British Social Attitudes Survey 1996). This demonstrates yet another example of the preference accommodation approach to policy-making. In opting for few policy developments, documents produced between 1994 and 1999 on Europe reflect this sense of caution. These sentiments are best expressed in the *Road to the Manifesto* document (Labour Party, 1996a):

> In many cases the structures and institutions of the EU will need to be changed. But institutional reform must be the servant of policy objectives, not an end in itself. A Labour government will therefore assess proposals for change against their ability to contribute to the attainment of its political priorities. (Labour, 1996a, p. 3)

In adhering to the continuum approach, Blair was rigorous in applying control on the party machinery, reducing the moves of his sternest opponents with their limited resources. More authority was lodged with the leader and his chosen appointees took tighter control of campaigning and the management of public relations. This was exemplified later by the lack of consultation over the *Road to the Manifesto* document and the removal of Clause Four from the party constitution. The new Parliamentary intake of 1992 also provided the leadership with more sympathisers, a reality confirmed by the 1996 study undertaken (Baker et al.) into the attitude of Labour MPs on Europe. This trend reinforced the moves towards programme accommodation with the broadening of party appeal not being resisted by the new membership, which contrasted sharply with the attitude of some party activists who have left the party since Blair's election (Cruse, 1998).

As regards trust, internal party memos from Gould (1998) indicate this continued to be a problem area, with the need to move the party from being imprisoned by its past. This was critical to the process of attracting switch voters in building a broad coalition of support whilst identifying economic aspirations as a virtue that a Labour Party supporter should identify. Though no rash promises were being sought, there was a need to build on previous reforms, winning over C1s and C2s, as the Fabian Society identified (*Southern Discomfort Series*, 1992–95). It was clear that in earning the trust of the electorate, the open conduct of the election campaign and 'a fairness not favours' approach to longstanding supporters was welcomed. Although these studies did not carry the message of the need to produce a substantial political idea, it was, however, clear that reform of Clause Four was likely to be well received (Heffernan and Brivati 2000) alongside the provision of identifiable, responsible and carefully budgeted benefits. These were linked to key principles, notably freedom and opportunity.

Europe did not feature on such a list of primary objectives, though in the broad sense, disregarding integration was perceived as internally damaging as well as creating a negative impression with continental allies. This was a further instance of the coating of camouflage on European policy in order to keep it out of the media fray and direct public attention. Too great an emphasis on electoral strategy could paradoxically reduce the appeal of the party, as policy detail would constantly be taking a back seat to electoral strategy. This was a tactic that had been warned against as early as 1994 by Bryan Gould: 'A Party that is seen to be preoccupied with elections, rather than government, may paradoxically reduce its appeal to the voters' (*New Statesman*, 3 June 1994, p. 20). This, however, was increasingly the case on the European issue.

Contribution of Europe to the policy agenda

Between 1994 and 1997, Labour under Blair chose not to address the European issue in any form of strategic fashion. The Maastricht Treaty, which now shaped the European question far more than the limited references of the Policy Review Process, had two distinct elements to its findings. In one sense, it indicated progress towards a democratic decentralised federal-style union, yet its contents also provided solace to those seeking to preserve a key role for the nation-state in decision-making. Nevertheless, the Council of

Ministers, an intergovernmental body, remained the ultimate decision-maker within the union. Thus, the nation-state was still very influential in respect of policy-making whilst allowing for the increasing power of the forces of globalisation and their impact on power relations. This suited the traditional centralist perception of subsidiarity, the received view within the British governing political elite.

Although a matter of serious conjecture, Europe was receiving little direct attention, a reality that was dictated by the fact that voters were not interested in such an abstract notion where rapid policy delivery was not achievable (British and European Social Attitudes Survey, 1998). However, it must also be said that the Labour leadership appeared ill-prepared to deliver a meaningful statement on where the party stood in this regard as the need to define its position was not viewed as politically important. More significantly, its generality was an electoral asset providing substantial leverage during campaigning.

In reality, Labour devoted little serious thought to Europe (personal interview with Charles Grant, 20 January 1998). Positive European sentiment was evident (Baker et al. 1996), yet moves towards creating a policy think-tank with a specific European brief were slow. The Centre for European Reform was only fully established at the start of 1998, although the need to create a body with a specific European brief, in contrast to the other newly established research bodies (most notable amongst these were IPPR, NEXUS and Demos) had been evident since 1996. It was only in 1998 that the Centre for European Reform published the influential *Can Britain Lead in Europe?* pamphlet which provided a focus for Labour Party thinking on the issue.

However, the degree to which Labour's economic policy has been shaped by the European question is often overlooked. Firstly, policy programmes were framed by increasing interdependence, yet beyond that, the commitment to Europe enhanced Labour's credibility as a party of sound economic management, showing itself willing to accept economic realities which it failed to do in the first half of the previous decade. As an increasingly modern social democratic party, this implied the need to accommodate the preferences of capital, thus forestalling any radical policy, a clear cost of neo-liberalism in the eyes of the more traditional party supporters. This was a reality already very evident under Smith. Beyond this macro-economic policy, solutions on offer were shifting the party in the direction of EMU (Daniels 1998). Europeanisation of the party was thus symbiotic with successful economic strategy and a means of reassuring key electoral, commercial and financial interests of the modernised nature and common sense of New Labour's conduct. In adopting a positive European stance, the party was taking on the accompanying strictures of economic discipline on monetary and fiscal matters as well as in respect of a counter-inflation policy. This transpired despite some existing internal opposition. Blair (1996) endorsed full recognition of the fact that much of the party's economic policy hinged on the European framework. Yet in keeping with his approach, this was underplayed.

In terms of examining policy behaviour on Europe from summer 1994 through to the 1997 election, Blair clearly did not want to lose any domestic support, yet he also realised the potential losses abroad with its consequent undermining of goodwill by pursuing a distant semi-detached European stance. This explains the emergence of the policy of 'constructive engagement', a reflection of political pragmatism giving due credit to the constraining factors affecting the management of interest rates, inflation and public sector borrowing. It also reflected a challenge to existing negative perceptions of Europe, even though Labour supported the government on its policy over the beef crisis (as late as 1996). At no point, however, was the party viscerally anti-European (Marquand, 1997).

The critical question requiring investigation was whether Blair understood how Europe could contribute to his agenda. He had to determine whether it could make a positive contribution by generating new opportunities for instilling increased popular support, or if it was still perceived as a legitimate issue, though one on which it was advisable to defer in respect of priorities because of its potential electoral damage. The issue was central to a wider policy dilemma: namely that of how to secure the best interests from a solid relationship with the United States at the same time as promoting and preserving pan-European integrity. Though demonstrating support for the EU social and employment charters, the party preferred the deregulatory models of the US Democrats on labour market issues. This appeared to fly in the face of the traditional perception that in supporting the European social model a party of the left was displaying its true credentials. This illustration conveys a strong sense of New Labour's policy thinking.

Blair (1996) was evidently keen to protect and promote a patriotic case for the UK, yet what remained unclear was the type of Europe in which he was keen to see Britain play a positive role. The issue of a preferred vision of Europe and how it was to be created continued to be avoided directly. After all, it also impacted on national identity, an issue close to the heart of the electorate and one that had been threatened by the withdrawal from the ERM in 1992 and the possible loss of the pound sterling. This represented a major influence behind increasing public scepticism over Europe (British and European Social Attitudes Report, 1998).

This whole issue can also be considered in terms of psephological concerns, with the need to respond to the important trends of class and partisan dealignment and the wish not to be consigned to the political wilderness for any longer: hence the justification for completing the process of moving the party from a class base to one with a broader electoral appeal (illustrating the ideas of Pannebianco, 1988). In practical and critical terms, this confirmed the creation of a populist party moving towards, in New Labour–speak, an 'inclusive approach' to politics that also recognised the importance of political symbolism. Labour was thus content to function largely within existing institutional arrangements in order to sustain trust and appear responsible. European perspectives were underpinned by what Shaw (1998) has termed an 'adjustive' non-critical approach, especially in respect of ideas regarding representation. This was all part of the desire to create consensus, albeit couched in New Labour terms of generating trust, appearing progressive, exuding sense and responsibility whilst also generating an atmosphere of national cohesion and renewal promoted by a non-radical party. In promoting the term *People's Party*, Labour was working on behalf of the whole population, jettisoning the old ideas of conflict between those with and those denied opportunity. Within this perspective, economic modernisation was underpinned by Europe, though on the overtly political questions it was a different matter, one on which it was possible to defer progress. The phrase *People's Europe* was used as the theme for the British presidency of the Council of Ministers in the first half of 1998.

Blair's attention to Europe was limited from the outset. According to Gould (1998) the 'policy framework' section of the 1994 *Statement of Principles* has few references to Europe. Those included are couched in global terms of reacquiring strength and influence. These were general statements that gave no indication of a crafted European strategy. In the leadership campaign, no time was given to the European policy, as it was not viewed as central to the process of national renewal. Nothing substantive was planned as Blair acknowledged the work of Kinnock and Smith and wished, wherever possible, to defer on the issue. This was in contrast to the approach Kinnock had developed, which ultimately helped to redefine his political thinking.

The party leader did not indicate any sense of wishing to take European matters beyond the remit of using them as a device to retain unity which, as M. Shaw (1994) notes, was enhanced through economic strategy. In other regards, European matters were subsumed into domestic politics. In *New Britain – My Vision of a Young Country* (1996) Blair also talked generously in terms of leading the reform movement in Europe rather than trailing behind. However, it was far from clear from these sentiments what this actually implied in respect of policy detail. Too often, speeches made by representatives of the leadership (Andrew Smith MP, Chief Secretary to the Treasury) veered towards broad statements, to the effect that Europe was at the centre of the party's concerns with domestic and international politics. This tactic confirmed that the party was still playing 'oppositional opportunism' (Rosamond 1994) and at the same time seeking to demonstrate to the electorate a sense of unity which was non-existent in the Major administration over European matters.

Blair did, however, establish a working group responsible to him, charged with the task of preparing Labour's position should it enter government during the Intergovernmental Conference reviewing the provisions of the Maastricht Treaty. This body consisted of some Shadow Cabinet members and a number of MEPs, some of whom held key positions in the European Parliament, notably David Martin, a Vice President of the Parliament, and Pauline Green, leader of the Socialist Group. This ensured a wide channel of communications extending to fellow colleagues in the socialist grouping in the Strasbourg Parliament and the Party of European Socialists.

However, in evaluating the government's approach, the policy needs to be qualified by the way in which it was simple to watch the Tories tear themselves apart over Europe. This schadenfreude was buoyed by the Maastricht Treaty which the party essentially supported. However, it was aware of increased public reservations over Europe and the threats to possible undermining of the relationship with the United States.

In considering whether there is an issue of continuity or discontinuity with respect to the handling of the European question, it is essential to unearth Blair's position on Europe in the context of agreed party statements in this area. From this, it is also possible to identify and explain any variations in approach. As early as October 1993 the party laid out its main thoughts on how to approach the Union (Labour Party, 1993). Although the impetus of the statement was an economic impulse driven as a consequence of an initiative of the then Commission President Delors to promote economic renewal, it provides a good marker for revealing party thinking. This document was presented to the 1993 party conference and duly accepted, although this has to be viewed in the context of the lack of reflection on the wider implications of the Treaty on European Union (which at this point had not been ratified) by every member state. The thrust of the document is populist in so far as it identifies attainable policy goals which the public could understand, though it also reiterates the party's commitment to true economic convergence if effective monetary union is to be realised. This message is reinforced in the party document *A People's Europe* (Labour Party,1995b), which is a clear effort to demonstrate the relevance of Europe to everyday life. Although it makes reference to the importance of the need for a European and international strategy, it uses language to represent the desire to advocate the winning rhetoric it believed to be necessary in securing its primary goal. It even goes so far as to say that it was not designed to present any reflective and strategic perspectives. This document could have been produced a year earlier as a tool for campaigning in the elections to the European Parliament. However, the party was too reticent to do this, as the new leadership preferred to establish itself by focusing on domestic matters. The party leadership was also content to endorse, in a general sense, the comments of the European

Commission Reflection Group led by Carlos Westendorp, which offered a range of proposals for EU institutional reform.

Many of the sentiments expressed in the aforementioned documents also featured in the critical 'A Fresh Start for Britain – Labour's Strategy for Britain in the Modern World', part of the *Road to the Manifesto* document (Labour Party, 1996a). This constituted the forerunner of the 1997 election manifesto, a party document designed to indicate clear policy commitments whilst also promoting the winning rhetoric the party so urgently required. It is this publication that explains why Britain needs to be a strong member of an integrated regional block so that it can hope to bring benefits to the population by using its new-found capacity to respond to problems stretching beyond the limits of national frontiers. As the document states: 'Nothing is doing more to undermine Britain's economic and political influence than the doubt being created about our commitment to Europe' (Labour Party, 1996a, p. 3).

As a pre-election document it presented the differences in the tone of approach between itself and the government, yet it failed to indicate how the party was going to play the stronger European role that it stated was necessary. This is a reflection of the party's lack of thinking and its fear of being too tightly locked into policy commitments which it believed could rebound on them. It represented a further example of programme accommodation, but in this instance, one based largely upon inaction. In tapping the populist strand of thinking, it opted to talk about the need to restore public legitimacy through the introduction of review and reform procedures into particular problem areas, notably the EU's institutional structure, its accountability, efficiency and agriculture policy. The familiar comments on EMU convergence targets were also evident, as was the reticence to declare itself wholeheartedly in favour of the single currency.

These documents reflect the mentality imprinted on the minds of the party leadership and in turn beg the question of the nature of leadership Blair and his Shadow Foreign Secretary were providing on this vital issue. Blair's speeches to the party conference in 1994, 1995 and 1996 were each full of positive messages on Europe. These were couched in terms of his message of renewal and in the latter, he spoke of the need to have the full consent of the people prior to moving towards monetary union.

Blair's address to the Friedrich Ebert Stiftung in May 1995 casts light on his approach. It also helps to understand the basis of the submission to the 1996 IGC and Labour's conduct at the first European summit which the Prime Minister attended following the election victory. This pragmatic statement is lacking in substantial reflection on the European question, though it makes plain Blair's belief in the role of nation-state and the retention of the veto on key issues. These included security, taxation, treaty changes and border controls on third-country nationals, ideas which his Foreign Secretary Robin Cook, was happy to endorse. The task was still relatively easy for him, in view of his previous record as a politician with considerable doubts regarding Britain's involvement with Europe. He also highlighted the issue of competition and the realisation of open markets, thus furthering his wish to make Europe more meaningful to the people and extending his vote-gathering base. Pooling of sovereignty remained problematic, though not irresolvable, as it could be conflated with European co-operation in a way destined not to threaten national identity. His close advisers, Mandelson and Liddle (1996), developed this line of argument in their text, which was the clearest indication of how New Labour may behave in government.

Nevertheless, it is the handling of the issue of monetary union that is critical in establishing New Labour's attitude to Europe, as it was this policy area that was developing most quickly during the decade. Undoubtedly, this had major implications for all European economies. The reality of the handling of this policy shows that the leadership was far from certain on how to cope with it, falling back wherever possible on the question of convergence criteria, or Conservative disarray as a means of evading direct confrontation.

Initially, much of the attention given to monetary union revolved around the political handling of it, more particularly the matter of holding a referendum. Although initially opposed to the idea, Blair came out in favour of holding one, thus showing his populist inclinations again whilst also pre-empting government thinking. As regards hard detail, Labour had moved from initial support in principle for monetary union to a position where it gave more qualified support. In December 1994, this amounted to a call for a politically accountable European Central Bank. No doubt this was inspired by the party's need to be seen to be distancing itself from the government policy that had contributed to the ERM crisis of September 1992. Eighteen months later the policy had altered to one of not being opposed in principle to monetary union. In 1996 the Shadow Chief Secretary to the Treasury Andrew Smith, in his speech to the Royal Institute of International Affairs, went further and revealed why it was necessary to join EMU if the conditions were right. Labour's position was thus one of not being opposed to EMU, although it was far from happy concerning the arrangements agreed by the other member states about making this possible, though also expressing wider anxieties regarding the workings of the Union. These weaknesses were not, however, exposed by the government and Labour felt no sense of urgency in rethinking its problematic policy prescriptions.

This weakness was placed under the microscope again, with the publication of the Lammers Schauble document in 1994 by two members of the Christian Democrat Party in the German Lower House. This was a significant document in so far as it represented German government thinking on the integration process. This paper suggested that a hard core of countries geared to greater integration should be strengthened and that further development of the Union should reconcile coherence, consistency and elasticity. This was a recommendation accepted by the Reflection Group which had been charged by the European Commission with the task of reviewing the performance of the Maastricht Treaty. Although the statement was more directly concerned with the pace of further integration, it did provide Labour with an opportunity to state its positive European thinking in response. This was expressed through constructive engagement.

Yet Labour had very little to offer for the reasons stated earlier, preferring to provide a shopping list of concerns which it wished to have aired at the IGC in 1997 (Labour Party, 1995c). The emphasis was again on populist ideas rather than a reflection of a considered review of the current and potential future state of the Union. Consequently, an opportunity to curry favour abroad was lost, whilst in domestic terms, the party had opted to remain low-key in its approach. As the election came closer, the party's position on Europe became increasingly cautious with the leadership recognising the need to promote a patriotic approach which ensured that the United Kingdom was not seen to be totally inward-looking by placing considerable emphasis on bilateral relations with the United States. However, there was also awareness that both France and Germany did not sense that their nationhood was lessened in any way by involvement with the EU (Blair, 1996). To translate this into practical and understandable electoral policy was a task that the leadership and its advisers showed no inclination to tackle, yet this was a serious dilemma for the Labour Party.

Conclusion

The campaign commitments were revealed in the 'War Book' which, as Gould (1998) stated, had three watchwords: namely 'remind', 'reassure' and 'reward'. Labour entered the 1997 election with a series of clear campaign pledges geared towards populist policy, in which Europe did not feature (personal interview with Lord Whitty, Labour Party European Policy Co-ordinator, 24 February 1998). This was in tune with the strategy that had been pursued by Blair throughout the period since his election as party leader.

In the desire not to be outflanked by the government, Labour was not prepared to take any unneccesary risks and appreciated the reality of public perceptions over Europe (British Social Attitudes Survey, 1996). In providing something tangible for the electorate, there was very little that they could offer besides stressing the benefits of expanded markets as a consequence of the liberalisation in areas such as in energy, telecommunications, social policy and employment. However, the European underpinning of economic policy could have been more overtly stated. In sharing with the Tories in the run-up to the Amsterdam Summit (IGC) a desire to retain the veto on tax, budget, defence, security, treaty reform and immigration, the PLP was also maintaining a populist and patriotic strand to its approach. This achieved little in distinguishing it from narrow English nationalism increasingly evident in Conservative Party ranks. Nevertheless, this satisfied the need to display responsibility and competence whilst generating trust, the catalyst for much New Labour policy programming in the Blair era.

The problem was reconciling the aspiration of international influence with disproportionate economic power which is all the more difficult to sustain with a public inclined towards introversion, or at best more sympathetic to American ideas and practices (Peterson, 1997). This implied reservations about certain elements of EU policy that conflict with key economic principles. Yet the election campaign was contested on the basis of attempting to appeal to both patriotic and pro-European sympathies. The latter had been confirmed as early as 1995 in the Party's new Clause Four that made reference to 'Co-operating in European institutions'. This represented another of Labour's positive intentions though couched in terms of a generality. Macshane refers to this as a policy of 'co-petition' (personal interview, 14 February 2000). This implied that wherever possible the government should promote the notion of competition, whilst also endorsing the principle of co-operation. In reality this represented constructive engagement with the EU. As this approach ran the whole gamut of policy concerns, it did little to reconcile the differing needs in appealing to continental and transatlantic policy-making traditions and ideals. This compounded the existing challenge of seeking to be patriotic and pro-European in actions and policy intentions. It also served to legitimise Labour's choice to defer on the issue of Britain's future political and economic destiny.

New Labour chose not to lead on Europe, determining that it was not fundamental to its primary goal, that of office-seeking, though it was an important contributory factor. It also realised that in pushing the Europe issue to the forefront of political decision-making, it may expose itself to Tory attack and some internal stirrings of discontent generated by longstanding reluctance concerning European integration. Continuing criticism of the government whilst in opposition provided a useful electoral stick with which to beat the floundering Conservatives. In promoting modernisation in both economic and political guises, the Labour leadership preferred to camouflage the issue, limiting public discussion through tight party management whilst waiting for the government to implode. It also realised full well that on the key issue of monetary union, there was no way in that even if it had so desired, the public and economy would be ready for entry into the first wave of monetary union. This even allowed for the programme of national renewal being advocated.

The manifesto (Labour Party, 1997) committed the party to entry, on the basis of overcoming the triple veto of Cabinet, Parliament and a referendum. (This, however, does not square with trust, the 'Blairite' catalyst identified throughout this chapter critical to the attaining of office.) Having deferred from constructing a clear policy strategy in opposition, the leadership failed to appreciate that although intentions may be positive, this does not help when the workload increases immeasurably and the demand to deliver on policy promises escalates. This was to have serious consequences for Labour and contributed, to some extent, to the disappointing results at the European Parliamentary elections in 1999.

6
In Power: Ending Triumphant Isolationism

In May 1997, the Labour Party achieved an electoral victory by broadening, rather than deepening, the party's appeal (Clarke, 1999). In contesting the election, it was careful to avoid any policy commitments to the EU that would bind it more tightly into the integration process. However, the party remained positive in its references to European integration (Labour Party, 1997). This reflected an appreciation of the problems attached to this policy issue, as misperceptions and misgivings on European integration had long since etched themselves into the minds of the electorate and those of their political representatives.

This was incontrovertibly in line with the focus group mentality which key strategists were imposing on the party (Gould, 1998). Polling evidence from MORI (*New Statesman*, 7 November 1997) shows that Europe was ranked as either the ninth or tenth most important issue in determining voting preferences, far behind issues such as health care, housing and law and order. This made it easier for the party to lessen its display of high-level overt support for European integration. The evident hesitancy did not mark a policy change, rather an identifiable need to continue to accommodate public opinion and to lessen discussion within the party, in case any threats to unity were provoked. It also provided an opportunity for a further display of leadership strength. Party divisions would only serve to create an unfavourable public impression, which could prevent the party attaining its primary goal.

With Europe being a lesser priority in policy terms, it followed that the government intended to devote less time to it, but as the

European issue had spilled over into so many areas of public policy, the party did not have this choice. Europe, though, was not the only New Labour policy where the new government had to be watchful of electoral scepticism: the introduction of the minimum wage represented another problem area (Kenny and Smith, 1997).

In working towards the electoral victory it desperately sought, the party opted to watch the Conservatives continue to fracture on an issue that was seeping ever more deeply into the domestic political debate. The reality of this, as Lodge (1998) indicates, draws national ministers increasingly into the responsibility for formulating and adopting European policies. In pursuing this course, Labour was helping to ease itself into power, capitalising on the multitude of weaknesses that the government was displaying. However, it was Europe that generated the greatest level of rancour within the Conservative party. This stemmed from decisions earlier in the decade to take sterling into the ERM at an inappropriate rate, the unwillingness to call a referendum on the Maastricht Treaty and, most critically, the strong element of Euroscepticism evident within party ranks (Worcester and Mortimore, 1999). All of this enabled Labour to defer on its detailed policy thinking on this important matter. Although it realised what it rejected, beyond the short term, it was unclear on the specifics and rationale of a carefully crafted policy. The policy documents, identified in the previous chapter, constructed whilst in opposition concentrated only on Labour's broad objectives.

For a party touting its claims of modernity and progressiveness in terms of stretching beyond the traditional social democratic canvas, this was a considerable omission. In desiring influence within the EU without wishing to take on some of the accompanying responsibilities (especially with regard to endorsing and participating in full monetary union and the Schengen Treaty), Labour was cautious in its approach. Monetary union was, and remains, the fundamental element of the ongoing integration process and a benchmark against which commitment to the EU has to be assessed. The party had agreed to hold a referendum on EMU in late 1996, yet it was unwilling to risk consulting the electorate on the very same area to which it had committed itself. Approval of EMU entry had become dependent upon overcoming the triple lock of support from the Cabinet, Parliament and the electorate.

These inconsistencies are at the heart of any analytical examination of Labour's performance on Europe in government, as the issue intersects with the two most critical concerns for the leadership, namely economic policy and party unity. These objectives had been achieved but had also to be sustained in government. As M. Shaw (1994) remarks, reconciling these twin pressures has been a constant struggle for previous leaders. Consequently, an examination of the realities and implications of these inconsistencies provides the pivotal element of this chapter in seeking to conceptualise and analyse the party's European policy in government until the European Parliamentary elections in June 1999.

This chapter will also explore the gap between the party's winning rhetoric and the range of constraints evident in policy formulation and its outcomes. Where possible, it will draw a distinction between perspectives on economic and political integration, as Labour has undoubtedly reflected more on the realities of the former. The party has, though, demonstrated hesitancy in both areas, albeit for varying reasons. This behaviour will be highlighted during the course of this evaluation by concentrating on the issues of overarching party strategy, policy towards EMU, foreign and defence strategy and the government's evolving leadership style. The latter will also be viewed in the context of the Presidency of the Council of Ministers, chaired by the government in the first half of 1998.

In seeking to address and work within the dual constraints of vote maximisation and media pressure, it becomes apparent that the party's performance ebbed and flowed between May 1997 and June 1999 due to policy-making constraints, domestic priorities and developments within the EU. This was despite the fact that the dominant leadership faction did not face any challenge to its position of strength or policy-making principles. It was determined, at all costs, to ensure that the European issue would not derail the party from the consensus it had attained in securing electoral success: as a consequence, policy discussion was limited by the party leadership who were inclined, wherever possible, to engage in populist policy choices. (personal interviews with N. Siegler and Dr D. Macshane 14 February 2000). The leadership showed itself to be unwilling to initiate considerable change and was loath to take any decision that would weaken its popular position. Ultimately, this implied that engagement in proactive policy was only possible when it believed that a positive outcome was certain. Between May 1997 and June 1999, Europe was deemed to be an adjunct to existing policies, in preference to being viewed as a distinct and leading policy issue, except in terms of defence strategy and, to a lesser degree, institutional reform. This became more evident from the second half of 1998.

The challenge presented in government

As Stephens has remarked (*Financial Times*, 15 December 1997), Britain has moved from a position of 'triumphant isolationism' in terms of its European policy, by virtue of electing a government in May 1997 fundamentally sympathetic to European integration. As a result of the renewal and modernisation process undertaken by Blair's two immediate predecessors, the issue became something of a unifying balm for the party and the Labour Movement (Young 1998). The origin of this rested in the imperative of finding an effective counter to the Thatcherite hegemony of the 1980s.

The challenge facing New Labour, Lloyd suggests (*New Statesman*, 2 January 1998), was to make an accommodation with the EU more palatable to the electorate. Yet in so doing, this was only satisfying one of the dual audiences that the government had to address. Beyond this, Labour was presented with the challenge of establishing a substantive European strategy defining an outcome beyond 'triumphant isolationism'. Critically, it overlooked the wider continental community which, following the period of acclimatisation, was soon disappointed by the new government's emerging European policy, in particular by the tone of the remarks made at the Malmo gathering of socialist colleagues immediately after the election. However, as this chapter will show, the policy pendulum had swung distinctly in favour of the domestic audience, especially with regard to the touchstone policy of European integration, monetary union (British and European Social Attitudes Survey, 1998). This was despite the need to repair relations with the EU partners following the difficulties generated by the handling of European policy by the Major government. New Labour's approach in government was typified in Blair's address to the French National Assembly (June 1998), when he remarked: 'You do not have to be a Eurosceptic, in any shape or form, to appreciate the deep concern amongst our peoples as to how to make sense and relate to the new Europe' (Blair, 1998, p. 4).

Cook, as Shadow Foreign Secretary laid out his broad objectives on European policy (Anderson and Mann, 1997) which reflected a continuation of an approach underpinned by preference accommodation. He also remarked in his mission statement as the new Foreign Secretary that he intended that the United Kingdom should be a: 'leading player in a Europe of independent states' (Foreign and Commonwealth Office, 12 May 1997).

Similar comments were made by the Prime Minister and the Chancellor of the Exchequer in the immediate post-election period (Kenny and Smith, 1998). However, populist motivations soon became more overt in party thinking as a response to the increasingly evident strain of anti-European attitudes within the electorate. As the British and European Social Attitudes Survey (1998) remarks: 'In recent years we have seen clear evidence of declining support for integration as people have linked their policy preferences on issues such as EMU to their attitude towards integration more generally' (British and European Social Attitudes Survey, 1998, p. 186).

Voter displeasure with the arguments in Conservative ranks did not prevent an ever-more sceptical European attitude developing within the electorate (British and European Social Attitudes Survey, 1998), though this did not equate with a sizeable increase in the numbers favouring withdrawal from the EU. This left Labour with a dilemma, in that it appeared compelled to inject a greater element of populism into its approach so as to retain the broad base of support it attracted in 1997 (Anderson and Mann, 1997). Blackburn (1997) identifies a whole range of distinct voting groups within the C2 and C1 categories from which Labour managed to secure support. Amongst the most noteworthy is the fact that it obtained 46 per cent of the votes of those paying mortgages compared with 29 per cent supporting the Conservatives.

None of this, however, constituted a grand vision comparable with much of the domestic policy programme, as this was not deemed essential for a second-order policy issue. However, it is interesting to note in the speech given by Blair in Aachen in May 1999, on the occasion of his receipt of the Charlemagne prize for his contribution to the promotion of European integration, that he infers that the challenge of advancing the policy to something distinct had not been taken up, much to his chagrin. However, this statement needs to be viewed in terms of the audience he was addressing at the time, as well as the tendency to continue to engage in winning rhetoric whenever the opportunity arose.

The underlying tone of what has transpired, is a sense of caution in the carrying out of European policy. This is underpinned by a response to public concerns, combined with a reaction to considerable political instability in Europe that emerged with the ending of a distinct era of leadership provided since 1981 by such major political figures as Mitterand, Kohl and Delors. A fear of detachment from the United States in the critical policy areas of defence and social regulation was also evident within the dominant leadership faction, which was keen to preserve the party's longstanding Atlanticist traditions. Thus, a constructive partnership with her European neighbours had to be combined with the traditional British emphasis on a global role.

Public anxieties over the direction of the EU, coupled with a desire to maintain the consensus secured in May 1997, had replaced positive expressions of European thinking in respect of overt commitment to the integration process. This approach must also be seen in the context of a government driven by a massive Parliamentary majority, increasingly aware of the needs to prepare for an elusive second consecutive election victory and to avoid alienating large sections of the domestic press (Anderson and Weymouth, 1999). Policy commitments were, by definition, likely to be limited and defined by domestic policy considerations and attainable policy outcomes. However, with an unusually large Parliamentary majority, the government did possess the capacity to mould public opinion and policy accordingly, though within the parameters of Westminster politics. Furthermore, the government was clearly disturbed by the nature of policy emanating from the EU that emphasised interventionism and social control in contrast to the neo-liberal tenets it was favouring. These ideas were anathema to the governing philosophy central to the appeal to the business community – namely flexible labour markets, welfare reform and free trade – that helped to garner votes and sustain support. Labour's concern with the European model reflected on the relatively poor economic performance of member states during the greater part of the 1990s, compared to Britain's more robust record.

However, as was the case with his predecessors, Blair had to be aware of not just addressing his electors, but the entire EU citizenry (Ludlow, 1998). This was a difficult task, though common to all elected heads of state within the EU, but the need to bridge divisions of domestic opinion may not have been as great in some other member states except, perhaps, in Denmark. Yet New Labour has been fortunate in that it has shared power with a majority of socialists and social democrats across the Union since entering government. Besides guaranteeing a largely positive initial reception, a reality that Foreign Secretary Cook was keen to exploit, this has helped domestically in displaying a sense of respect and international credibility for the party leadership.

In balancing the demands of competing audiences, the protection of national interest has understandably remained dominant. Through the demonstration of a pro-European position, the government has shown itself throughout to be at the forefront of promoting reform within the EU, though this has become more evident with its recent attention to defence issues (see party documents referred to in the previous chapter). This marks a contrast with Blair's immediate predecessors in government, and at times the extolling of these has generated ill-feeling. This dimension to policy- thinking was evident as early as 1996 in *The Blair Revolution* (Mandelson and Liddle), notably in speeches by Blair (Malmo, 1997) and Mandelson (Florence, January 1998). The former, in particular, caused short-term difficulties as this was at a meeting of fraternal allies, the party of European Socialists Congress, within three weeks of Labour's election success. The difficulties at Malmo were also partly caused by the tone as much as by the content of what was conveyed (personal interview with Charles Grant, 20 January 1998).

New Labour perspectives

It was clear to Blair from the outset of his leadership that the sympathetic European disposition formulated under Kinnock had to be continued, as this had contributed substantially to the regeneration of the party and its new-found unity. Kinnock had chosen to locate the party within the European political and economic mainstream and had largely succeeded in this objective. The party was now increasingly viewed as safe, pragmatic and prudent by the electorate. However, most crucially of all, it had constructed an acceptable non-controversial economic policy, fundamental, as Norton comments, to its acquiring the attributes of a party of governance (King et al., 1998). Yet Blair has always been aware that despite the enormous Parliamentary majority, his party only secured 44 per cent of the popular vote. As Brivati indicates (*New Statesman*, 19 February 1999) this was an approach in which European interests were only promoted when they coincided with national interest (Blair, 1997). Understandably, this policy approach was applied to the issue of monetary union, particularly as the public was expressing increasing reservations concerning progress towards EMU (British and European Social Attitudes Survey, 1998).

In contesting the 1997 election, the PLP sought to maximise its strategy which, as Saunders comments (King et al., 1998), played on three elements. These were the need to display competent party leadership, fiscal and monetary conservatism demonstrating policy convergence with the Conservatives, and a clear determination not to favour any special interests. Europe did not figure in the priority area defined by careful budgeting linked to existing spending targets or in the five key election pledges identified by the party leadership. However, it did feature in respect of an overall pattern of cautious commitment. After all, as Shaw (1998) comments, New Labour thinking was and has continued to be attuned to programmatic transformation in order to secure and retain office. Impressed by the performance of the Democrats in the United States in the 1992 and 1996 elections, as well as the Labour Party in Australia under the leadership of Hawke and Keating (Butler and Kavanagh, 1997), the PLP leadership appropriated the language of change and renewal. This was used to good effect in the conduct of their election campaign. Although the European issue could prove helpful in portraying influence beyond the domestic shores, the need to underplay the European dimension to policy, aside from where it bolstered national interest, was triumphant. This fitted in with the overarching strategy of consistency and the continuing status of Europe as a lesser issue in policy-making terms.

The Labour Party election manifesto was marked by its circumspection over Europe, which needed to consider public opinion carefully. This was reflected in the British and European Social Attitudes Survey (1998) which confirmed that voters from all main parties became more Eurosceptic between 1992 and 1997. The similarity of the statements between the two main party manifestos on European strategy is striking, with their comments on Britain playing a central role in European affairs. This was particularly the case regarding a negotiating position, the desire for economic convergence and the holding of a referendum. As the campaign unfolded, Labour revealed a more sceptical approach, patriotism being used as a vehicle (such as the use of a bulldog called Fritz in a party political broadcast on 15 April 1997) to promote respect. National interests had to be served at all times and it was even hinted that isolationist tactics would be used if these interests were threatened (*Independent on Sunday*, 20 April 1997). Even the declared aim of joining the Social Chapter was couched in terms that did not threaten the competitiveness of British business or Labour's desire to be the party of business. Policy aspirations were clearly being coloured by political constraints and the defining of essential priorities as articulated by the electorate.

On his election as Prime Minister, the strength of the Eurosceptic atmosphere was evident, yet the language expressed by Labour was different in tone from that expressed by the Major government. The Foreign Secretary, Cook, was keen to identify the sense of purpose given to European policy, exemplified by his participation in an intense range of meetings across Europe. These were supplemented by discussions involving Douglas Henderson, the government's first Minister for Europe.

Cook came to office claiming some distinct elements to his European policy issues, having opted to implement a European policy in which Britain was to play the role of a constructive yet pragmatic partner within the EU, rather than seeking fully to enact its rhetoric. These were the expectations of comradeship from fellow colleagues of the left, that Britain could lead or be one of the leading members of the Union and the fact that entry into the first wave of EMU was unlikely (*New Statesman*, 16 May 1997). These sentiments were endorsed by the Chancellor of the Exchequer, who also made reference to 'Third Way' ideas, notably the need to play a strong role in a changing Europe (*European Access*, August 1997), building on ideas outlined by Blair (1996). In this approach, the government was seeking a middle course between European social democracy and the principles of neo-liberalism. It also suggested

that the United Kingdom could offer a distinct set of policy principles which could be blended with traditional and evolving social
democratic virtues. This was based on the view that the existing
European model stifled growth through its tendency towards an
over-regulation of business. It was at this juncture that the government spoke in terms of Europe benefiting from Britain's experience
and its belief in promoting economic flexibility. This was a reverse
of the more traditionally cautious party perspective, yet, critically, it
helped to placate the domestic audience resentful of the constant
imposition of European rules and standards, though the European
audience was less impressed. This was perceived as further evidence
of the vitality of the economic as well as political relationship with
the United States, amounting to a further manifestation of populist
politics reinforcing the party's national status.

Caution was manifest in the handling of economic, employment,
common foreign and security policy issues, whilst outright resistance was evident on issues that were deemed damaging to national
interests, such as the abolition of border controls and tax harmonisation. In areas where clear policy outcomes were attainable, the
perspective was positive, notably in respect of the single market,
crime and environmental matters. These policy perspectives are
traceable in the positions taken at meetings in Noordwijk (a
preparatory meeting for the Amsterdam Summit) and at
Amsterdam. At the latter, the government was able to present the
agreed democratic improvements as acceptable to the British people
as part of what was to be promoted as a *People's Europe* during the
British Presidency of the Council of Ministers in the first half of
1998.

The pro-European rhetoric of New Labour in power was evident
from the outset. Whilst visiting his French counterpart in Paris,
Cook remarked: 'It is our commitment that we will draw a line
under the sterile, negative and fruitless confrontation which was the
policy of the previous government' (Anderson and Mann, 1997,
p. 114).

However, there was a tendency to couple this with critical anti-
European Commission comments on economic principles. These
were driven by the belief in promoting competition, the profit
motive and private enterprise as motors of a strong economy.
Deregulation was being encouraged in the name of promoting flexi-

bility and currying the support of the business community. Having learnt a lesson at Malmo regarding tone and presentation, the approach at Amsterdam was more conciliatory. Cook continued to speak in clear and ambitious terms about Britain playing a positive role in the Union (Budapest Speech, 26 November 1997). However, the positive European rhetoric always made reference to the need for Europe to change, notably in terms of economic policy and institutional reform. The latter again appealed to the populist instincts of the electorate. This was exemplified by Cook when he commented that: 'The EU seems to spend too much of its time discussing things that do not touch the people's lives, abstractions and institutions rather than a concrete agenda' (Cook, 1998, p. 3).

The fact that the speeches made by Cook and his government colleagues were mostly given outside the United Kingdom – represents a clear tactical move. In the wider European strategy it revealed a government seeking to take attention from a potentially troublesome domestic policy area, at the same time as giving some positive signals to its European neighbours. It also indicates a desire to placate the European policy audience. At no point, however, was Europe to be used to the same degree as a vehicle for strongly promoting or underpinning the policies of New Labour as had been the case with Kinnock, as wherever possible the government preferred to concentrate on attainable domestic policy outcomes.

EMU entry

Confirmation of the significance of the monetary union issue in understanding the Labour government's approach to European policy is best summed up by McElvoy (*Independent*, 25 June 1998) in her remarks that: 'Searching questions about the suitability of EMU for Britain are questions about the UK's interests and the kind of Europe we wish to forge' (*Independent*, p. 23).

The key test of commitment to the integration process is the issue of EMU membership. Party thinking on this is both revealing and consistent in terms of policy perspectives and public expressions of intentions. It reveals a great deal concerning the process of rebuilding relations with the other EU member states following the recent Conservative government, as positive concrete action, rather than vague declarations of intent, remains the most persuasive way of securing and sustaining their support. This, in turn, begs an investigation of how the government handled the EMU issue and what has actually transpired since 1997.

Monetary union is the policy area in which the government can lay to rest the old perceptions of the United Kingdom acting as the awkward partner (George, 1992), for EMU represents the essential building-block for the realisation of the single market and provides a crucial impetus for deeper integration. As McElvoy (*Independent*, 25 June 1998) hints, it becomes very difficult for the UK to realise its European objectives outside the framework of full EMU as well as to establish a popular reputation for competence crucial to the retention of electoral support. This approach also confirmed that Labour in government is prepared to repudiate previous policy measures, particularly tools of economic management. However, in responding to this challenge, the issues of the UK's political and economic destiny, combined with the protection of national interest, remain the critical issues requiring resolution.

The abandonment of the ERM in 1992 severely damaged the Major government and established the parameters for Labour in the conduct of the policy critical to its primary goal and related multiple objectives. From this point until the election, this issue dominated the domestic political debate, but it did not represent a real debate on the virtues of European integration. Rather, as Worcester and Mortimore (1999) point out, Europe played a role as an 'Image Issue' rather than as an 'Issue Issue'. Europe constantly served to remind the electors how divided the Conservatives were, rather than focusing discussion on the broader strategic question of Britain's economic and political destiny. This certainly suited New Labour, especially in terms of short- and medium-term objectives. Furthermore, it confirmed that Blair adhered to Labour's inclination towards programme accommodation, developed in the previous decade as part of the party's rehabilitation.

Following the election victory, the government sought to initiate a wider debate on the EMU issue, having laid out its desire to put in place a stable long-term monetary framework in which the granting of independence to the Bank of England was central. The debate, however, appeared to trigger volatility in the financial markets with the media seeking to maximise the subtleties from comments made by Cabinet members (Kampfner, 1998). In view of this uncertainty, the government, through the Chancellor, chose to clarify its position in a major statement to the House of Commons on 27 October 1997 (Volume 29, No. 55 Cols 583–9).

What the Chancellor achieved was a subtle balancing act in terms of reconciling the competing strands of domestic opinion on this vital issue. Although he indicated that Britain would not be part of the first wave of EMU entrants, he did declare the government's willingness to participate, with the proviso that certain conditions were met. However, Blair had already declared this intention in the House of Commons as far back as March 1995 (*New Statesman*, 31 October 1997). The difference between the two occasions was that in 1997 the government stated there were no constitutional bars to entry, and in this instance, laid out economic criteria to be met. However, the proclaimed tough choice that the Chancellor declared necessary was avoided. The five economic tests set down were such that obtaining clear and unambiguous responses was going to be difficult due to the subjective nature of the criteria set. The government, in accepting that domestic factors acted as possible policy constraints, was apparently being over-ruled by them, notably in respect of the Conservative-leaning press and the large elements of the Eurosceptic tabloid press (Anderson and Weymouth, 1999).

If there was a desire to provide leadership within the EU, the tone of the Chancellor's statement put an end to this. He opted for a domestic, in preference to a European route, using the issue to consolidate and build public goodwill, acknowledging the longer-term objective of having to adjust public opinion on the whole issue. This was part of the process of what New Labour language refers to as 'Reconnecting with Europe', a key component of a populist agenda. This was another phrase that government spokespeople frequently used in the press and public discussion during the British Presidency of the Council of Ministers in 1998. It confirmed that the government preferred to play a reactive role and this cast doubt on its policy ambition.

The statement appeared to satisfy all shades of opinion in the party and indicated that the proclaimed tough decision which the Chancellor had to make was, in effect, deferred. In placating the varied interests and opinions within the Labour Movement, the Chancellor chose to use language which left his policy options open. However, for wider public consumption, the policy was couched in terms in his House of Commons speech (27 October) which declared that the economic benefits of joining for business and industry were clear and unambiguous.

At this juncture, the domestic agenda was perceived to be the greater imperative and the government chose not to identify in explicit terms the link between Europe and the domestic constraints created by the need to fulfil the Maastricht convergence criteria for EMU entry. These could have undermined popular support in the short-term, though over the longer period it may well have helped in reshaping public opinion on Europe and the Euro in particular. This would have represented a decisive step in the government's efforts to win the battle of ideas with the Eurosceptics. In many respects, this attitude seemed to suggest that the strongest argument that the pro-Europeans could muster was that the single currency was an inevitable development.

Despite the claims of modernity and progressiveness, Europe was not the issue on which the PLP chose to underpin its policy pro-gramme. This represented a case of preference accommodation securing a victory over preference shaping, with European matters still being viewed as peripheral to vote maximisation, or at least whilst public opinion was being shifted from its sense of misgiving over Europe. In playing to the confrontational domestic gallery, the government chose to overlook the wider economic, political and commercial implications of its decision. This reflected a choice to view the issue only through the lens of domestic policy tests. In so doing, the government was proving itself to be far more concerned with the domestic agenda, in preference to treading on potentially dangerous ground as far as the electorate was concerned. The gov-ernment was thus responding to, rather than leading, opinion. The caution that characterised this position reflected a leadership that chose to respond to an external environment instead of helping to shape it.

Following the October statement, the government opted to use its Council of Ministers Presidency to display its sympathetic European credentials on issues other than EMU. In his address to the French National Assembly (1998), Blair reminded his audience that British entry into full EMU was dependent upon economic convergence. However, he also made the case for advancing integration on a functional basis. The centrality of EMU in EU discussions soon came back into focus during the Brussels summit of 1 May, which determined the participants for the first wave of EMU. Although the deal eventually struck kept the EMU timetable on course and resolved the issue of who was to be the governor of the Central Bank following a protracted dispute involving France and Germany, the government emerged from this experience humbled. Blair had chaired a meeting which approved a further key stage in European integration, one that confirmed Britain's distance from this process. The outcome of the summit revealed a clear gap between positive New Labour rhetoric on Europe and substantive achievement on the critical issue of commitment to real integration. The coincidence of this meeting falling on the first anniversary of the election victory helped calm domestic fears, though it did little to satisfy growing concerns about the plans of the government in a number of European capitals. The crucial external arena in which New Labour was keen to play a leading part was not being nurtured and promoted.

Besides the difficulties of the Brussels meeting and public apprehension, there remained the issue of the tests. A Treasury Select Committee (HM Treasury, 1998), examining all the tests, declared that it would be difficult to judge whether EMU was a success for five years. In reality this merely confirmed that the tests are subjective economic guidelines as opposed to objective standards. This was more a case of the government providing an effective escape route, should one be required, if EMU proved to be a failure. In adopting this approach, the government was seeking to display further competence in its desire to sustain support and be viewed as the country's natural economic manager (Kenny and Smith, 2001). Over the longer term, this was deemed a means of easing public reticence on Europe. This again indicates the need to ensure that Europe did not endanger the party's domestic electoral standing.

The more positive tones on EMU expressed by the Prime Minister in his address to the European Parliament (June 1998) and at the 1998 Cardiff European Summit a few days later, indicated a change in tone and language. With the July Cabinet reshuffle characterised by the placing of stronger European advocates in key posts (Quinn and Mandelson at the Foreign Office and the Department of Trade and Industry respectively), a new sense of confidence was generated, spurred on by a series of government-inspired seminars focusing on

European strategy. This marked one of the first instances of the Labour government devoting considerable time to the European policy question, albeit having been inspired to do so by the difficulties in Brussels.

Following the decision not to join the first wave of EMU, the government sought membership of the ECOFIN Council group (provisionally known as the Euro X committee). If this proved to be impossible to attain, its secondary objective was to limit its brief. However, at the Luxembourg Summit in December 1997, it had to accept that it was debarred from membership. Britain was far from happy with this decision and displayed considerable arrogance in its displeasure at being excluded (personal interview with Charles Grant, 20 January 1998). In so doing, the government was confirming its desire for influence without wishing to take on the commitment of responsibility, a reality that distressed many of Britain's European neighbours. On the domestic level, the government was cheered for doing its best in seeking to protect its diplomatic and economic status, but the problem of addressing differing and important policy communities remained.

Yet through 1998, with German support, Blair was able to obtain assurances that the committee would only concentrate on internal EMU affairs. In exploiting the anti-French sentiment stirred in Brussels, Blair had a further success in ensuring that non-EMU member states were involved in preparations for meetings and in confirming the primacy of the Council of Economics and Finance Ministers of the EU (ECOFIN) in economic policy.

Aside from the Euro X difficulties, the consolidation of a more positive position on EMU continued with the emergence of a National Changeover Plan introduced by Blair in February 1999. In this document, reference was made to a change of gear, though the emphasis remained on a strategy of *Prepare and Decide*. The Changeover Plan marked a realisation by the Blair leadership (Chicago, April 1999) that the country had to be prepared for the Euro, once a decision was made. The statement, though, was far more concerned with political realities than with changing economic and monetary conditions in the UK. In reality, this was another measure to boost the profile of competence it wished to confirm at every opportunity. Failure to undertake a plan would have represented a denial of reality. The Euro was being taken more seriously and the dangers of isolation were being recognised (*Independent*, 24 February). With support being given to the joint socialist manifesto for the European Parliamentary elections, which the Foreign Secretary played a key role in drafting (personal interview with Dennis Macshane, MP, 14 February 2000), a change in policy was evident. EMU was being touted as a device that could provide economic benefits and enhance UK power and influence through the pooling of sovereignty. However, the results at the European elections proved to be a setback for the party, confirming serious public disquiet over EMU (*The Guardian*, ICM Poll, 8 June 1999). Nevertheless, EMU remains the one issue capable of undermining the government's electoral position, as it gives the Conservatives one issue where they enjoy a commanding lead.

With Blair rather than Brown presenting the National Changeover Plan to the House of Commons, the Prime Minister was indicating his thinking to his broad-based domestic audience, which included a number of business leaders and Conservative party supporters. However, at all times he stressed the need for economic changes in European economies based on neo-liberal tenets and he was showing himself to be consistent in advocating the virtues of his national approach. The domestic constituency was being reassured and unnecessary risks were avoided. For fellow EU members, a critical policy community that had to be addressed, the real advance was that the government had played a key part in drawing up a policy document in which support for the future of the Euro was endorsed. This was sufficient for the time being to offset the ongoing British reluctance on issues of tax harmonisation and the withholding tax, even allowing for the fact that, formally, government policy had not changed.

The handling of entry into the EMU demonstrated the caution with which the PLP views Europe. With the party quickly made aware, once elected, of the danger in trying to progress from some of the very careful statements made in the election manifesto (Labour Party, 1997), prudence was evident. Public debate was increasingly dominated by the issue of the Euro with wider debate concerning integration stifled (British and European Social Attitudes Survey, 1998). The traditional misgivings regarding Europe returned to the surface, preventing calm and rational debate. As Gamble and Kelly (2000) claim, it was a case of members of the dominant leadership faction either subscribing to enthusiastic or pragmatic policy perspectives on EMU, though the latter appear to have been victorious. The government believed that it made more political sense to place the emphasis on macro-economic stability. The governing orthodoxy had become one where inflation is the biggest economic evil, government borrowing unwise and progressive taxation an electoral millstone.

Although the extreme Eurosceptics fared badly at the polls, obtaining 3.1 per cent of the vote (Young, 1998), much of their thinking entered into the political mainstream and was latched on to by the Conservatives and sections of the media. The leadership, desperate to retain consistency in its actions and the backing of its newly recruited supporters, was thus limited in its policy options, particularly as the party from Kinnock onwards had rejected the use of external influences as the driving policy impulse. Consequently, the government sought to make a more positive impact on the EU in other areas.

Foreign policy and defence influences

As Wallace remarks: 'Instinctively New Labour looks to America first, and across the Channel ... second.' (Wallace, 1998, p. 32). This reality is borne out by its unwillingness to confront the issue of whether the United Kingdom's ultimate destiny rests in the transatlantic link, the European theatre or somewhere between these poles. Furthermore, this approach is endorsed by the instinctive Atlanticism which Blair infuses into the party's strategy, helping to shape the vision of Europe that he prefers (Young, *The Guardian*, 24 November 1998). In pursuing this traditional Labour policy, Blair has shown himself to be more suited to consulting with the US, with a tendency to preach American virtues domestically as well as in Europe, particularly in respect of economic thinking. This was notable from the outset of the government in his address to fellow socialists and social democrats at Malmo in May 1997. However, between May 1997 and June 1999, there is evidence of New Labour learning from the dangers of too close an alliance with the US. In the first half of 1998, this occurred in the handling of the Iraq crisis, with the agreed military response between the US and the UK coming at the expense of co-ordinating policy responses with EU colleagues.

Undoubtedly, the issue of European policy ties into concerns over foreign and defence policy, though it has been transposed into more of a domestic concern underpinned by anxieties over insecurity, national pride and retention of sovereignty. This implies that the issue has to be viewed within a context of a wider set of changing international priorities and obligations, as well as against a rapidly changing international political system in which the UK is involved. This is at a level beyond her status as a middle-ranking power with a role at the UN Security Council and as a member of the group of industrialised countries (G8).

In seeking to explain the behaviour of Labour in power in relation to foreign and defence concerns, a historical context is required. Long-term strategy dating back to the last century involved the manoeuvring of strong states against each other reducing the level of possible weakening that the UK may have inflicted on its status as a world power. At the same time, this implied that any conflict would more likely involve smaller, less-threatening states, while British interest in Europe was directed by the principle of maintaining a balance of power. Britain continued unchallenged as an empire builder, or, as Parker (1997) suggests, a lion in the world, though a mere sheepdog within Europe.

This position was legitimised by geopolitics which ensured Britain's peripheral status in relation to the European landmass and the desire to remain on cordial terms with the United States. Over a long period they had provided an external support structure, conferring a range of economic and political benefits on the United Kingdom. These ranged from support in providing a defence capability unrivalled in western Europe to providing support for the pound sterling as an international reserve currency. For the Labour leadership, this provided a tool for undermining the claims of those within party ranks demanding a stronger ideological basis to the conduct of foreign policy.

In the postwar era, the UK has faced the dual problem of reconciling its decline on the world stage and its subsequent retreat from colonial glory with the rise of the Common Market and the emergence of the EU. In response, the two main political parties have chosen to bask in the nation's global reach and military strength. As a consequence, governments have been too preoccupied with the perception that Britain matters more diplomatically, economically and politically than it really does.

From the early days of membership, besides the Heath administration, Britain has not had a government prepared to endorse vigorously the merits of European integration to the public. The reality has been one in which the fear of exclusion has won out over a genuine lack of enthusiasm and conviction. It is against this backdrop that the Blair record has to be assessed. Positive European rhetoric and the desire to restore strong relations with EU colleagues marks a willingness to change position, yet what has followed clearly shows a policy constructed with US influence in mind. As Grant (1998) notes, picking up on the comments of former US ambassador to the UK Raymond Seitz, when Britain's voice is less influential in the key European capitals, its influence in the US will also decline.

Since the election victory, the government has sought to repair the damage caused by the previous government's largely anti-European behaviour. In containing and removing anti-European rhetoric, it has remained locked into the Atlanticist mind-set that has dictated much postwar strategy in foreign and defence policy across the political divide. In the context of the central thrust of this chapter, this confronts the paradox of wishing to be progressive but being guilty of traditional thinking and over- caution. Rather than helping to shape the environment, the display of ambivalence shows a party keener to play a reactive role. The Foreign Secretary remarked on the critical significance of this at the end of the Council of Ministers Presidency (*The Guardian*, 30 June 1998).

Even in this interview, he commented on the importance of the British relationship with the US. Once the immediate obligations of the government were dealt with in respect of the preparations for, and the meeting of, the IGC and the Presidency, the government began to engage in some wider thinking regarding the transatlantic relationship. In seeking to demonstrate its new thinking, the government was prompted by two elements. These were the criticism levelled at the handling of the first Iraq crisis in early 1998 and the wish to address defence matters. In the case of the latter, the desire to engage in agenda setting was also inspired by the need to recover some of the ground lost in dealing with the EMU issue.

In handling the first Iraq crisis of 1998, the government chose not to promote a common EU position, preferring to formulate a strategy with the US. What transpired was the acting out of the role of the loyal Washington ally. This generated considerable European discontent, with the Dutch Foreign Minister, Van Merlo, criticising Britain publicly for neglecting her duties as European Council President (*The Guardian*, 25 February 1998). This was symptomatic of the lack of thinking on Europe (personal interview with Charles Grant, 20 January 1998), the inherent caution mentioned earlier and the influence of the positive personal and political relationship between Blair and the US President. The outcome was that the close military and security alliance with the US was unchallenged and that NATO remained a pivotal organisation in the preservation of Europe's defence interests, even though the *raison d'etrê* of NATO was coming increasingly into question. This was as a result of the reshaping of Europe following the collapse of communism. Yet this approach was pursued at the same time as the UK was attracted to elements of Europe's economic integration agenda (with reservations over the currency and regulatory aspect). Foreign policy thinking in a European perspective was acceptable, provided that it did not clash with anything the US wished to promote. This made the UK position more difficult to sustain, particularly in the context of continuing ambivalence over other elements of the integration agenda. Although on defence and security matters, the UK has tended to side with the US, with the consequent danger of identifying the European role as insignificant as far as the UK public is concerned, this was starting to present a problem in building support and legitimacy for the EU domestically. This was particularly the case as the EU was keen to strengthen the common foreign and security policy created by the 1992 Treaty of European Union. Moreover, a common defence strategy clearly provides the public with an identifiable policy programme: one in a sphere identified with a sense of British strength, tradition and reputation. Britain's potential role was further buttressed by the considerable element of firepower that could be deployed on NATO's behalf.

During the spring and summer of 1998, a series of seminars were staged by the Labour Party with the aim of devoting more time to European issues, and defence became an area where it was clear that the UK was keen to play a distinctive role. For Britain and, more especially, Blair, this represented a means of appealing to the US and European policy communities whilst assisting in the appeal to populist domestic intentions central to New Labour thinking. In European terms, by generating debate beyond the question of burden sharing, the government was displaying leadership.

The brokering of the St Malo Defence Declaration with France in December 1998 shows a development from tone into substance, with the message conveyed by the government important in demonstrating a positive European image through a concrete achievement, designed to complement the transatlantic alliance and strengthen NATO. For the EU, it was significant in helping to identify a clear European defence strategy in which the EU must possess a capacity for autonomous action (European Council Declaration, June 1999).

This represented a positive achievement for the government, despite the contradictions that appeared to characterise its thinking. It also added impetus to NATO's support for an initiative that France had been advocating for a long time as part of an evolving Common European Foreign and Security policy. It implied the need for Europe to develop its own capabilities in the spheres of intelligence, strategic transport and command and control facilities. However, Britain and her European neighbours were still working very much within a NATO structure, though one that granted them more freedom whilst guaranteeing French involvement. The Labour government's substantial involvement in this development enabled them to address the European policy community at the same time as acknowledging the continuing importance of the ties with the United States and displaying a sense of domestic political strength in a manner with which the voter could identify.

Political leadership

In examining the record of Labour in power, it is important to recognise that in the first six months of 1998 Europe emerged as an issue in its own right in the domestic context. During this period, when the government had begun to rebuild its relations with its EU partners, it was faced with a serious problem, as Blair had to chair a key meeting in Brussels on 1 May to determine the number of states entering the first wave of EMU. In deciding which countries were going to enter the EMU at its inception, Blair, according to Young was playing the role of: 'Umpire and not player' (Young, 1998, p. 495).

On this touchstone policy, his position was constrained by the existing commitments on EMU. However, this event proved to be a chastening experience as although the policy paradoxes identified earlier remained, the evidence indicates the start of a period of reflection and first principle thinking on a range of broader European questions (personal interview with Charles Grant, 20 January 1998). The rhetoric on EMU altered, whilst the populist message of the Presidency was reinforced at every available opportunity. This was geared to addressing the needs of both domestic and external audiences.

After an eight-month acclimatisation period, taking on the mantle of Presidency of the Council of Ministers provided the government with an opportunity to display possible leadership strategy. In preparing itself for this challenge, it had to accept that the Union was facing two of its sternest challenges, monetary union and enlargement. Furthermore, it had to confront these at a time when the legitimacy of the EU was increasingly being questioned by the electorate, not just in the UK, but also in some other EU member states (British and European Social Attitudes Survey, 1998).

Although this chapter has traced the government's handling of the European question in terms of identifying a clear trend in behaviour, the Presidency provides a distinct focus for leadership inclinations to be observed. However, it must be stated that the office also has clear limitations in terms of what is achievable within a six-month time period. Much of the agenda is determined in advance, thus the priority of the office holder is to try to make an impact through effective chairing of meetings and agenda setting. In terms of one of the main arguments in this study, leadership is taken to imply the development of ideas and initiatives which others follow, combined with the ability to influence and possibly control the actions of others (O'Connell, 1997). This generated an opportunity for a government to extend its actions beyond the matter of presentation of issues, the retention of internal party discipline and the constraints imposed by preference accommodation. Yet it appeared that the government had chosen to impose limits on its policy actions based on the criteria of what it perceived the public would tolerate and, more critically, support. At the very least, Labour could move away from the minimalist approach of the previous government. Any sign of leadership thus implied little more than the normalisation of relationships that had been so badly strained in the middle of the 1990s.

The leadership question is best conceptualised by considering the issue in two ways. Firstly, this can be done by examining the aspirations set down by the Presidency, viewed in the context of the inheritance of the actions of the previous government and the declared policy objectives of the PLP. Secondly, the impact of domestic politics on the leadership's aspirations and the identifiable outcomes sought by the dominant faction in the party must be considered.

During the first six months, the government exploited the welcomes and expressions of goodwill from across the continent (aside from the negative reaction to Blair's speech at Malmo in May 1997). It also made its presence felt in EU bargaining processes, extolling a more positive perspective on a number of issues. Dynamism was apparent at the outset of the new government, as demonstrated earlier in the chapter. However, this was largely driven by the need to dispel the legacy of the past, whilst also seeking to serve as wide a political constituency as possible. This constituted a gesture to the notion of inclusive politics proclaimed by New Labour as one of its guiding principles. Trading on the domestic political dynamic, the Foreign Secretary spoke of the position of strength enhanced by internal unity from which the party could work (Anderson and Mann, 1997).

The Foreign Secretary outlined a broad set of objectives in his address to the European Parliament (January 1998). In addition to piloting the course of EMU and enlargement through the EU policy-making machinery, he made it clear that the UK wished to create an effective and inclusive Union. Central to this was the promotion of attainable objectives, including policy reforms that would help to address the decline in public regard for the Union. Many of the sentiments had been expressed in the build-up to the Presidency but in less specific terms (Cook, September 1997). Commitment to the EU was reaffirmed at every available opportunity, despite the near inevitability of not entering with other member states into the first wave of EMU.

The constraints and limitations of domestic politics were evident throughout the period. As a consequence, they inspired the essence of the government's programme. Regardless of the many declarations of belief in the European ideal, the government was keen to ensure that acceptance of further commitment to European integration had to be accompanied by internal reforms within the EU, predominantly on policy matters. This had the twin objectives of furthering some of the government's policy preferences and serving to placate public apprehension.

In addressing the European Parliament (June 1998), Blair identified two strands of opinion on Europe. These constitute outright opponents of the Union and individuals who, although broadly supportive, worry about the direction and priorities of the Union. It was the latter that the government wished to reach, realising full well that radical actions were neither appropriate, nor in the remit of the party's policy programme. The government understood public misgivings over Europe, but had clear policy priorities, determined by public opinion as well as a series of key pledges in the manifesto. Europe, however, did not feature amongst these, despite the government's rhetoric. This is best exemplified by the remarks of the first Europe Minister in his comments about making Europe more relevant to the electorate: '... Breaking a corrosive pattern of sterile debate and empty caricatures in the UK, and working with our partners to show how the Union serves the interests of ordinary people' (Henderson, 1998, p. 564).

By the same token, the government knew it had to act on European matters and was keen to do so, though the shadow of a partly Eurosceptic media was ever present. This was a major concern for a government enthused by the media, yet worried about the damage it could inflict on the domestic consensus which it had worked so hard to establish and was adamant to sustain.

Central to the European challenge was the need to communicate a sense of commitment to those being led. Party unity made this far easier, as the number of Labour MPs displaying misgivings on Europe was declining (Baker and Seawright, 1998). This was in line with the findings of the survey that demonstrated large majorities in all three main parties faithfully supporting their respective leadership's policy. The new Labour MPs elected in 1997 showed themselves to be broadly more pro-European than those in previous surveys. The survey evidence did, though, indicate some differences over the extent of market-driven solutions to economic and social problems, as well as caution concerning granting extra powers to non-elected EU institutions. On technical policy detail, some differences emerged concerning the role of the European Central Bank. These findings reflect and confirm both the changing nature of the PLP and its broader appeal and the lack of divisiveness in party ranks.

Interestingly, the survey also identified a strand of thinking within party ranks which suggested that the leadership was tightly controlling the agenda of discussion on Europe, leaving little opportunity for effective internal debate. For those keen to protect constituencies with wafer-thin majorities, this did not present a problem, but in other respects, it served to confirm the strength of the leadership and its ability to impose a top-down model of leadership. This style of management was confirmed by the decision initially to suspend and soon after to expel two Labour MEPs, Ken Coates and Hugh Kerr, in early 1998 for public criticism of government policy. This action did not, though, generate any major dissension in party ranks. The dominant party faction had a clear policy agenda which the European issue could not afford to disturb, though Europe was starting to receive slightly higher priority status. This was reflected in the fact that the initial brainstorming discussions on developing European policy included Mandelson, but not the Chancellor or Foreign Secretary. It also involved consultations with political figures across the political divide as well as with a range of academics. Mandelson however, continued to play an important informal role as an unofficial European liaison officer following his departure from the Cabinet at the end of 1998.

The Council of Ministers Presidency gave the government an ideal opportunity to display its European credentials. Party unity provided the opportunity to conduct a positive pro-European line without generating internal dissent. Firstly, the party could consolidate the pan-European welcome received and, secondly, enunciate some of its European policy ideals. An examination of events indicates that in many respects, this opportunity came too soon in the life of the government. The lack of serious policy attention devoted to Europe until the second half of 1998 was proving to be costly in terms of the scarcity of new initiatives on offer. This was allowing for the limitations of the office, and the fact that much of what is achievable in a six-month period is moulded by existing obligations and established agendas. Britain, in this respect, was fortunate, as one of the main elements of its six months was to launch successfully a wide-ranging set of negotiations for enlargement of the Union. Critical work in this area during the previous Council Presidency had already been undertaken by Luxembourg (Ludlow, 1998). In terms of EMU, the agenda was equally clear and with the countries selecting themselves for the first wave of entry, the government was free to create its own distinct agenda. With the Foreign Secretary choosing not to make a major speech on Europe in the UK, the influence of domestic political concerns was again shown to be apparent. The reality is that the focus was on the normalisation process: 'Britain has come a long way in the past year in its relations with the rest of the EU' (Blair, June 1998, p. 10). In other regards, attention was devoted to the delivery of outcomes geared to raising the legitimacy of the EU in the minds of the electorate.

Although it is argued that the Presidency left a good impression (Ludlow, 1998) which can be attributed to the efficiency of the operation, this does not equate with leadership according to the criteria set out by O'Connell (1997) earlier in the chapter. However, within this evaluation, considerable attention is placed on the attention to detail paid by government officials in preparation for meetings along with the acknowledgement of the need for symbolism as demonstrated best by the Prime Minister's address to the French National Assembly (1998).

In overall terms, despite the evident criticisms of the Presidency, it did boast a series of creditable achievements (*The Guardian*, 9 June 1998). Domestically, the government endeavoured to sell the idea that internal economic policy principles could bring benefit to other member states. Yet the claims of the Minister for Europe (Henderson, 1998) that the domestic European debate had been transformed to a more perceptive level of discussion are untrue except in terms of an elite policy agenda. It was becoming increasingly evident from the thinking which occurred through the summer of 1998, that it was no longer possible to assume that charisma and economic ideals were the correct means of believing that one could determine the pace of events. As Stephens points out

(*Financial Times*, 13 November 1998), Blair was recognising the need to desist from making claims of leadership within the Union, opting for a less ambitious and high-profile diplomatic approach. This was the underlying theme of the remainder of the period until June 1999, combined with calls for institutional reform and the need to strengthen the Union's defence capability.

Other achievements of the Presidency included the lifting of the ban on the export of British beef, setting out detailed plans for reform of the Common Agricultural Policy and bringing in a ban on drift-net fishing, whilst through the work of senior Treasury Civil Servant Sir Nigel Wicks, Britain was able to retain a role in the Euroclub meetings. This did not, though, preclude making criticisms about Europe from the perspective of advocating, whenever possible, US-oriented economic and social policy ideas.

Normalisation was achieved in the context of repairing damaged diplomatic relations, yet to have expected more from the administration was not realistic. However, this was not the intention conveyed by the government and its media handlers who were guilty of displaying arrogance and insensitivity to continental political allies (personal interview, Dr D. Macshane, 14 February 2000), particularly with reference to the notion of providing some form of leadership within the EU (as evidenced by the behaviour at Malmo). This was one of the Foreign Secretary's identifiable objectives. Even in the address to the French National Assembly (1998), the Prime Minister called for a new political vision of Europe without clearly declaring the nature of the political framework to endorse this, although he did indicate developments to which he was opposed. This indicates a failure to take up the challenge highlighted at the outset of the chapter. Furthermore, he also draws attention to the modest achievements. The populism on display was not just short-term and only began to lessen with the willingness to engage in reflection and policy. This altered the political language to one where the government began to speak more openly about seeking alliances, in line with the domestic emphasis on a new form of inclusive politics.

The Presidency concluded with the Cardiff Summit, a gathering that lacked a major agenda: the member states opted to wait for the outcome of the German election prior to beginning the complicated bargaining on enlargement and budgetary management issues. For the government, it provided an ideal opportunity quietly to conclude the Presidency with Blair expressing an increasingly positive tone towards the EMU process. Tactically, he could do little else following the Brussels confusion, though he had no desire to forsake his European ideals. The evidence of a positive tone towards Europe was identifiable in Blair's speech to the European Parliament: 'The single currency brings with it huge structural economic changes. Change is necessary, beneficial even. But we must be honest with our citizens that change there will be. And we must prepare for it' (Blair, June 1998, p. 2).

The Presidency gave a clear boost to reflection on European policy and evidence of leadership in discrete policy areas was soon evident. However, as this study shows, this was limited to areas where the United Kingdom had distinctive strengths and where agreement across the political spectrum was easy to sustain. Diplomatic relations with other EU member states were repaired and in addition to the St Malo declaration, the government formulated a policy agreement with Germany on 'Third Way Politics' (*Die Neue Mitte*). The overarching question of the UK's future destiny, however, was left unresolved. True leadership was not desired and only possible if the government chose to lead public opinion and engage in preference shifting as opposed to preference shaping. This constituted a self-imposed policy constraint that the government wished to retain whilst waiting to see how the key touchstone of integration, the Euro, performed. However, free from the public glare of the Presidency, the government made some progress in clarifying its thoughts from the summer of 1998 onwards. Overall, any conclusions on leadership can only be drawn from a wider political context, but the Presidency has provided the only opportunity for the European issue to be considered in full public view by New Labour. Lessons were learnt during the six months and a change in government mood was manifest but the pace of change permitted was limited, with policy advocacy deemed less important than the retention of popular support. The controversy over tax harmonisation at the end of 1998 served, however, to sour progress, showing the government in a poor light (interview with Charles Grant, 20 January 1999).

The 1999 European elections

Labour campaigned in the 1999 elections on a pan-European platform drawn up by the party of European Socialists, a preparatory
process that involved the Foreign Secretary to a considerable degree
in its preparation. This document, whilst supporting some of the
government's broad objectives, also proclaimed the strength of the
European social model to which it was far less attracted.
Furthermore, it also warmly endorsed the introduction of the Euro
which: 'should make a significant contribution to promoting sustainable growth, low inflation and high levels of employment'
(Party of the European Socialists, 1999, p. 8).

   In endorsing this programme, the party was admitting to the
dangers of holding an isolated position and recognised the need to
work more closely with its continental brothers. Retaining the
support of key allies, it recognised that its credibility would be protected by its ability to argue for change inside a formal political
grouping. With the bulk of the document focusing on issues that
concerned the party long before its election victory, the programme
was deemed worthy of support. The document also conveyed a
more Anglo-Saxon tone in its content than anything previously produced collectively by left-of-centre parties in Europe, a reflection of
the influence Cook may have had as chairperson of the group formulating the document. In so doing, the leadership was retaining
the support of political colleagues, appealing to its important external audience and furthering some of its most fundamental principles. However, most importantly, following the St Malo declaration,
it was showing itself to be actively involved with European issues.

   The decision to campaign on a pan-European platform confirmed
the strength of the Labour leadership and its willingness to display a
more overtly European dimension to its behaviour. Although Blair had
no intention of taking great political risks, he was openly declaring the
difference between the two main parties on a range of European
matters, whereas before he had preferred to point towards broad consensus. For the first time since 1997, there were very clear policy differences between the two main parties. The level of risk to which Blair
was willing to subject the party was confirmed, however, by the decision largely to disengage himself and the higher levels of the party
from the rigours of the campaign. In practical terms, this resulted in

the decision not to appoint a leading strategist to orchestrate the election campaign.

Undoubtedly, the Kosovo crisis was taking up much of the leadership's attention, though for Blair, it provided an opportunity to project and play a leadership role on the international stage. It also enabled him to demonstrate his capacity to learn lessons from previous foreign policy episodes in ensuring that the 'special relationship' with the US did not damage relations with European partners, as was the case following the first Iraqi air raids of 1998. In its approach to the election, Labour chose to view the poll as more of a referendum on domestic performance. The outcome of this was to illustrate in a vote how far the government could go in its policy programme before unsettling its supporters. Deep down, however, there was the realisation that executive power was not at stake and this lessened the importance of the exercise for politicians and voters. In fact, the whole campaign was lacklustre. Furthermore, electoral turnout had always proved disappointing in European elections and the indications were that this was not likely to alter.

The lack of professional campaigning when compared with the efforts of the previous three General Election campaigns gave party supporters little reason to vote. Rather than preparing the ground for the eventual referendum, this approach heightened the risk of the referendum, making its timing even more problematic. The outcome was to strengthen the hand of the range of parties fighting on an anti-Euro platform, stirred by an effective single-issue campaign launched by the Conservative party leader. The results damaged the party's hard-won image of a tough and professional machine and represented the first notable setback since 1992.

As Macintyre remarks (*Independent*, 15 June 1999), the result was dismaying for Labour, with its vote slumping to 28 per cent, and only 6 per cent of the total electorate voting Labour and 8.3 per cent Conservative in a turnout of 23.1 per cent (Cowling, 1999). As compared with the 1997 election, Labour only managed to secure 21 per cent of their vote, in contrast to the Conservatives who retained 37 per cent (Cowling, 1999). The Tories did relatively poorly for all their focused efforts, yet this was more to do with the distinct lack of interest in the institution being voted for, rather than the focus of their campaign. Labour's campaign resulted in many of its traditional heartland supporters choosing not to vote, displaying a sense of 'Euroagnosticism' rather than Euroscepticism. This also confirmed the common electoral characteristic of choosing to vote as a means of registering discontent. The anti-single currency lobby capitalised on Labour's caution and the deep-seated issues that remained unresolved regarding the party's longer-term destiny and its perception of the integration process.

Trying to establish whether the handling of the election campaign represented a tactical error or a deeper-seated failing by the party, it is important to consider how crucial success on Europe was seen to be in terms of the overall party record in government. If judged against the manifesto pledges of 1997, it was a secondary concern. However, when viewed in terms of a progressive and modernising government keen to resolve outstanding concerns impacting on the nation's future destiny, as Blair proclaimed in Aachen in May 1999, the perspective changes, with an element of paradox once again evident.

In determining a judgement, the key factor appears to be the degree of risk Blair was willing to take. What is evident from the early weeks of the Labour government is that in not seeking to address the European issue in a strategic vein, the party was unwilling to direct and lead public opinion. The preferred route was one in which the electorate would change its thinking of its own accord, discarding its misgivings about European integration, conceding that membership of the Euro was inevitable. Ironically, this strategy is high risk for a government which has caution writ large over much of its behaviour. It is because it does not follow that the Prime Minister could speak on his supporters' behalf as successfully in this case as on other populist causes, a suprising course of action for a government keen to eliminate obstacles to future electoral success. Furthermore, there was also the danger of a misjudgement that could result in the Conservatives dictating the European agenda at the next election. In taking this line, Labour was nevertheless confirming that policy advocacy had an inferior status in comparison to vote seeking, thus confirming the relevance of Strom's (1990) views to this study. Europe was not going to be allowed to endanger the wider electoral concerns nurtured so carefully by Kinnock, Smith and Blair. Despite the potential weakness of the approach on this one policy, New Labour strategists remain keenly aware that this need only be, in the worst case, a chink in the policy armoury used to fight the main opposition party at the next election. This is despite the fact that it remains the Conservative Party's chief weapon of political combat.

The 1999 result, when placed in context, reveals a suprising lack of foresight by the government. In playing down the election, Labour was ignoring the wider European question and was playing into the hands of the opposition, albeit a lame one. Yet Labour's dominant leadership faction was able to distinguish between the electorate's broader interest in the EU and the general disinterest in its institutional framework. The problem, though, of legitimising the importance of Europe in the eyes of traditional party supporters remained. This represented a failure on the part of the leadership and even an element of complacency.

Conclusion

Paradox and circumspection have been evident in the actions of New Labour in government in their handling of the European question. Undoubtedly, their behaviour, to some extent, can be explained by acknowledging the lack of preparation by the Blair leadership on this issue prior to May 1997. The exploitation of their chief opponent's broad-based antipathy to the Union, coupled with the constant attention to short-term political advantage and the wish not to appear radical in any way, has resulted in a mixed performance on Europe. In government, Labour was consolidating, rather than building, on the achievements of Kinnock, though from the second half of 1998 onwards, there have been positive signs of a more defined set of European policy objectives evolving.

This more favourable tone has to be qualified by the poor showing in the 1999 elections to the European Parliament, that served to rekindle doubts concerning the degree to which the party was willing to chance advocating a pro-European policy stance. Overall, a cooling-off in its endorsement of Europe is evident, although this appears to have been motivated by essentially domestic policy concerns. Isolationism has been replaced by normalisation, though beyond this, doubt remains about the real desire to remould a dynamic European vision, especially in terms of the key measure of commitment to integration, EMU membership.

The appeal to national interest, combined with the playing of the Atlanticist card, hover persistently in the background, retaining in the eyes of continental allies a potent set of constraining factors on deeper UK involvement in the integration process. This was further complicated by Blair's displeasure at the continental tendency towards social protection and anti-competitive behaviour within economic strategy, exemplified in his leader's speech at the Corn Exchange (April 1997). In domestic terms, this ties in with the limited objectives which the government set itself on Europe, recognising the lack of priority it receives in respect of voter attention, though this contrasts with the government's public outpourings and claims of modernisation and progress, hence the attention given to the highlighting of this paradox within the assessment.

Though the constraints on the government are wide-ranging, the reality of moving to something far-sighted and carefully conceived beyond triumphant isolationism has to rest with the Cabinet, the depth of its conviction towards European integration and its willingness to act on such sentiments. From examining events, the sense of conviction appears to be far greater in economic than political terms. This can be explained by the identification of defined economic gains generated by integration that can be translated into attractive and concrete positive policy outcomes for the coalition of supporters that voted Labour. At the same time, this was combined with the promotion of New Labour economic strategy within member states, under the guise of 'Third Way' thinking. With regard to EMU membership, the government's National Changeover Plan symbolises the wish of the party hierarchy to place Britain in a more central position in the debate concerning the future of Europe in an appropriate set of economic circumstances. Thus, as Baker and Seawright contend: 'Blair regards European co-operation as primarily a means to practical and popular ends' (Baker and Seawright, 1998, p. 225).

A true test of progress would indicate more than movement away from a legacy of bitterness based on charges of illegitimacy and betrayal (Cowling, 1999). The process of normalisation which has continued has ensured the end of 'triumphant isolationism', yet it took some twenty-six months for Blair (*The Guardian*, 27 July 1999) to make his first speech to a British audience devoted entirely to the European question. As Young remarks, New Labour remained:

> determined to relegate the question of the Euro to the technical realm, as if its only political significance lay in its capacity to desta-

bilise his government rather than its central import to a political leader claiming as strenuously as he does to be a British European. (*The Guardian*, 27 July 1999)

In seeking to prepare the political ground for the moment when the economic conditions are appropriate for EMU entry, Blair has not moved the discussion, in domestic terms, beyond the admission that Europe no longer revolves around a zero-sum strategy. This confirms the status of the policy as one defined more by image than issue. A clear alternative for a progressive government would have been to use EMU entry and membership of the Euro as an opportunity to enter into widescale political reform that could sweep away tribal political concerns, securing power for the pro-European centre and centre-left. Although the Foreign Secretary laid out a clear basis for a positive European policy on his appointment, the results have been limited, but the notion of constructive engagement has produced more than mere rhetoric. The approach is nevertheless marked by consistency in adhering to limited specific intentions.

Britain is not a leader in Europe, as she lacks the resources and policies to succeed in this (*New Statesman*, 2 January 1998). However, she can recover the ground lost with her continental allies. To achieve this objective whilst retaining substantial domestic support is a difficult challenge. Yet this is not beyond a strong government with a distinct vision shared by a dominant leadership faction with the courage of its convictions. As the processes of monetary union, enlargement and the creation of a common foreign and security policy continue to create a new European configuration and set of dynamics, New Labour has a definite opportunity in the latter of these policies to play a very constructive role. This would also remove the central paradox at the centre of the government's actions, as well as convincing its supporters and doubters that it is offering a distinct policy stance based on domestic needs. At the same time, it would represent an upholding of a pan-European policy perspective, a reflective and considered style guaranteed not to alienate opinion amongst important allies in other European capitals, confirming the end of British isolationism and New Labour's international credentials. In confronting this challenge, the leadership would appear to think that it is going beyond its remit, particularly in using a second-order issue to threaten much of what it has achieved domestically in respect of policy and attracting a broader electoral base from which to draw its support.

7
Concluding Remarks

During the 1980s and 1990s, it became increasingly obvious to many in the Labour Movement that without a positive European policy it was going to be more difficult to exploit the growing frailties of the Thatcher and Major governments. Hattersley (1997) suggests that the transformation of Labour into the European party was rational, as this change was inspired by the evolving nature of the EC: however, as this study reveals, the explanation and justification of the reversal have far deeper and more complicated roots.

Despite the variations in the level of enthusiasm for Europe as a pivotal element of party strategy during the period examined, a very significant departure has occurred for a party which had long experienced deep division over how to approach this sensitive policy area. These difficulties can be largely attributed to internal policy differences, the state of party competition and intense debates surrounding the issues of sovereignty and socialism (Grahl and Teague, 1988).

The preceding chapters have sought to show how, in undergoing a major policy reversal, the PLP, once Kinnock had established his authority as leader, used the European issue as a springboard for its renewal and modernisation. This conclusively demonstrated Labour to be the more European of the two main British political parties. This text has argued that Europe was critical to the leadership, as it interlocked with the twin concerns of economic policy and party unity, identified by M. Shaw (1994) as crucial elements in the rehabilitation of Labour following the electoral humiliation of 1983. Not only did these two issues concern the party internally, but they were also fundamental to any hope of altering the public's perception of it. Furthermore, in conducting this study and placing the emphasis on the European question as a means of explaining Labour's rebirth, the intention has been to fill a gap in the existing literature on the renewal and modernisation of the party, by focusing on an issue often ignored or underestimated. Much of the existing literature (Hay, 1999; Rosamund, 1990, 1993, 1994; M. Shaw, 1994; Shaw, 1995; and Wickham-Jones, 1995) focuses on other policy areas, notably the party's relations with the unions, ideological concerns and economic matters, whilst Europe is treated as a subsidiary concern. Consequently, Europe is not perceived as an issue forcing change and underpinning policy. In some cases, it is viewed simply as a tool for the conduct of adversarial politics (Rosamund, 1994).

Suprisingly, the reversal generated little anger, even though it was not an obvious vote-winner for a party with a vote-winning agenda. Yet, with the recognition of increasing Europeanisation of domestic decision-making, the issue could not be ignored as it was critical to the party re-establishing credibility and respect. Over time, this helped to fashion a strong and implicit basis for an array of policy statements. Above all else, the PLP had to ensure that it could prove its competence in handling the economy: this required the reversal of economic policy as soon as Kinnock had consolidated his position. The question was how the party would handle Europe and what priority status the issue would receive in its search to move from being a four-time election loser to a decisive victor.

In seeking to add a new dimension to the wide-ranging discussion on the renewal and modernisation of Labour, this study has used Harmel and Janda's 'Integrated Theory of Party Goals and Party Change' (1994). This sets out a clear process for the conduct of policy change within a political party. Although reference is made to the work of Downs (1957) and Kircheimer (1966) in explaining the process of policy change, they are both limited in the explanations that they can provide. As a consequence of applying the Harmel and Janda (1994) model, it has become clear that the European issue emerged as a central element underpinning Labour's efforts to attain its primary goal: securing electoral victory. This was also the case with its associated multiple goals on the path to gaining political power. The dominant party faction that the afore-mentioned academics identify played a critical role in determining the party's future course which, as a result of increasing strength of the party leader from the mid-1980s, enabled it to pursue a clear strategy.

In explaining and placing these changes in a theoretical setting, this study also makes reference to what Strom (1990) has referred to as a vote-seeking party, a concept that links with Harmel and Janda's (1994) primary goal approach. The exploration of this policy change in respect of its rationale and wide-ranging implications also demands a consideration of the programmatic appeal that Labour was seeking to make. This study clearly reveals a consistent approach based on the concept of preference accommodation as outlined by Dunleavy (1991), in which the party, in its desire to appeal to a wider section of the electorate, was careful not to over-extend its enthusiasm for Europe. However, during the period of study, it is evident that the party leaders differed in their perception of the possible pace and extent of changes, as well as its central role in the party's appeal to a broader electoral base.

Explaining the change

Throughout the body of t185his work, what is evident is that, once achieved, the policy reversal on Europe has been unquestioned. This has provided the foundation for the behaviour of the PLP and the Labour Movement in its recovery from the three-fold crisis identified by Whiteley (1983).

In tracing the evolution and development of the policy, this study shows how, in seeking to widen its appeal to realise its vote-seeking objective, an increasingly assertive leadership used domestic political factors to drive the response to broader political developments. In responding to electoral losses and public support for the Conservative party, Europeanisation of the political process became the underlying impulse to promote the necessary changes to make the party more respectable. However, it was not viewed as a purely external influence, thus confirming one of the key elements of the Harmel and Janda (1994) thesis.

As Europe interlinks with the crucial concerns of party unity and economic policy, it has shown itself to be a vital element in the rebuilding process. However, over the sixteen-year period considered, the degree to which individual leaders have stressed the centrality of this issue has varied according to prevailing internal and external political circumstances and priorities, as defined by the dominant leadership faction of the time. Electoral considerations have, at times, resulted in the European issue being given lower priority status, most notably after 1994, though the extent of Europe's influence on the domestic political process has continued to expand since the ratification of the Treaty on European Union. This has occurred particularly in areas such as economic management, trade, investment, environment and defence.

Thus, it was more than a tool of party management but a perspective which the party leader and dominant faction were keen to utilise. In exploring the differing priorities set and the behaviour that has ensued, the findings show policy consistency, though its ranking in overt priority terms has varied. Public proclamation of this approach has therefore had inferior status compared to the underpinning role it has clearly had. What has emerged, despite the focus of much of the aforementioned literature, is a policy approach driven by more than electoralism. The evidence points to an accompanying sense of conviction based on the realisation of the value and inevitability of increasing European influence as part of a longer-term strategy to restore credibility and gain supporters. This was a conviction which Kinnock acquired through the mid-1980s, whilst Smith had long possessed it and Blair's populist instincts ensured that there was continuity of approach, more especially since the second half of 1998.

In order to appreciate fully the extent of the policy reversal and its wide-ranging implications, this study makes reference to the bitter internecine strife and deep introversion that catapulted the PLP into such a strong anti-European stance in its 1983 manifesto. Charting the policy reversal, Chapter 2 illustrates how far the party moved on the European issue between the 1983 defeat and the consolidation of Kinnock–Hattersley's leadership authority in the mid-1980s. At this point, it was able to introduce the ideas contained in *Fabian Tract* 509 (1985), focusing on shifting attitudes, altering the presentation of policy and broadening electoral appeal, albeit in an undemonstrative fashion. This required new positions to be found on issues including sovereignty, ideology, party structure and, most critically of all, economic policy. Important elements of the trade union movement and the TUC subsequently played a prominent part in helping the leadership to secure its objectives. The PLP could not, of course, afford to offend the Unions, as control of the party revolves around: 'an accommodation between the Trade Union and Parliamentary leaderships' (Keating, 1999, p. 101). With their support, the party leader could deliver the policy changes desired. However, the role and influence of the Unions has been lessened by the reforms of Kinnock and Smith.

The severe lessons of the 1983 defeat had to be fully digested and this necessitated the jettisoning of unpopular policy and the re-establishing of party unity, which links with M. Shaw's (1994) argument. As early as 1985, Kinnock began to move the party away from its commitment to nationalisation. Primary research (personal interview with Neil Kinnock, 2 December 1996), as well as evidence in a range of publications, demonstrates his awareness of the need to move in this direction as soon as his position was more secure. Throughout, however, he recognised the electoral sensitivities of so doing, even allowing for Europe's low voter saliency. Consequently, he chose to use the European issue as a pivot for renewal and modernisation by driving it forward as an internal response to external change, part of the strategy of preference. The internal party reaction to a newly-emerging EC policy agenda helps to explain the tactics used in the 1984 European elections and the positive statements made by Kinnock, including the call for a new Messina Conference.

The reality was that change was stimulated by effective party management, grounded in a clear conviction regarding the future path which the party should take. In restoring credibility, the need to reform economic policy, which John Edmonds General Secretary of the GMB described as untenable (personal interview, 13 June 1995), was imperative. This implied replacing the AES with an internationalist policy upholding the principles of economic integration and accepting the pooling of sovereignty of which some unions fully recognised the value. These factors contributed to the forging and sustaining of party unity, helping to sustain the primary goal identified. Furthermore, in going beyond the work of M. Shaw (1994), Shaw (1996) and Grahl and Teague (1988), the European issue is proven as an agent of change, rather than accepted as a given in explaining the process of change.

Having carried out the most necessary policy reforms, secured his position and identified a distinct primary goal, Kinnock was ready to undertake a wide-reaching policy overhaul to convince the electorate that a credible alternative government existed. Following the poor showing in the 1987 election, in which the party still only secured 30.8 per cent of the poll, it was vital for the Labour Movement that a public exercise was conducted to convince the wider electorate of Labour's extended programmatic appeal. The campaign had been derailed over the issues of defence and taxation. As Norris remarks: 'Kinnock began a course of action between 1987 and 1992 which was designed to remove the image of Labour both as an extremist and divided Party' (Norris, 1994, p. 124).

The subsequent Policy Review Process, as Chapter 3 illustrates, marked an important stage on the path of reform begun during Kinnock's first four years as party leader, though it largely confirmed much of what had already been stated in interviews, speeches and publications. It laid particular stress on the final burial of AES, the greater acceptance of neo-liberal ideas and overcoming remaining doubts over EC membership. The latter had been very much in evidence in the party's handling of the Single European Act at Westminster. However, European issues received little specific attention in the official review documents, although they implicitly featured in the party's plans as a vehicle for promoting change in other areas. They helped to provide a critical component of the new model party which was being created (Hughes and Wintour, 1990). According to Laybourn (2000) the changes: 'collectively abandoned many of Labour's established shibboleths.' (Laybourn, 2000, p. 124).

The review represented an internal response to a raft of influences and was orchestrated firmly by a more assertive leadership setting its own agenda. The European issue was implicit in this, with the domestic political discourse increasingly shaped by Europe, notably in the areas of economic and social policy. European matters were no longer viewed as separate from the dominant political culture, as they were perceived as a means of capitalising on the party's newfound unity and economic competence. This was a reflection of the desire to seize new opportunities, as well as applying political craft marked by a lack of ideological underpinning, helping to earn respect and generate wider appeal, as outlined in *Fabian Tract* 509 (1985). In moving to a more inclusive non-ideological path as a means of legitimising Kinnock's programme of reform and managerial leadership, the party was not divesting itself of its past traditions, but seeking a return to a consensus, albeit with an adaptation of traditional ideas. This constituted a key element of its eagerness to portray the right image and maintain the electoral priority which was boosted by the 1992 British Social Attitudes Survey recording a noticeable increase in pro-European sentiment between 1986 and 1990. Although the party was successful in securing forty-five seats in the elections to the European Parliament in 1989, the significance was more symbolic than a verdict on Labour's record. The result represented the first major political reversal at national level for the Conservative Party leader since 1979.

Securing electoral victory

With the completion of the Policy Review Process outlined in Chapter 3, Labour was keen to confirm its suitability for government. Even though the later-than-anticipated election in 1992 proved to be a disappointment, the party's European policy certainly did not contribute to the defeat. Despite the assertion of clear leadership by the dominant faction in the party, the electorate was not keen to endorse Kinnock as a national leader. Having won the internal battles over Europe, he still had to recast the party and European policy into a mode likely to unsettle the electorate. This resulted in domestic policy considerations becoming the dominant influence and the implementation of the tactic of opportunism, a deferring ploy, which Smith and Blair utilised to full effect. This represented a strategy of exploiting the weakness of the government, though in each instance this was sustained by party unity pursuing a consistent approach based on pro-European sentiment, coupled with the presentation of policy documents confirming the party's thinking.

Smith's brief tenure as party leader did not provide sufficient opportunity or time to recast opinion more firmly towards economic and political integration, despite his strong pro-Europe pedigree. In part, the situation was due to the PLP favouring the contents of the European Communities Amendment Bill. The ERM crisis of 1992 presented the party with something of a dilemma, as it did not wish either to revise the policy position it formulated on the basis of the first challenge to its legitimacy, or to threaten the continental support it had been nurturing since the middle of the previous decade. Opposition to the Bill from within the party did not prove troublesome to the extent of threatening unity, as Chapter 4 indicates, though it cast light on policy perspectives upon which the party may have dwelt longer.

The defeat at the polls focused the party almost totally on electoral concerns and although progress on Europe was unaffected, the party opted to concentrate on a domestic agenda to help secure its primary goal: acquiring office. Deferring detailed policy discussion and watching a weak government create more problems for itself, particularly over Europe, suited the PLP leadership.

Until the election of Blair, European policy was not advanced during the 1990s, though there was no variance from the past either and the steadying hand of George Robertson, the party's European spokesman remained as an influential element (personal interview with Regan Scott, National European Communities Co-ordinator, TGWU, 3 July 1995). This was despite the fact that Smith gathered around him a different team of advisers from Kinnock. The distinctive policy on the social dimension remained, marking out a clear policy variation between the PLP and the Conservatives, whilst the European case could be used as a means of furthering British interests and influence by directing the discussion of European concerns beyond the confines of Westminster. This was not attempted, as it was thought to be risky and the Policy Review Process had not defined a set of parameters for such a debate. A constructive discussion could have been used to build up the case of Labour competence despite voter disinterest, yet even if it had so desired, being in opposition prevented Labour from being able to shape voting preferences effectively. This was because of the policy-making constraints imposed on it by the political process.

Although Europe was still defining policy parameters for Labour in so far as the sympathetic position on Europe determined policy-making, it was not performing the role of lynchpin in defining party strategy. The approach taken suggested a sense of complacency with a victory for pragmatic forces. In the handling of the European Communities Amendment Bill, detailed in Chapter 4, Labour chose not to engage in confrontation with the government, as it perceived this would threaten its hard-earned respectability and involve the party in tough policy decisions. This was something in which it was unwilling to involve itself, particularly as the EC was proclaiming ideals sympathetic to social democratic thinking. It preferred to help make the passage of a piece of European constitutional law a domestic success. Attention was focused on the opt-out clauses and this was deemed sufficient to distinguish itself from the government, preserving credibility and providing an identifiable voter base. In exploiting the government's contradictory stance regarding the desired central European role and the lack of commitment to key policies, the PLP was able to put aside longer-term policy considerations. Reticence and pragmatism slowed the evolution of European policy but did not and could not remove the issue from party strategy, as this analysis maintains throughout. What the period beyond the Policy Review Process indicated was consolidation, whereas the Policy Review itself provided a public confirmation of the achievements of Kinnock and Hattersley in setting out a future strategy and starting to realise it by restoring credibility and authority to the party leadership.

With the election of Blair, it was soon evident that the new leader was going to act as an agent for continuing change in the party, building on the foundations in place. The message of national renewal contained little specifically on Europe but did not contradict the achievements of Kinnock and Smith. As with the populist strand manifest in Blair's manner, the party's behaviour was marked by the promotion of values in preference to policy detail wherever possible. Europe was not destined to be used as the primary device for promoting change to the same degree as previously, yet neither was it deemed as an external influence on the domestic body-politic, or in any way irrelevant due to the continuing Europeanisation of domestic politics. The overlap with domestic concerns, most notably over sovereignty, was recognised, with an overt acknowledgement of the value of pooling sovereignty (Mandelson and Liddle, 1996) in solving transnational problems.

Throughout the period from Blair's election in 1994 to the General Election in 1997, as Chapter 5 shows, office-seeking and active vote maximisation strategies dictated that the issues of trust and public identity were paramount. Careful economic policy, combined with protection of national interests, were primary concerns: elements which satisfied the demands of party unity and competent economic policy. However, there was an important difference between Smith and Blair regarding Europe: namely, that the latter, particularly through Cook, was prepared to sketch out a framework of thinking geared to creating a set of more substantive European policy intentions. Nevertheless, this was based on the forging of winning rhetoric and the caution that was central to this. As the election approached, it also provided leverage for the development of policy, primarily in the sphere of economic issues that veered from the EU, though it was important to domestic voters and endorsed patriotic sentiment. This was a response to the Conservative use of the nationalist card in which the role of the nation-state was emphasised, alongside the retention of the veto on key issues. In attaining these ends, Blair was happy to continue the process used by Kinnock, transferring power from sovereign institutions to a core elite that constituted the new dominant faction.

However, Blair was also aware of the mistakes made by socialist and social democrat governments across Europe during recent decades in their handling of economic policy, as well as the need to camouflage the full realities of Europeanisation so as to appear credible in the eyes of an electorate still apprehensive about European integration. Europe was not the prime symbol of change: the real challenge remained in the domestic forum, despite Europe directly impinging on this. The determination of policy had to reflect on where national interests lay and votes could be accumulated. This was manifest in the handling of social policy when it appeared that business competitiveness might have been threatened by new legislation. The reality of Blair's approach was to advance policies inclined towards populism and adjustment (Shaw, 1998), favouring economic efficiency and social justice. These made reference to past eras, yet Blair was keen to update traditional ideas whilst stressing renewal in respect of realising desired goals such as revising the relationship between capital and labour.

The party opted increasingly for consensus policies, appeals to inclusiveness and the demands of psephology formulated by senior policy advisers determined to accommodate voter preferences. The ultimate challenge rested in devising policy prescriptions that were different from the government, but which appealed to segments of the electorate who previously voted for them. As far as Europe was concerned, Labour's unwillingness to expound in substantive policy terms on its future ideals for the EU provided the party with leverage when election campaigning began. Rather than viewing Europe as a positive device for generating new opportunities which would instil popular support, the PLP erred on the side of caution, particularly where there were possible dangers to the transatlantic relationship (personal interview with Lord Whitty, 24 February 1998). Whereas sovereignty could be shared in economic terms, in political terms this was harder to promote, despite the rhetoric. Thus, a party portraying itself as modern was not willing to advance European policy beyond using it as a device to retain unity, aside from terms of grand rhetoric exploiting the openings generated by the tactic of mere opportunism. Ironically, this also creates the impression of uncertainty, with a party expressing the national desire to retain and exert influence, whilst acknowledging a tendency towards introversion on the grounds of pragmatism and caution. On the other hand, the similarities with the approach of the Conservatives possibly served to placate voters.

Labour in government

Having secured victory with a 10.8 per cent increase on the vote received in 1992 through a campaign laying greater emphasis on positive references rather than commitments on Europe, the government hoped to devote less time to the European issue. This was a decision based on its perception of electoral sensitivities and the need for caution reflected in the election manifesto (personal interview Dr D. Macshane MP, 14 February 2000). The force of preference accommodation was taking precedence over long-term policy ideals in the search to realise the party's primary goal – office seeking.

Yet, the paradox identified whilst in opposition remained, with Labour unwilling to present detailed policy responsibilities though content to have influence on major issues confronting its fellow EU members. In focusing on the limited areas of monetary union, foreign and defence policy, party strategy and leadership, Chapter 6 charts the ebb and flow in terms of the governments's practical moves towards European integration between 1997 and 1999. This is explained by examining its domestic priorities and EU policy developments. The strength of the leadership enabled it to concentrate on its need to continue a stable economic policy and preserve party unity, demonstrating consistency with the work of Kinnock and Smith. However, the element of evident populism exceeded that of the aforementioned leaders and Europe featured more as an adjunct to existing policy except in the case of defence strategy. What was lacking was a clearly conceived set of detailed objectives declaring more than a collection of broad policy intentions. This would have taken the government well beyond the rhetoric of triumphant isolationism of the previous government by declaring its European credentials. These characteristics only began to emerge during the summer of 1998 after Britain's Presidency of the Council of Ministers, when informal discussions began at a range of political, diplomatic and academic gatherings (personal interview with Charles Grant, 20 January 1998).

The challenge was to construct a European policy to which the electorate would warm, extending beyond that of the previous government, especially as its electoral appeal was now far more broadly based. At the same time, the PLP needed to impress other EU member states and their entire citizenry of their commitment to the integration process. This required the party leadership to direct public opinion, yet this would have constituted going beyond preference accommodation. The government's response was circumspect: it stressed that caution was not synonymous with Euroscepticism, as illustrated by Blair's address to the French National Assembly (June 1998). The grand vision was oriented to domestic concerns, central to an active vote maximisation strategy and the preservation of the strong ties with the US. In focusing on these relations, Blair was not only maintaining Labour's Atlanticist traditions, but was also keen to preserve a link which fostered ideas contrary to some of those emerging from the EU. This applied, in particular, to those stressing interventionism and increased social control and regulation. These were anathema to the dominant leadership faction in New Labour favouring flexible labour markets and adaptation to change.

Where possible, the government sought to cash in on attainable goals, such as in relation to extending provisions on the single market and the environment. It attempted, where it could, to keep European issues out of the domestic focus with EMU being the exception. This explains the tendency of the party leadership to feel more comfortable addressing foreign audiences about Britain's role in the EU.

As regards EMU, the government failed in a critical test regarding its commitment to integration by opting not to undertake an active role in contributing to the successful implementation of the strategy. The choice made by the Chancellor in playing to the domestic gallery in his statement to the House of Commons on 27 October 1997 was to ignore the wider implications, responding to, rather than leading, opinion. This constituted a further manifestation of preference accommodation. It reflected the paucity of real debate over the European issue (Baker, Gamble and Seawright, 1999), with the party leadership fearing a further airing of the traditional public misgivings concerning Europe. The government did not favour total exclusion from EMU and attempted involvement, albeit on its own terms, and introduced the National Changeover plan in preparation for EMU entry.

Critically, this was the one policy that could undermine the government, yet in its desire to go beyond the Chancellor's 27 October 1997 statement a cautious government was taking an enormous risk deferring on the date of a referendum. This was done in the hope that public opinion would alter without a major government campaign to orchestrate this – a further manifestation of preference accommodation. In seeking to avoid a decision on EMU, the government was doing its utmost to ensure that Europe did not damage its future electoral prospects. Yet it appeared, paradoxically, to be both acknowledging deeper Europeanisation of domestic politics and overlooking the potential damage the opposition could cause.

The handling of foreign policy also revealed caution and the maintenance of the Atlanticist tradition, with the issue of Britain's political, economic and diplomatic destiny remaining unresolved. Yet after the EU Presidency, evidence of reflection on EU strategy resulted in defence policy being selected as an area where the United Kingdom could play a positive role within the EU. This was an astute move, focusing on populist tendencies and it satisfied domestic, United States and European audiences. It was useful as a further delaying tactic for a government keen to avoid confrontation with a difficult issue.

The limited use of the Presidency, outlined in Chapter 6 as a means of moving from the evident caution, was partly due to this opportunity coming too early for the government. However, in retaining the broader-based support for which it had fought so long and hard, the dominant faction had little option but to limit its ambition and retain its policy programme framed around preference accommodation. Despite the evident disappointment which this induced in other European capitals, Blair was simply continuing an approach that had shown itself to be successful. However, at this juncture, the position of the leader was stronger than at any point in the previous sixteen years and this enabled him to determine and manage the party agenda free from any meaningful challenge (Cowley, 1999). This was all the more significant as the dominant faction began to think more seriously about a second consecutive election victory. Policy advocacy was clearly losing its battle with the desire to accumulate votes. Even the considerable input to the party of European Socialists manifesto for the 1999 European elections was not supplemented by a co-ordinated domestic campaign. This partially contributed to New Labour's very poor performance, confirming its fears, yet demonstrating its desire to accommodate and placate as many interests as it possibly could.

Final reflections

The Labour Party's policy reversal on Europe constitutes one of the most significant events in recent domestic political history. As this study shows throughout, in marrying the twin objectives of restoring party unity with competent economic policy, it was paramount that the party resolved its position on Europe. In so doing, it embarked on its slow path to political rehabilitation by appearing to be a rational and relevant organisation in voters' perceptions. Each of the leaders, in his own style, influenced by the conditions of the time and public opinion, recognised the virtues and gains of this strategy. Consequently, the European issue became a central, though not always explicit, element of party strategy geared to seeking a clear primary objective: securing political office. In reality much of the Conservative Party's political clothing had been stolen by Labour in its bid to reassure the electorate that a vote for change did not represent either a vote for instability or lunacy.

By the end of June 1999, the PLP proved both its economic competence and confirmed its unity (Baker et al., 1999), critical outcomes attributable to the need for its policy reversal on Europe. The party no longer resembled the rebellious, fractious and troublesome body which Kinnock inherited in the summer of 1983. Europe did not represent an obstacle to the party leader in his efforts to retain unity. It now represented a central component of policy-making, even if not always the most pivotal. This was in total contrast to the situation in both the early 1980s and much of the 1970s (Wilson, 1979).

Furthermore, there are signs that once a second term is secured some of the inherent caution of New Labour in its European policy will begin to evaporate, with the party having proved its economic competence and unity. Yet as Stephens remarks: 'For the past three years, Mr. Blair has made Britain's case in Europe. It is time to make Europe's case in Britain' (*Financial Times*, 17 November 2000).

Capitalising on the inevitability that is felt regarding membership of the Euro (ICM Research, January and November 1999), the government realises that it needs to convince doubters of the practical reality of combining the role of diplomatic and economic bridge between the United States and Europe, whilst nurturing a positive long-term relationship with its European partners. In securing victory in this battle of ideas which has been intensified by the Danish referendum result in September 2000, the government does not wish to be associated with a clearly unpopular policy.

However, in seeking to obtain a more prominent role in Europe sharing sovereignty, the underlying rationale remains pragmatic, fostering British power and influence, whilst also proclaiming patriotism. This is promoted on the basis of it being a saleable concept in the domestic environment most notably when combined with proposals for institutional reform and the strong endorsement of EU enlargement as the Prime Minister outlined in his speech in Warsaw (6 October 2000).

While the economic case for entry into EMU, the touchstone of true commitment towards integration, could be resolved through a positive referendum result, the political management involved in the timing of this has become more difficult. In moving to the pragmatic centre (Jones, 2000), Labour has acknowledged the lessons of its 1980s electoral defeats, yet the party needs to match the rebuilding of Britain's position in Europe with the regeneration of an equal sense of pro-European conviction amongst the electorate. The government needs to find the appropriate language to capitalise on the reality that a divorce from Europe appears not to be a strongly held view as compared with the growing sense of inevitability surrounding the acceptance of the Euro. It is in this light that the government now proclaims its new mantra on the future of the EU as a superpower – not superstate. This provides a firmer indication of what the government desires, though it leaves plenty of flexibility surrounding its commitment to particular aspects of EU policy and the means by which it seeks to immerse itself fully within the European project. This is a reality that will become evident in the run-up to the 2004 EU Intergovernmental Conference. However, as a party, Labour is unstinting in its desire to be immersed in Europe and the EU, though it prefers to display caution wherever and whenever it can. The present leadership, however, remains inclined to pragmatism in its handling of the European question as the electorate continues to display a strong sense of 'Euroagnosticism', as the 2001 election campaign has demonstrated.

Bibliography

Alderman, K. 'Legislating on Maastricht', *Contemporary Record*, Vol. 7, No. 3 (1993), 499–521.

Anderson, P. and Mann, N. *Safety First: the Making of New Labour* (London: Granta, 1997).

Anderson, P. and Weymouth, A. *Insulting the British Public? The British Press and the European Union* (Harlow: Addison Wesley, 1999).

Baker, D., Gamble, A., Ludlam, S. and Seawright, D. 'Labour and Europe: a Survey of MPs and MEPs', *Political Quarterly*, Vol. 67, No. 4 (1996), 353–71.

Baker, D. and Seawright, D. *Britain For and Against Europe* (Oxford: Clarendon Press, 1998).

Baker, D., Gamble, A. and Seawright, D. 'The Sounds of Silence: New Labour Party Management and the European Union'. Paper presented to the Political Studies Association, Annual Conference, Nottingham (1999).

Baker, D., Gamble, A., Seawright, D. and Bull K. 'Europe: Enthusiasm, Circumspection or Outright Scepticism?' in Fisher, J., Cowley, P., Denver, D. and Russell, A. (eds), *British Elections and Parties Review Volume* (London: Frank Cass, 1999).

Bale, T. and Buller, J. 'Island in a Sea of Consensus: Exploring the Differences Between the Conservative and Labour Parties over the Social Chapter'. Paper presented to the Annual Conference on Elections, Public Opinion, and Parties Conference, Manchester (1995).

Bale, T. *Sacred Cows and Common Sense: the Symbolic Statecraft of the Political Culture of the Labour Party* (Unpublished Ph.D., University of Sheffield, 1997).

Barber, L. 'UK Tests Domestic Voters on EMU', *Financial Times* (17 June 1998), 2.

Benn, T. *Conflicts of Interest: Diaries 1977–80* (London: Arrow, 1991).

Bilski, R. 'The Common Market and the Growing Strength of Labour's Left-Wing', *Government and Opposition*, 12 (1977), 306–31.

Blackburn, R. 'Blair's Velvet Revolution', *New Left Review*, 223 (1997), 3–16.

Blair, T., 'Forging a New Agenda', *Marxism Today*, October (1991), 6–9.

Blair, T. 'Why Modernisation Matters', *Renewal*, Vol. 1, No. 4 (1993), 4–11.

Blair, T. 'Let Us Face the Future', 1945 Anniversary Lecture, *Fabian Pamphlet 571* (London: Fabian Society, 1995a).

Blair, T. Mais City Lecture, City University, London (22 May 1995).

Blair, T. Speech to the Friedrich-Ebert Stiftung (30 May 1995).

Blair, T. *New Britain – My Vision of a Young Country* (London: Harper Collins, 1996).

Blair, T. Speech to the Corn Exchange (6 April 1997).

Blair, T. Speech to the Congress of the Party of European Socialists, Malmo (6 June 1997).

Blair, T. Speech to the French National Assembly, Paris (28 March 1998).

Blair, T. Speech to the European Parliament, Strasbourg (18 June 1998).

Blair, T. Speech to the Economic Club of Chicago (22 April 1999).

Blair, T. Speech on Receipt of the Charlemagne Prize, Aachen (13 May 1999).

Blair, T. 'Superpower – not Superstate, *The Federal Trust* (October 2000).

Blair, T. and Schroder, G. *The Third Way* (*Die Neue Mitte*) (London: Labour Party, 1999).

Bocev, P. 'Britain and Europe', *Le Figaro* (30 June 1998), 15.

Bomberg, E. and Peterson, J. 'Policy Transfer and Europeanisation: Passing the Heineken Test'. Paper presented to the Political Studies Association Annual Conference: London (2000).

British Social Attitudes Survey *9th Annual Report* (Aldershot: Gower, 1992).

British Social Attitudes Survey *13th Annual Report* (Aldershot: Gower, 1996).

British and European Social Attitudes Survey *15th Annual Report* (Aldershot: Gower, 1998).

Brivati, B. 'New Labour is Just Child's Play', *New Statesman* (19 February 1999), 28.

Brown, G. 'Commentary', *European Access*, No 4. August (1997), 9–12.

Buller, J. 'New Labour's Foreign and Defence Policy: External Support Structures and Domestic Politics', in *New Labour in Government*, ed. Ludlam, S. and Smith M. (Basingstoke: Macmillan 2001).

Bulmer, S. and Birch M. 'The Europeanisation of Central Government: the UK and Germany in Historical Institutionalist Perspective', in Aspinwall, D. and Schneider, M. (eds), *The Rules of Integration* (Manchester University Press: Manchester, 2000).

Butler, D. and Kitzinger, U. *The 1975 Referendum* (Basingstoke: Macmillan, 1975).

Butler, D. and Kavanagh, D. *The British General Election of 1983* (Basingstoke: Macmillan, 1984).

Butler, D. and Kavanagh, D. *The British General Election of 1987* (Basingstoke: Macmillan, 1988).

Butler, D. and Kavanagh, D. *The General Election of 1992* (Basingstoke: Macmillan, 1992).

Butler, D. and Kavanagh, D. *The General Election of 1997* (Basingstoke: Macmillan, 1997).

Callaghan, J. *The Retreat of Social Democracy* (Manchester: Manchester University Press, 2000).

CDU/CSU, 'Fraktion des Deutschen Bundestages', *Reflections on European Policy* (Bonn: September 1994).

Clarke, P. *A Question of Leadership. From Gladstone to Blair* (London: Penguin, 1999).

Cook, R. Speech to the Overseas Club and Senate, Hamburg (9 September 1997).

Cook, R. Speech to the Hungarian National Assembly, Budapest (26 November 1997).

Cook, R. Speech to the European Parliament, Strasbourg (14 January 1998).

Cook, R. Speech to the Royal Institute of International Affairs, London (25 June 1998).

Costello, N., Michie, J. and Milne, S. *Beyond the Casino Economy* (London: Verso, 1989).

Cowell, N. and Larkin, P. 'New Labours: The Recurrent Transformations of the Labour Party'. Paper presented to the Annual Elections, Public Opinion and Parties Conference, Northampton (1999).

Cowley, P. 'Europe in the House of Commons', *Discussion Paper Series No. 99/5* (Brunel University European Affairs Unit, 1999).

Cowling, D. 'A Yawn for Europe: the 1999 European Elections', *Journal of Representative Democracy*, Vol. 36, No. 3 (1999), 224–31.

Crewe, I. (1993), 'The Thatcher Legacy', in King, A., Crewe, I., Denver, D., Newton, K., Norton, P., Sanders, D., and Seyd, P., *Britain at the Polls 1992* (Chatham, NJ: Chatham House, 1993).

Crossland, A. *The Future of Socialism* (London: Jonathan Cape, 1956).

Crouch, C. 'The Terms of the Neo-Liberal Consensus', *Political Quarterly*, Vol. 68 (1997), 352–60.

Cruse, I. 'New Labour and Modernisation: Using Change as a Resource'. Paper presented to the Political Studies Association Annual Conference, Keele (1998).

Curtice, J. and Steed, M. (1992) 'The Results Analysed', in Butler, D. and Kavanagh, D., *The British General Election of 1992* (Basingstoke: Macmillan, 1992).

Daniels, P. 'From Hostility to Positive Engagement: the Europeanisation of Labour', *Western European Politics*, Vol. 21, No. 1 (1998), 72–96.

Davies, A. *To Build a New Jerusalem: the British Labour Party from Keir Hardie to Tony Blair* (London: Abacus, 1996).

Delors, J. *Europe, Embarking on a New Course in Contemporary European Affairs and After* (Oxford: Pergamon Press, 1989).

Downs, A. *An Economic Theory of Democracy* (London: Harper Collins, 1957).

Driver, S. and Martell, L. *New Labour: Politics after Thatcherism* (Cambridge: Polity Press, 1998).

Dunleavy, P. *Democracy, Bureaucracy and Public Choice* (Hemel Hempstead: Harvester Wheatsheaf, 1991).

Duverger, M. *Political Parties* (London: Methuen, 1954).

Eatwell, J. 'The Development of Labour Policy 1987–1992', in Michie, J. (ed.), *The Economic Legacy 1979–1992* (London: Academic Press, 1992).

Elliott, G. *Labourism and the English Genius: the Strange Death of Liberal England?* (London: Verso, 1993).

Featherstone, K. *Socialist Parties and European Integration: a Comparative History* (Manchester: Manchester University Press, 1988).

Falla, S. 'A Europe of the Peoples? New Labour and Democratising the EU', in Hoskyns, C. and Neuman, M. (eds), *Democratising the EU – Issues for the Twenty-first Century* (Manchester: Manchester University Press, 2000).

Freeden, M. 'The Ideology of New Labour', *Political Quarterly*, Vol. 70, No. 1 (1990), 42–51.

Fukayama, F. *The End of History and the Last Man* (London: Hamilton, 1989).

Gallie D., Penn, R. and Rose, M. *Trade Unionism in Recession* (Oxford: Oxford University Press, 1996).

Gallup, *Gallup Political and Economic Index* (London, 1984–92).

Gamble, A. 'The Labour Party and Economic Management', in *The Changing Labour Party* (London: Routledge, 1992).

Gamble, A. and Kelly G. 'The British Labour Party and Monetary Union', *Western European Politics*, Vol. 23, No. 1 (2000), 1–26.

Gamble, A. and Payne, A. (eds) *Regionalism and Economic Order* (London: Routledge, 1996).

Gardiner, N., 'No No Yes, Labour's Post-War European Policy', *Renewal*, Vol . 14, No. 1 (1996), 54–61.

Garner, R., 'Labour's Policy Review: a Case of Historical Continuity', *Politics*, 10 (1) (1990), 33–39.

Geddes, A. 'Labour and the European Community 1973–93', *Contemporary Record*, Vol. 82, No. 2 (1994), 370–80.

George, S. *An Awkward Partner: Britain in the European Community* (Oxford: Oxford University Press, 1992).

George, S. 'Britain and the EU', *European Access*, No. 6 December, (1998), 12–13.

George S. and Haythorne, D. 'The British Labour Party', in Gaffney, J. (ed.), *Political Parties and the European Union* (London: Routledge, 1996).

George, S. and Rosamund, B. 'The European Community', in *The Changing Labour Party*, ed. Smith and Spear (London: Routledge, 1992).

GMB, *Journal* (London: August 1988).

Goldblatt. D. and Held, D. 'Bring Back Democracy', *New Statesman* (10 January 1997), 24–7.

Gould, B. *A Future for Socialism* (London: Cape, 1989).

Gould, B. 'Courage is Best', *New Statesman* (3 June 1995), 20–1.

Gould, B. *Goodbye to All That* (Basingstoke: Macmillan, 1995).

Gould, P. *The Unfinished Revolution: How the Modernisers Saved the Labour Party* (London: Little Brown and Company, 1998).

Grahl, J. and Teague, P. 'The British Labour Party and the European Community', *Political Quarterly*, Vol. 59, No. 1 (1988), 72–88.

Grant, C. 'Can Britain Lead in Europe?', *Centre for European Reform* (London, 1995).

Grice, A. and Coyle, D. 'Blair Gears Up to Ditch the Pound', *The Independent* (24 February 1999) 2.

Hain, P. *Ayes to the Left* (London: Lawrence and Wishart, 1995).

Hall, S. and Jacques, M. (eds) *New Times* (London: Lawrence and Wishart, 1989).

Harmel, R. and Janda, K. 'An Integrated Theory of Party Goals and Party Change', *Journal of Theoretical Politics*, 6 (3) (1994), 259–87.

Harris, M. 'The Ideology of New Labour', *Political Quarterly*, Vol. 70, No. 1 (1999), 42–53.

Harrison, M. *Trade Unions and the Labour Party Since 1945* (London: Allen and Unwin, 1960).

Hattersley, R. *Choose Freedom: the Future of Democratic Socialism* (London: Penguin, 1987).

Hattersley, R. *Fifty Years On: a Prejudiced History of Britain since the War* (London: Little Brown and Company, 1997).

Hay, C. 'Labour's Thatcherite Revisionism: Playing the Politics of Catch-Up', *Political Studies*, Vol. 42, No. 4 (1994), 700–7.

Hay, C. *The Political Economy of New Labour* (Manchester: Manchester University Press, 1999).

Hayward, P. 'It's the Culture Stupid – Deconstructing the Blair Project', *Talking Politics*, Vol. 11, No. 1 (1998), 42–6.

Healey, D. *The Time of My Life* (London: Michael Joseph, 1989).

Heath, A. and Jowell, R. 'The Decline of Class Voting', in Denver, D. and Hands, G. (eds), *Issues and Controversies in British Politics* (Hemel Hempstead: Harvester Wheatsheaf, 1992).

Heffernan, R. 'The Labour Party, Political Communications and the Enhancement of Leadership Power'. Paper presented to the Annual Elections, Public Opinion and Parties Conference, Sheffield (1994).

Heffernan, R. *Ideology, Practical Politics and Political Consensus: Thinking about the Process of Political Change in Great Britain* (Contemporary Political Studies, 1997).

Heffernan, R. *New Labour and Thatcherism: Political Change in Britain* (Basingstoke: Macmillan, 2000).

Heffernan, R. and Brivati, B. *The Labour Party: a Centenary History* (Basingstoke: Macmillan, 2000).

Heffernan, R. and Marquasee, M. *Defeat from the Jaws of Victory: Inside Kinnock's Labour Party* (London: Routledge, 1992).

Henderson, D. 'The UK Presidency: an Insider's View', *Journal of Common Market Studies*, Vol. 36, No. 4, (1998), 563–77.

Holden R., 'Labour's Transformation: the European Dynamic', *Politics*, Vol. 19, No. 2 (1999), 103–8.

Holland, S. *Out of Crisis: a Project for European Recovery* (Nottingham, 1983).

House of Lords Select Committee, European Union Session (1984/5).

Hughes, C. and Wintour, P. *Labour Rebuilt: the New Model Party* (London: Fourth Estate, 1990).

ICM Monthly Poll, *The Guardian* (8 June 1999).

Jann, D. and Hahn H. 'The New Rhetoric of New Labour in Comparative Perspective: a Three Country Discourse', *Western European Politics*, Vol. 23, No. 1, (2000) 26–46.

Jenkins, C. *All Against the Collar: Struggles of a White Collar Union Leader* (London: Routledge, 1990).

Jones, A. 'UK Relations with the EU, and Did You Notice the Elections', *Talking Politics*, Vol. 12, No. 2 (2000), 312–17.

Jones, B. and Keating, M. *Labour and the British State* (Oxford: Clarendon Press, 1985).

Jones, T. *Re-making the Labour Party: from Gaitskell to Blair* (London: Routledge, 1996).

Kampfner, J. *Robin Cook* (London: Phoenix, 1998).

Keating, M. *The Politics of Modern Europe: the State and Political Authority in the Major Democracies* (Cheltenham: Edward Elgar, 1999).

Kellner P. 'Labour's Adaptations Since 1979 in Adapting to Post-War Consensus Symposium', *Contemporary Record*, November (1989), 13–15.

Kenny, M. and Smith, M. '(Mis)Understanding Blair', *Political Quarterly*, 68 (1997), 220–30.

King, A. *New Labour Triumphs: Britain at the Polls* (Chatham House: New Jersey, 1998).

Kinnock, N. *Which Way Should Labour Go?* (London: Labour Party, 1980).

Kinnock, N. 'A New Deal for Europe', in Curran J. (ed.), *The Future of the Left* (Cambridge: Polity Press, 1984).

Kinnock, N. 'The Future of Socialism', *Fabian Tract 509* (London: Fabian Society, 1985).

Kinnock, N. *Reforming the Labour Party* (London: Labour Party, 1994).

Kircheimer, O. 'The Transformation of the Western European Party System', in Palombara La J. and Weiner, M. (eds), *Political Parties and Political Development* (Princeton, NJ: Princeton University Press, 1966).

Labour Party, *Labour's Programme* (London: Labour Party, 1982).

Labour Party, *Labour's Plan: the New Hope for Britain* (London: Labour Party, 1983a).

Labour Party, *Report of the Eighty-Second Annual Conference of the Labour Party* (London: Labour Party, 1983b).

Labour Party, *Myths of Withdrawal* (Labour Party Research Department, London: Labour Party 1983c).

Labour Party, *Reports from the National Executive Committee* (June, September and December, 1983d).

Labour Party, *Report of the Eighty-Third Annual Conference of the Labour Party* (London: Labour Party, 1984a).

Labour Party, *Joint Manifesto with Confederation of European Socialists* (London: Labour Party, 1984b).

Labour Party, *Report from the National Executive Committee* (December 1984c).

Labour Party, *Report of the Eighty-Fourth Annual Conference of the Labour Party* (London: Labour Party, 1985).

Labour Party, *Report of the Eighty-Fifth Annual Conference of the Labour Party* (London: Labour Party, 1986).

Labour Party, *Britain Will Win: Labour's Manifesto* (London: Labour Party, 1987a).

Labour Party, *Report of the Eighty-Sixth Annual Conference of the Labour Party* (London: Labour Party, 1987b).

Labour Party, *Democratic Socialist Aims and Values* (London: Labour Party, 1988a).

Labour Party, *Report of the Eighty-Seventh Annual Conference of the Labour Party* (London: Labour Party, 1988b).

Labour Party, *Meet the Challenge, Make the Change* (London: Labour Party, 1989a).

Labour Party, *European Parliamentary Election Manifesto* (London: Labour Party, 1989b).

Labour Party, *Look to the Future* (London: Labour Party, 1990).

Labour Party, *Opportunity Britain: Labour's Better Way for the 1990s* (London: Labour Party, 1991).

Labour Party, *It's Time to Get Britain Working: Labour's Election Manifesto* (London: Labour Party, 1992).

Labour Party, *Labour's Economic Approach* (London: Labour Party, 1993).

Labour Party, *European Parliamentary Election Manifesto* (London: Labour Party, 1994a).

Labour Party, *Report of the Ninety-Third Annual Conference of the Labour Party* (London: Labour Party, 1994b).

Labour Party, *A New Economic Future for Britain* (London: Labour Party, 1995a).

Labour Party, *A People's Europe* (London: Labour Party, 1995b).

Labour Party, *The Future of the European Union, Report on Labour's Position in Preparation for the Inter-Governmental Conference* (London: Labour Party, 1995c).

Labour Party, *Report of the Ninety-Fourth Annual Conference of the Labour Party* (London: Labour Party, 1995d).

Labour Party, *The Road to the Manifesto* (London: Labour Party, 1996a).

Labour Party, *Report of the Ninety-Fifth Annual Conference of the Labour Party* (London: Labour Party, 1996b).

Labour Party, *New Labour, Because Britain Deserves Better* (London: Labour Party, 1997).

Laybourn, K. *A Century of Labour: a History of the Labour Party 1900–2000* (Stroud: Sutton Publishing Limited, 2000).

Lent, A. 'Labour's Transformation: Searching for the Point of Origin', *Politics*, Vol. 17, No. 1 (1997), 9–15.

Leys, C. 'Still a Question of Hegemony', *New Left Review*, 181 (1991), 119–20.

Lloyd, J. 'European by Default', *Marxism Today* (October 1990), 22–4.

Lloyd, J. 'Beyond the Mission Statement', *New Statesman* (16 May 1997), 22.

Lloyd, J. 'A Very British Lead', *New Statesman* (2 January 1998), 16–17.

Lodge, J. 'Cook with the Wrong Recipe for Europe', *Parliamentary Brief*, November (1998), 5–6.

Ludlam, S. and Smith, M. *New Labour in Government* (Basingstoke: Macmillan, 2001).

Ludlow, P. 'The 1998 UK Presidency: a View from Brussels', *Journal of Common Market Studies*, Vol. 36, No. 4 (1998), 571–83.

Macintyre, D. 'All the Excuses Cannot Disguise This Anti-European Majority', *The Independent* (15 June 1999), 18.

Macshane, D. 'Trade Unions and Europe', *Political Quarterly*, Vol. 66, No. 1 (1991), 351–64.

Macshane, D. 'Trade Unionism and Europe', *Political Quarterly*, Vol. 62, No. 3 (1992), 252–7.

Macshane, D. 'Europe's Next Challenge to British Politics', *Political Quarterly*, Vol. 16 (1995), 231–5.

Macshane, D. 'Ending Tory Hegemony', *Renewal*, Vol. 40, No. 2 (1996), 87–91.

Mandelson, P. Speech to European University Institute, Florence (30 January 1998).

Mandelson, P. and Liddle, R. *The Blair Revolution: Can New Labour Deliver?* (London: Faber and Faber, 1996).

Manufacturing, Science and Finance Union, *Europe 1992* (London, 1988).

Marquand D. *The Progressive Dilemma: From Lloyd George to Kinnock* (London: Heinemann, 1991).

Marquand D. 'After Euphoria: the Dilemma of New Labour', *Political Quarterly* , Vol. 68 (1997), 335–43.

Martin, D. 'Bringing Common Sense to the Common Market: a Left Agenda for Europe', *Fabian Tract 525* (London: Fabian Society, 1988).

McElvoy, A. 'Watch Out Tony – The Left Fears the Euro', *The Independent* (25 June 1988), 4.

McSmith, A. *John Smith* (London: Verso, 1994).

Merkel P. 'After the Golden Age: Is Democracy Doomed to Decline?' Paper presented to the Institut de Ciences I Politiques Conference on Socialist Parties in Western Europe, Barcelona (1990).

Minkin, L. *The Contentious Alliance: Trade Unions and the Labour Party* (Manchester: Manchester University Press, 1991).

Mitchell, A. and Heller, R. 'New Labour, New Deal', *New Statesman* (26 July 1996), 10.

Nairn, T. 'The Left Against Europe', *New Left Review* (September/October 1972).

Newman, M. *Socialism and European Unity: the Dilemma of the Left in Britain and France* (London: Junction Books, 1983).

Norris, P. 'Labour Party Factionalism and Extremism', in Heath, A., Jowell, R., Curtice, J. and Taylor, B. (eds), *Labour's Last Chance? The 1992 Election and Beyond* (Aldershot: Dartmouth, 1994).

O'Connell, J. 'The Integration of Europe: the Role of British Leadership'. Paper presented to the Thirteenth Lothian Conference, London (1997).

Panebianco, A. *Political Parties: Organisation and Power* (Cambridge: Cambridge University Press, 1988).

Parker, N. 'From Lion to Sheepdog: the Ex-Imperial State in the European State System'. Paper presented to the Thirteenth Lothian Conference, London (1997).

Party of European Socialists, *21 Commitments for the Twenty First Century* (Brussels: Party of European Socialists, 1999).

Perryman, M. (ed.) *The Blair Agenda* (London: Lawrence & Wishart, 1996).

Peterson, J. 'Britain Europe and the World', in *Developments in British Politics Volume 5,* ed. Dunleavy P., Gamble A., Holliday, I. and Peele, G. (Basingstoke: Macmillan, 1997).

Radice, G. 'Southern Discomfort', *The Fabian Society* (London: Fabian Society, 1992).

Radice, G. and Pollard, S. 'More Southern Discomfort', *The Fabian Society* (London: Fabian Society, 1993).

Radice, G. and Pollard, S. 'Any Southern Comfort', *The Fabian Society* (London: Fabian Society, 1995).

Rentoul, J. *Tony Blair* (London: Little Brown & Company, 1995).

Reubinstein, D. 'A New Look at New Labour', *Politics*, Vol. 20, No. 3 (2000), 161–7.

Richards, S. 'Eurosceptics and Europhiles are Still Smiling', *New Statesman* (31 October 1997) , 7.

Riddell, P. *The Thatcher Government* (Oxford: Oxford University Press, 1983).

Robertson, G. *Labour Party News*, Labour Party (London: January/ February 1992).

Rosamond, B. 'Labour and the European Community. Learning to be European', *Politics,* 10 (2) (1990), 41–8.

Rosamond, B. 'The Labour Party, Trade Unions and Industrial Relations', in Smith, M. and Spear, J. (eds), *The Changing Labour Party* (London: Routledge, 1992).

Rosamond, B. 'National Labour Organisations and European Integration. British Trade Unions and 1992', *Political Studies,* Vol. 41 (1993), 420–34.

Rosamond, B. 'The Labour Party and European Integration', *Politics Review,* Vol. 3, Part 4 (1994), 21–3.

Ryan, A. 'Labour's Conundrum', *The Times* (14 July 1987), 20.

Sanders, D., 'New Labour, New Machiavelli: a Cynic's Guide to Economic Policy', *Political Quarterly,* Vol. 67, No. 4 (1998), 290–302.

Seyd P. *The Rise and Fall of the Labour Left* (Basingstoke: Macmillan, 1987).

Seyd P. 'Labour: the Great Transformation', in King, A., Crewe, I., Denver, D., Norton, P., Sanders, D. and Seyd, P., *New Labour Triumphs: Britain at the Polls 1997* (Chatham NJ: Chatham House, 1997).

Seyd, P. 'New Parties/New Politics. A Case Study of the British Labour Party', *Party Politics,* Vol. 5, No. 3 (1999), 383–405.

Seyd, P. and Whiteley, P. *Labour's Grass Roots* (Oxford: Oxford University Press, 1992).

Shaw, E. *Discipline and Discord in the Labour Party* (London: Routledge, 1988).

Shaw, E. *The Labour Party Since 1979: Crisis and Transformation* (London: Routledge, 1994).

Shaw, E. 'Programmatic Change in the Labour Party 1964-1999'. Paper presented to Conference on Party Politics in the Year 2000, Manchester (1995).

Shaw, E. *The Labour Party Since 1945* (Oxford: Blackwell, 1996).

Shaw, E. 'The Determinants of Programmatic Transformation of the British Labour Party'. Paper presented to the American Political Science Association Meeting, Boston (1998).

Shaw, M. 'Towards a Global Policy for Labour', *Renewal,* Vol. 4, No. 4 (1994), 28–37.

Smith, A. Speech to the Royal Institute of International Affairs, London (20 March 1996).

Smith, A. Speech to the Board and Partners of the Osterreichische National Bank, Vienna (24 May 1996).

Smith, M. and Spear, J. *The Changing Labour Party* (London: Routledge, 1992).

Smith, M. 'Understanding the Politics of Catch-Up: the Modernisation of the Labour Party', *Political Studies,* Vol. 42 (1996), 708–15.

Smith, M. 'Neil Kinnock and the Modernisation of the Labour Party', *Contemporary Record*, Vol. 8, No. 5 (1995), 555–6.

Smith, M. and Kenny, M. 'Reforming Clause IV: Tony Blair and the Modernisation of the Labour Party'. Paper presented to the Political Studies Association Annual Conference, Glasgow (1997).

Sopel, J. *Tony Blair: the Moderniser* (London: Bantam, 1995).

Stephens, P. 'The Goal is Set', *Financial Times* (13 November 1988), 20.

Stephens, P. 'Clearing the Fog on Europe', *Financial Times* (15 December 1997), 23

Stephens, P. 'Return to the Bunker Mentality', *Financial Times* (17 November 2000), 27.

Strom, K. 'A Behavioural Theory of Competitive Party Politics', *American Journal of Political Science*, Vol. 34, No. 2 (1990), 565–98.

Tawney R. *Equality* (London: Allen and Unwin, 1931).

Taylor, A. *Trade Unions and the Labour Party* (Beckenham: Croom Helm, 1987).

Taylor, G. *Labour's Renewal? The Policy Renewal and Beyond* (Basingstoke: Macmillan, 1997).

Taylor, G. *The Impact of New Labour* (Basingstoke: Macmillan, 1999).

Taylor, R. 'Trade Unions and the Labour Party: Time for an Open Marriage', *Political Quarterly*, Vol. 58 (1987), 424–37.

Taylor, R. *The Trade Union Question in British Politics* (Oxford: Blackwell, 1993).

Teague, P. 'The British TUC and the European Community', *Millennium Journal of International Studies* , Vol. 18, No.1 (1989), 29–45.

Teague, P. 'The Alternative Economic Strategy: a Time to go European', *Capital & Class*, Vol. 26, Summer (1989), 43–70.

Thorpe, A. *A History of the British Labour Party* (Basingstoke: Macmillan, 1997).

Tindale, S. 'Learning to Love the Market', *Political Quarterly*, Vol. 2, No.1 (1992), 276–300.

Treasury Select Committee, *The UK and Preparations for Stage Three of EMU* (1998).

TUC, *Report of the Proceedings of the 113th Annual Trades Union Congress* (London: TUC, 1981).

TUC, *Report of the Proceedings of the 114th Annual Trades Union Congress* (London: TUC, 1982).

TUC, *Report of the Proceedings of the 115th Annual Trades Union Congress* (London: TUC, 1983).

TUC, *Report of the Proceedings of the 116th Annual Trades Union Congress* (London: TUC, 1984).

TUC, *Report of the Proceedings of the 117th Annual Trades Union Congress* (London: TUC, 1985).

TUC, *Report of the Proceedings of the 118th Annual Trades Union Congress* (London: TUC, 1986).

TUC, *Report of the Proceedings of the 119th Annual Trades Union Congress* (London: TUC, 1987).

TUC, *Report of the Proceedings of the 120th Annual Trades Union Congress* (London: TUC, 1988a).

TUC, *Maximising the Benefits. Minimising the Costs* (London: TUC, 1988b).

Walker, M. 'An End of Term Report on the Head Relaxed Cook has Feel for Europe', *The Guardian* (30 June 1998), 15.

Walker, M. 'Britain's EU Presidency Boy', *The Guardian* (9 June 1998), 20.

Wallace, W. 'Where Uncle Sam Leads', *New Statesman* (24 April 1998), 32.

Wendon, B. 'British Trade Union Responses to European Integration', *Journal of European Public Policy*, Vol. 1, No. 2 (1994), 1–20.

Whiteley, P. *The Labour Party in Crises* (London: Metheun, 1983).

Wickham-Jones, M. 'Recasting Social Democracy: a Comment on Hay and Smith', *Political Studies*, Vol. 43 (1995), 698–702.

Wilson, F. L. 'The Sources of Party Change: the Social Democratic Parties of Britain, France, Germany and Spain', in *How Political Parties Work: Perspectives from Within* (London: Praeger, 1994).

Wilson, H. *Final Term: the Labour Government 1974–76* (London: Weidenfeld and Nicolson, 1979).

Wilton, I. 'Labour Policy Review: Is it a Break with the Past', *Contemporary Record*, 4(1) (1990), 14–15.

Wincott, D., 'The Conservative Party and Europe', *Politics Review*, Vol. 1, No. 4 (1992), 12–16.

Worcester, R. *British Public Opinion. A Guide to the History and Methodology of Political Opinion Polling* (Oxford: Blackwell, 1991).

Worcester, R. 'Follow the Polls – Go for EMU', *New Statesman* (7 November 1997), 21.

Worcester, R. and Mortimore, R. *Explaining Labour's Landslide* (London: Politico's, 1999).

Wright, T. 'Who Dares Wins – New Labour – New Politics', *Fabian Pamphlet 579* (London: Fabian Society, 1997).

Young, H. *This Blessed Plot – Britain and Europe from Churchill to Blair* (Basingstoke: Macmillan, 1998).

Young, H. 'Swimming with Bill', *The Guardian* (24 November 1998), 24.

Young, H. 'Blair is a European. He Must Speak Now', *The Guardian* (27 July 1999), 20.

Interviews Conducted

Dr Roger Berry MP Backbench Labour MP, 13 December 1999

Charles Clarke Neil Kinnock's Private Office, 30 June 1995

John Edmonds General Secretary, GMB Union, 13 June 1995

David Foden Director, European Trade Union Institute, 20 September 1996

Charles Grant Director, Centre for European Reform, 20 January 1998

Rt Hon Neil Kinnock Leader of the Labour Party 1983–1992, 2 December 1996

Dr Dennis Macshane MP Member of Labour Government Foreign Affairs Team, 14 February 2000

Joyce Quinn MP Shadow Europe Minister, 3 July 1995
Regan Scott National European Community Co-ordinator, TGWU, 3 July
   1995
Nick Siegler International Secretary, Labour Party, 14 February 2000
Lord Whitty Labour Party European Union Co-ordinator, 24 June 1999

Index

Note: most references are to the Labour Party (including New Labour from 1994) and the PLP, except where otherwise indicated. **Emboldened** pages indicate chapters

Ollscoil na hÉireann, Gaillimh

3 1111 40071 4802